Working Women and Labour Laws

About the Author

Dr. Malkit Singh is HoD and founder member of the Post Graduate Department of Human Rights in D.A.V. College for Girls, Yamuna Nagar. He is the person who designed the syllabus of Post Graduation in Human Rights of Kurukshetra University, Kurukshetra as his college was the first college to introduce Human Rights at the Post Graduate level under the Kurukshetra University, Kurukshetra.

He decided to work on the human rights conditions in Punjab during the militancy and got scholarship from the International Institute of Human Rights Strasbourg (France) to attend Summer Human Rights Course, in July 2005 and July 2007. He is a prolific writer and researcher. He wrote 2 books on the position of human rights in Punjab during the Militancy and also contributed many articles on human rights and women rights in the reputed national and international research journals. He has keen interest in Indian Philosophy and he is also founder member of Gandhian Studies and Nehru Studies Centres of the college, established under the (Epoch Making Social Thinkers of India) by UGC, New Delhi.

During the teaching of the human rights to PG classes in a women college he came across the various problems of working women. He observed that even the much educated women are paid less in private and semi-government sectors than their counterparts.

The abysmal position of the working women at workplace and no regard of the women's work at home forced him to initiate his further research on this serious issue. He decided to work on the women labour and labour laws in India and initiated this work with his Post Graduate students, simultaneously applied a major project to UGC, New Delhi for financial assistance.

Fortunately he got the Major Research Project from UGC. This book is outcome of his years of hard work with his Post Graduate Students as well as the three years of Major Research Project sanctioned by UGC.

Working Women and Labour Laws

An Analytical Study

Malkit Singh

CONCEPT PUBLISHING COMPANY PVT. LTD.
NEW DELHI-110059

ISBN-13: 978-93-88937-08-5

First Published 2020

Published and Printed by

Concept Since 1974

Concept Publishing Company Pvt. Ltd.
A/15-16, Commercial Block, Mohan Garden,
New Delhi-110059 (INDIA)
T : 91 11 25351460, 91 11 25351794
E : publishing@conceptpub.com; *W* : www.conceptpub.com

Cataloging in Publication Data--Courtesy: D.K. Agencies (P) Ltd. <docinfo@dkagencies.com>

Malkit Singh (*Lecturer on human rights*), **author.**
Working women and labour laws : an analytical study / Malkit Singh.
pages cm
Includes bibliographical references and index.
ISBN 9789388937085

1. Women—Employment—Law and legislation—India. 2. Women—Employment—Government policy—India. I. Title.

LCC KNS1278.W58M35 2019 | DDC 344.54014 232323

Preface

Women continue to participate in labour markets on an unequal basis with men. Globally, women are paid less than men. Women in most countries earn on average only 60 to 75 per cent of men's wages. Contributing factors include the fact that women are more likely to be wage workers and unpaid family workers; that women are more likely to engage in low-productivity activities and to work in the informal sector, with less mobility to the formal sector than men; the view of women as economic dependents; and the likelihood that women are in unorganised sectors or not represented in unions. Women perform 66 per cent of the world's work, produce 50 per cent of the food, but earn 10 per cent of the income and own 1 per cent of the property.

Their struggle for gainful employment was started in West with the advent of modernisation and industrialisation and now it is expanded across the globe. The ever expanding economy has created the demand for more workers and women joined their counterparts to meet the demand of the economy, however, they are facing many challenges and discrimination on the part of payment and working conditions at the workplace.

The socio-psychological, economic and political barriers created many hurdles in their way to get equality in the sphere of work; they were prohibited to get the higher jobs and education just by giving the logic that women are physically, emotionally and intelligently weak. To cross the barrier of patriarchy women not only proved the iron at the workplace but also catered their duties towards the family and society.

This work presents the struggle of women labour at national and international level in a historical perspective. It linked the struggle of Indian women labour with the women labour and labour laws in the other parts of the world.

A careful analysis of the government initiative, the policy making process for the development and empowerment of women in India is done along with the analysis of the international framework for the development and empowerment.

The rise in the level of women education and their entering into the professional life and mainstream economy has been analysed along with its socio-economic and political impact on the Indian society.

This book presents the critical analysis of the labour laws, institutional mechanism and government initiatives taken by the government to improve the employment and condition of working women in India.

Malkit Singh

Acknowledgments

During my study I have worked with a large number of people whose contribution in assorted ways to my research endeavour and particularly in making of the research project deserve special mention. It is a pleasure for me to convey my gratitude to them in a humble way.

In the first place I would like to record my deepest gratitude to University Grants Commission, for approving my research proposal and giving me the financial assistance to work on the one of core issues of women rights.

I am grateful to all my teachers Professor. Ashutosh Kumar, Professor Pam Rajput, Bhupinder Brar, Prof. Ujjwal Kumar Singh, Prof. Sanjay Chaturvedi, Prof. Ronki Ram, Prof. Anupma Roy, Prof. Deepak K. Singh, Prof. Pampa Mukherji and Dr. Navjot Kaur at the Deptt. of Political Science, Panjab University, Chandigarh, who have contributed in their own way to the shaping of my vision about research. I am really thankful to them because they contributed to enrich my knowledge as a Master's Degree student and subsequently as a researcher.

I am also thankful to the other eminent scholars like Dr. Sushma Arya, (former) Principal, D.A.V., College for Girls, Yamuna Nagar, Dr. Vishav Mohini (former Director Women Studies Centre) D.A.V., College for Girls, Yamuna Nagar. Dr. Indrani Mazumdar, Senior fellow, Women Development Studies Centre, New Delhi, Professor Asha Kaushik (Rtd), Director, Women Studies Centre, University of Rajsthan, Jaipur, Dr. Anil Dutta Mishra, Former Deputy Director, Gandhi Memorial Museum and Libraray, New Delhi.

My Wife Dr. Shikha Saini and my Son Yugansh Singh deserve the special thanks for their constant support and inspiration in the completion of this work. I am also thankful to Ms. Sakshi, Research Associate in this project for her support and handwork which made to complete this project along with me.

I am grateful to all the staff members of DAV College for Girls, Yamuna Nagar for their moral support and inspiration.

Malkit Singh

Contents

List of Tables and Figures

LIST OF TABLES

LIST OF FIGURES

Abbreviations

APWW	: Asia Pacific Women's Watch
ASEAN	: Association of South East Asian Nations
BPFA	: Beijing Platform for Action
CEADAW	: Convention on the Elimination of All forms of Discrimination Against Women
CEBC	: Chief Executive Board for Coordination
CL-CM-CP	: Child Labour, Child Marriage, Child Prostitution
CSO	: Central Statistics Office
CSW	: Commission on the Status of Women
CSWB	: Central Social Welfare Board
CSWI	: Committee on the Status of Women in India
D&A	: Domestic and Allied
DAW	: Division for the Advancement of Women
DAWN	: Development Alternative With Women
ECOSOC	: Economic and Social Council
EPZ	: Export Processing Zone
FNB	: Food and Nutrition Board
FWCW	: Fourth World Conference on Women
FWPR	: Female Work Participation Rate
GAD	: Gender and Development
GDP	: Gross Domestic Product
GoI	: Government of India
ILO	: International Labour Organisation
IFAD	: International Fund for Agricultural Development
IME	: Information and Mass Education
IMR	: Infant Mortality Rate
INSTRAW	: International Research and Training Institute for the Advancement of Women
IPC	: Indian Penal Code
IRDP	: Integrated Rural Development Programme

LFPR	: Labour Force Participation Rate
MDGs	: Millennium Development Goals
MGNREGA	: Mahatma Gandhi National Rural Employment Guarantee Act
MKSP	: Mahila Kisan Sashaktikaran Pariyojana
NEP	: New Economic Policy
NGOs	: Non-Governmental Organisations
NREGS	: National Rural Employment Guarantee Scheme
NRHM	: National Rural Health Mission
NSS	: National Sample Survey
NSSO	: National Sample Survey Office
OSAGI	: Office of the Special Adviser on Gender Issues and Advancement of Women
PNDT	: Pre-natal Diagnosis Test
POA	: Programme of Action
PS	: Principal Status
PSSS	: Principal Status and Subsidiary Status
PWPR	: Paid Worker Participation Rate
RMK	: Rashtriya Mahila Kosh
SAP	: Structural Adjustment Programme
SAW	: South Asia Watch
SEZ	: Special Economic Zone
SGSY	: Swarnajayanthi Gram Swarozgar Yojana
SHGs	: Self Help Groups
SLL	: Special and Local Laws
SSK	: Sahajani Shiksha Kendra
STEP	: Support to Training and Employment
UN SWAP	: UN System-wide Action Plan
UNDP	: United Nations Development Programme
UNIFEM	: United Nations Development Fund for Women
UNO	: United Nations Organisation
UPS	: Usual Principal Status
VRS	: Voluntary Retirement Scheme
WAD	: Women And Development
WCP	: Women Component Plan
WFC	: Workers Felicitation Centre
WHO	: World Health Organisation
WIA	: Women's Indian Association
WPR	: Work Participation Rate
WPR	: Worker Population Ratio
WPRS	: Women Participation Rate Survey

Chapter 1

Introduction

Thinking about Women Labour and Labour Laws

Report of UN Conference 2006: Since ages women have been facing domination, subjugation and oppression due to patriarchal nature of society. However, the social scenario has undergone changes but it has not yet reached the goal of providing equal status for women. Series of changes through processes like industrialisation, modernisation and globalisation have created entirely new set of conditions. This in-fact brought rise in the proportion of women's engagement in gainful employment.[1]

> "Women represent one half of the world's population. They constitute one third of the work which is performed in the world, receive only one tenth of world's income and own less than one hundredth of the world's property."[2]

The aggregate of all human physical and mental effort used in creation of goods and services is called Labour. In the modern phraseology it is strictly an energetic work, though in general it implies hard work but mostly it is confined to the industrial work done by the working class.[3] According to the Marxist view labour is a primary factor of production. The size of a nation's labour force is determined by the size of its adult population and the extent to which the adults are either working or are prepared to offer their labour for wages.[4] Any work whether manual or mental, which is undertaken for a monetary consideration is called labour. Sometimes, the term labour is used in a very broad sense of total working force or labour force which includes all persons who work for living as distinguished from those who do not or are not expected to work for a living such as children, specially-abled and old persons etc.

Labourer is a person who owns labour and sells his or her labour in market.[5] In classical economics, labour is one of the three factors of production, along with capital and land. Labour can also be used to describe work performed including any valuable service rendered by a human agent in the production of wealth, other than accumulating and providing capital. Labour is performed for the sake of production in modern economic life, for the sake of a share of the aggregate product of the community's industry. The price per unit of time, or wage rate, commanded by a particular kind of labour in the market depends on a number of variables, such as the technical efficiency of the worker, the demand for that person's particular skills and the supply of similarly skilled workers. Other variables include training, experience, intelligence, social status, prospects for advancement and relative difficulty of the work. All these factors make it impossible for economists to assign a standard value to labour. Instead, economists often quantify labour hours according to the quantity and value of the goods or services produced.[6]

Economist start from the premise that resources such as labour, capital, land, time and personal income are scare, this means that everybody must make choices–for example, workers have to choose between having more leisure time and having more income from employment. Economist key assumption is that people make these choices rationally. They weigh up the costs and benefits of each option and select the one that will make them richer (maximise their wealth) or make them happier (maximise their utility) or satisfy more of their preferences, so, if a worker opts for more leisure time, an economist would infer that he or she values the benefits of leisure more highly than extra income to be obtained from working longer hours. Moreover, economist commonly assume that people's basic preference remain *stable over time,* so that if the economic environment changes, their behaviour will change too, in response. If wages raise, the leisure–loving worker might decide to reduce his or her working time even further, because the same income can be generated in fewer hours.

Labour lawyers commonly think about their subject in perspective to the workers' rights, economic efficiency for firms or for market as a whole and social justice for workers. Their ideas have been changing with the change in the dynamics of socio-economic and political set-up. Although at the early stage of industrial revolution the sociological perspective of lawyer could not make much sense due to the old socio-economic and political set-up. But with the rise of democracy and the passing of new labour laws as the positive initiatives of state to secure the social-economic and political justice for all citizens have not only changed the status of work-force but it has also lead to the new scenario in case of the payment of labour in context of production, profit and economic efficiency.

In the historical context we choosed the United Kingdom as the suitable country to trace the development of labour laws and political intervention of the state to secure the rights of workers and ensure the economic efficiency of the country after reviewing the literature in context of workers' struggle and development of the labour laws. To understand the theoretical paradigms in the historical context a review of the literature of two prominent thinkers of U.K. Otto Kahn-Freund and H. Collins is comprehensively done.

The work of Otto Kahn-Freund has exercised, and continues to exercised, a considerable degree of influence over labour lawyers thinking. Writing in 1950s, he drew on industrial relation theory, a branch of sociology in order to understand the law.[7] This was essential because anyone using 'black-letter' approach–in other words, looking solely at legal materials—would have acquired a wholly misleading knowledge of the relationship between employer and employees. For example there were few legal control on the circumstances in which employee could be dismissed. At common law, the contract of employment could be terminated if employer gave notice. The court did not inquire into whether or not employer had a good reason for dismissal. There was no statutory intervention in this area until 1971. But this did not necessarily mean that, in practice, employer had an unfettered power to dismiss their employees. Where trade unions were present in a workplace, they were often able to use their collective strength to protect individual employees against arbitrary dismissal.

Drawing on sociology, Kahn developed a sophisticated theory of labour law called 'collective laissez-faire'. His insight was that in Britain, the law play very minor role in industrial relations, particular in comparison with other industrialised Western nations. There were relatively few statutes obliging employers to treat individual workers in particular ways or even to promote collective barraging between trade unions and employers. Instead, employers and trade union were left to regulate their own affairs. It was this policy of 'non-interference' that Kahn labelled collective laissez-faire.

But collective-laissez-faire did not mean that the laws played no role at all. In the nineteenth and early twentieth century, the common law courts were hostile to the trade unions. The courts cast doubt on the legality of trade unions by declaring their aims foul of doctrine of restraint trade.[8] And they set about developing various economic torts—conspiracy, inducing breach of contract, interfering with trade or business—which exposed strike organisers to civil liability. In the infamous *Taff Vale case of 1901*, the House of Lords held that union could be sued in tort in their own name and held liable for actions of their officials.[9] Collective barraging could not easily take place under these conditions. Successive governments therefore intervened with statutes which removed the common law obstacles to collective barraging. *The Trade Union Act, 1871*[10] declared that the doctrine of restraint of trade did not apply to unions. *The Trade Dispute Act, 1906*[11] protected unions from tort liability and provided that strike organisers could not be held liable for torts of conspiracy, interference with business or inducing breach of contract.

But collective laissez-faire was more than just a description of the law, Kahn and Freund also saw it as an ideal for the law to strive towards, for three main reasons. First, he argued that legal intervention was unnecessary because collective bargaining was an effective way protecting workers. The presence of unions successfully redressed the power imbalance between workers and employers. Second, he claimed that workers' rights were more secure if they were acquired through collective bargaining rather than through constitutional or legislative guarantees. He believed that if the government had not granted the rights in the first place, it could not take them away. Third, he thought that collective laissez-faire was more flexible than legislation because it allowed unions and employers to decide things for themselves and to respond to changing circumstances.

The Demise of Collective Laissez-faire

It was in 1960s and 1970s, government in UK became increasingly interested in promoting workers' rights and managing the economy more actively. They also wanted to reduce the level of strike action—partly for economic reason and partly because strikes came to be seen as problem in their own rights. People began to question the system which relied almost entirely on collective bargaining to protect workers. In the eyes of its critics, collective bargaining suffered from two major flaws. First, it did not cover all industries or workplaces. In 1967, it was estimated that only 50 per cent of manual workers and 30 per cent of white-collar workers were union member and majority was not covered under the collective laissez-faire policy. The condition became worst in comparison to male female membership of trade union. In 1951, only 27 per cent of women workers were union members in comparison to 56 per cent of men workers.[12]

One major statutory response to the first of these concerns was the unfair dismissal legislation, introduced in 1971. The concern that unions might not protect all sections of the workers was addressed in the anti-discrimination legislation, The Equal Pay Act 1970, an another important step came with the enactment of the Sex Discrimination Act 1975, which tackled the many other respects in which employers might discriminate: in recruitment, in training, promotion and so on. It also tackled unions against members and application for membership. The government intervention at this stage could be seen as a way regulating unions, not just supporting their activities. We could therefore view this legislation of the late 1980s and 1990s as the beginning of a shift away from collective laissez-faire. Either way, this period marks the emergence of workers' rights as a central concern of modern law in UK which has impacted the other countries also.

The other major problem faced by government in the 1960 and 1970 was the high level of strike action. In 1964-66 for example, 190 working days per 1,000 employees were lost because of strikes.[13] Unions were in a relative powerful position because unemployment was low. Employers could not ignore the demands of workers who could easily move to jobs elsewhere. Strikes were cause of concern for two reasons. First, it was thought that they were contributing to UK economic problems. If UK firms were hit by high level of strike action, they might not be able to deliver product to purchasers on time. This would give them a reputation for unreliability which would harm their chances of exporting goods abroad. Second there was a growing feeling that the high level of strike action was a sign that unions were out of control. Davies and Freedland suggest that the high level of strike action at that time produced a crisis of truly constitutional proportions.[14] Those on the right of the political spectrum in particular began to argue that the trade unions were running the country not the government.

In 1965, the Labour government set up a Royal Commission, to investigate the strike problem.[15] Much of the evidences given to the commission advocated a stronger role for the law in regulating industrial relations. By the time the commission reported, the strike problem worsened and it became a major issue in the electoral politics. The new development like the issue of rights of the worker as an individuals and reducing of strikes along with to control the inflation in UK has remained a challenge for the every upcoming government from 1960s to 1980.

Individualism and Deregulation—1980s and early 1990s

The year 1979 saw successive conservative governments adopting a novel approach to labour law. The three themes were identified for promoting workers' rights, tackling the strike problem and promoting economic growth. The ideological commitment of the conservative government was individualism and the individual rights were emphasised instead of the strong labour union. The new legislation like *Employment Act 1988*, reduced the importance of as it give the individual worker a right against employer, not to be dismissed or subjected to detrimental treatment on the grounds that they were not trade union members.[16] The section 15-16 of this Act took away the union blanket immunity and subjected them to the immunity rules governing strike organises instead.

In a green paper published in 1991, the government claimed that its attempt to reduce the power of union has succeeded.[17] The labour government was elected in 1997 brought a new approach to labour law. It remained concerned with two themes, the workers' rights and prosperous economy along with fairness at workplace.

The Gender Division of Labour

The method the work is divided between male and female according to their gender roles instead of their efficiency is usually referred as the 'gender division of labour'. It is not only concerned with the paid employment, but more generally the work, tasks and responsibilities that are assigned to women and men in their daily lives. This also effects their turn and participation in labour market along the gender lines. The gender division of labour is often linked with biological traits; but nowadays if we notice that in some society's women perform tasks and jobs that in some other societies are traditionally considered as men's jobs, and *vice versa*, we see the division of labour has much to do with what each society perceives as appropriate for both sexes.

The absolute majority of women perform the house chores like cooking, washing clothes, cleaning, and everything that is necessary to sustaining the household like fetching water or fuel. Simultaneously, they also work at the small scale agriculture, cottage industry and unorganised sector of the economy as suits to their role in the family or near the home. On the other hand, more technical house-hold tasks, like dealing with electrical or mechanic equipment, is traditionally a man's job.

The gender division of labour is not fixed for all time; it changes in response to the demand of labour in context of time and space. For example, men and women follow different migration patterns, and engage in different occupations when they migrate. Migration may also result in men taking on tasks that they would not normally consider within their socially ascribed role, like having to cook for themselves. Some migrants often have to accept occupations for which they are overqualified. The employment of immigrant women in industrialised countries, as maids or care-providers, may not make it possible for them to advance their professional area of work.

Labour market is the place where workers and employees interact with each other. In the labour market, employers compete to hire the best labour at low price and the workers compete for the best pay and satisfying job. The labour market in an economy functions with demand and supply of labour. In the market, labour demand is the firm's demand for labour and supply is the worker's supply of labour. The supply and demand of labour in the market influence the bargaining power of labour and employer.[18] The demand and supply matrix of the market may create a situation where a worker can be forced to sell his/her labour at the very low rate due to the oversupply of labour and lack of work. Simultaneously, the low supply of labour can create a situation under which labourer can increase their labour arbitrary. The matrix of the demand and supply can create the situations under which the functioning of the economy can be paralysed. So it becomes necessary to regulate the labour not only for the welfare of the working class but also for the socio-economic and political stabilisation of any nation.

Unfortunately, the labour market (as well as education and training) is segregated along the gender lines with differences between regions and cultures. Some generalisations about the gender divisions in the labour market are quite truthful, men dominate certain sectors, which are considered being highly paid and tough. On the other hand, women concentration is in services and of men in manufacturing. By sub-sector there is also a gender division: in manufacturing, for instance, there are more women concentrated in the electronics and garments industries and men in the car industry. This is called 'occupational segregation', which is commonly split into a horizontal and a vertical dimension.

In the context of gender, horizontal segregation refers to the extent to which men and women are located in different occupational sectors. Women are usually highly concentrated in the sectors that require lesser skills (e.g. agriculture), that promise little chance for career advancements (e.g. services) and that are related to care-giving (e.g. Nursing), which often coincide also with low wages. On the other hand, vertical segregation refers to the extent to which men and women occupy different hierarchical positions within the same occupational sector. Within the same sector, women tend to occupy the lower ranks of the hierarchical ladder (and consequently the lower salary ranges). Statistics show that the higher the position, the wider the gender gap, so that on average women hold less than 5 per cent of the top jobs in corporations

As the bargaining between the employee and employer over the labour rate for the production and working conditions are not a onetime process or it doesn't happen at the time of recruitments only, it is a continuous and very complex phenomenon. It involve a set of rules, regulations and laws to regulate the service benefits of the workers and the working conditions of the workers along with behaviour of the labour force in collective as well as in the individual form. The development of trade-union and the trade organisation have not only created two competing pressure groups under the democratic governance of the world but also provided two responsible parties who have been committed to the welfare of the population of their nation and world.

Under the democratic governance, the labour regulations and the market strategies to maximise the profit have been claimed to be designed for the greater good of human society. The principles of sustainable development, environment economy, women empowerment along with the old concept of social-justice have been dominating the mainstream politics since the 1980s. However, the Gender and Marxist perspective has been continuously opposing the capitalist and patriarchal set-up of the economy and they have been continuously advocating for radical transformation of the national and international economic order. They are advocating for the gender sensitive and social justice based economic order.[19] The diverse perspectives on the labour, production and distribution of the resources have impacted the socio-political set-up of the society that resulted into the development of different perspectives on the political governance. Labour and labour laws has been on the core of political governance since the ages of human civilisation and the change in the mode of production has always been followed by the change in the labour laws and working conditions. The question of inclusion and exclusion of women in the labour market have been also influenced by the political governance and the demand of the labour at the national and international levels. Simultaneously, the special legal provisions for the welfare of women and child labour have been also influenced by the demand of labour and the political governance at national and international levels.[20]

Law is usually understood to emanate from legislatures, to be administered by state officials, interpreted by the state judges, and enforced by the state's coercive power. However, in many accounts of the origins and operation of labour law, labour and management are said to play a significant role in its enactment and administration.[21] Indeed, this role has sometimes been described as 'constitutional'. Moreover, even when labour laws are enacted by the state, they are often interpreted and applied by specialised public, private or hybrid agencies and tribunals, staffed by non-legal experts including labour and management representatives. These bodies do not simply adjudicate; they use other strategies—rule-making, education, and inspection, and mediation, negotiation—to secure compliance and reinforce relationships. When they do adjudicate, they typically employ evidentiary and interpretative rules, modes of reasoning and remedial powers.[22]

Finally, the labour law which regulates workplace relations often differ from state laws partly because the state concedes the parties considerable latitude in defining their relationship, partly because it lacks the capacity to enforce its law in countless workplaces, and partly because of the irrepressible tendency of workplaces to generate their own indigenous law that is sometimes explicit (contracts, collective agreements, standard operating procedures), sometimes implicit (customs, usages and patterns of behaviour imbricate in routines of work) but always powerful.

To sum up, it can be said that the labour law is different from other legal fields because it is so often promulgated through non-legal (i.e., political, social, and cultural) processes, expressed in the form of 'non-legal' (i.e., non-state) norms and administered through 'non-legal' forums operating with 'non-legal' processes (i.e. those not normally employed by conventional courts). Indeed, labour law—as it functions in actual workplaces—has often been used by legal scholars not only to challenge the hegemonic claims of state law and legal institutions, but also to initiate alternative approaches to law such as legal pluralism, reflexive law and critical theory.

An important distinction that is popularly made nowadays in all discussions relating to labour legislation is between workers in the organised/formal sector and those in the unorganised/informal sector. Many who make this distinction do so with motives to mobilise the public opinion to regulate the working conditions and wages of workers in this sector. As the absolute majority of workforce in developing countries is working in the unorganised sector of the economy and near about 94 per cent of the total work-force in India is working in the unorganised sector.

At the outset of the debate over the rights of the workers in the unorganised sector is that the state must have to intervene through the welfare measures and workers have to organise themselves. It is said that the workers must have to remember that the organised sector of today economy was also unorganised once. Moreover, many rights, benefits and practices, which are popularly recognised today as legitimate rights of the workers, are those that have accrued as a result of the struggles carried out by the earlier generation of workers. The other argument is that the workers should be conscious of the hidden agendas of the ruling and managerial class of pitting one section of workers against the others.

The advent of globalisation and the opening of the economy of developing countries like India have led to the rapid technological change and expansion of industrialisation which resulted into the creation of new opportunities. The expansion of the communication net-work and easy accesses to the knowledge and information has created a world which is more connected than ever before, as approach to the latest information in any part of the world is just a click away. The integration of world economy and the global linkage of various socio-cultural organisations have been working as agents for integrating local cultures and creating a global culture.

Some of the policy-makers, academicians and researches argue that the global agenda of liberalisation, privatisation and globalisation has been posing new challenges to the people living in the developing countries particularly the groups that were earlier supported by the state welfarism. The Structural Adjustment Programme (SAP) and New Economic Policy (NEP) to which the developing countries adopted in the early1990s have been posing new challenges to the political governance of the respective countries. The widening of gap between the rich and the poor, environmental concerns, the protests of the local people against mega projects and the gender issues have become the major concern of national and international governance. Attempts have been made both at the national and international level to rationalise the economic development and to find alternative strategies and techniques for inclusive and sustainable development.

The spread of modern information technology has been supporting the movements at the local level by providing them opportunities to interact and share their experiences with the marginalised groups in different parts of the world. The global connectedness of the local groups, particularly of women and other marginalised sections of society like tribals, landless labourers etc. has led to the creation of a new hope of the widening and strengthening of democracy and democratic culture across the globe. The recent upsurge against the dictatorial regimes and Arab Spring are viewed as the global upsurge for democracy and human rights. The interaction and network of the human rights groups from local to global level have further enhanced the capacity of human rights groups to put global pressure on the national governments for implementing the human rights laws under their territorial jurisdiction.

The promises and the efforts of global governance are aimed to improve the condition of women across the globe. There is an emerging trend of linking women rights with human rights, which demands equal and universal rights of women across the globe. The present international view holds that women shall be considered as one group, irrespective of their caste, colour, creed, language, socio-political status and nationality and all the human rights shall also be provided to the women as they are provided to men. The post-war efforts of the United Nations and the democratisation of the world have led to the development and empowerment of women across the globe. The emphasis of the national and international governments has been on the deepening of democracy and expansion of the human rights to each and every deprived section of society. The old concept of the national government and political control of the nation is now being transformed into the new concept of human governance, which aims at the inclusion of the deprived sections of the society into the socio-economic and political mainstream of the nations and expansion of the human rights to every citizen.[23]

A unique mechanism for the development and empowerment of women at the international level came into existence under the United Nations Organisation (UNO) and Division for the Advancement of Women (DAW), International Labour Organisation (ILO). The Commission on the Status of Women (CSW) was also established under the auspices of United Nations Economic and Social Council (ECOSOC) in 1946. CSW is dedicated exclusively to gender equality and the advancement of the status of women. It is the principal global policy-making body, meeting annually to evaluate progress on gender equality which identifies challenges, sets standards and formulates concrete policies to promote gender equality and the advancement of women worldwide. CSW prepares reports and recommendations to call the immediate attention of the countries all-over the globe towards the promotion of women rights in all fields of the socio-economic, political and educational activities, and present the same before the ECOSOC.[24]

The convention on the Political Rights of Women (1954), Convention on the Elimination of All Forms of Discrimination Against Women (1979), International Research and Training Institute for the Advancement of Women (INSTRAW) (1976), Office of the Special Adviser on Gender Issues and Advancement of Women (OSAGI) (1997) and United Nations Development Fund for Women (UNIFEM) (1976) are worth mentioning to the credit of United Nations.[25]

Especial efforts of International Labour Organisation (ILO) have been continuously helping the working class to organise themselves and sell their labour with human dignity. Although the very beginning and the preamble to the constitution of ILO clearly states that "Universal and lasting peace can be established only if it is based upon on social justice. Hence, the basic objective of the organisation is to help and improve social conditions throughout the world. The following examples of concrete measures "urgently requires" are specifically mentioned in the preamble: regulation of the hours of work, including the establishment of maximum working day and week; regulation of labour supply: prevention of unemployment; provision of adequate living wage; protection of worker against sickness, disease and injury arising out of his or her employment; protection of children, young persons, and women; provision for old age; protection of the interests of workers when employed in countries other than their own; recognition of the principle of freedom of association.

International action in these matters was required; the preamble makes clear, because "the failure of any nation to adopt humane conditions of labour is an obstacle in the way of other nations which desire to improve the condition in their own countries." Finally, in agreeing to the ILO constitution, the member governments declare in the preamble that they are "moved by sentiments of justice and humanity as well as by the desire to secure the permanent peace of the world."[26]

Although the principle of the gender-justice and equal pay for equal work were on the agenda of President Woodrow Wilson's Fourteen Points at the platform of action during the war years. However, ILO took long time to consider the special requirement and provisions for women labour and it was in 1958 when adopted it first convention on the rights of working women. After the initiation it made many efforts and conventions to protect the rights of working women across the globe? The worth mentioning are: ILO Discrimination No. 111 (Employment and Occupation Convention) 1958, ILO Recommendation No. 111 Discrimination (Employment and Occupation) 1958, ILO Convention No. 156 Workers with Family Responsibility 1981, ILO Employment Policy Convention (No. 122) 1964, ILO Private Employment Agencies Convention (181) 1997, ILO Human Resource Development Recommendation No. 150, ILO Human Resource Development Convention (No. 142) 1975, ILO Domestic Workers Convention (No. 189) 2011, ILO Equal Remuneration Convention (No. 100) 1951, ILO Recommendation No. 90: Equal Remuneration 1951, ILO The Minimum Wage Fixing Convention No. 131, 1970, ILO Convention No. 110—Plantation Convention, 1958, ILO Convention No. 183 Maternity Protection 2000, ILO Recommendation—191 Maternity Protection Recommendation 2000, ILO Maternity Protection Convention No. 103 (Revised), ILO R-095 Maternity Protection Recommendation 1952, ILO Maternity Protection (Agriculture) Recommendation, UN General Assembly Resolution of Declaration on the Elimination of Violence against Women, Discrimination (Employment and Occupation) Convention of 1958, ILO Employment Policy Convention (No. 122) 1964, ILO Private Employment Agencies Convention (181) 1997, ILO Human Resource Development Recommendation No. 150, ILO Human Resource Development Convention (No. 142) 1975.

In a significant development, human rights discourse has been extended to private domain. Now the major societal issues like gender justice, domestic violence and child rights are no longer being considered a matter of individual prerogatives as argued earlier. The violation of women rights inside and outside the walls has become an issue of political governance in the globalised world. The socio-economic and political initiatives have also been taken to curb the menace of violence against women and children both at the national as well as at the global level.

The important debates on the impact of globalisation on women and their labour rights is moving around the socio-cultural, economic and political aspects of their lives in these days. The development of information technology that connected feminist movements across the globe has been viewed as a new hope for the development of socio-economic and political rights of women across the globe. Late 1980s and early 1990s not only witnessed the rise of women movements at the global level but they also saw a global understanding among the women groups for the socio-economic and political development of women across the globe.

The development of industry and trade in the developing countries is also viewed as a positive development for women employment; the global industry is finding women as suitable employees. The free-flow of knowledge and information is also considered as a positive development to enhance the education and skills of women. They provide the new horizons of knowledge and information to the women to which they were lacking earlier. Now women can share their work experience with the other women and the democratic and global governance will help to develop and implement the policies which favour women at the local and global levels.

The other argument is that the globalisation will enhance the exploitation of women as privatisation and liberalisation are solely guided by the principle of maximisation of profit. The employment opportunities which will be provided by development of industry and trade will not help women as it will be guided by the logic of maximisation of profit and minimisation of labour cost. The new opportunities and employment of women will only be provided only if the women prove themselves as cheap labour in comparison to male labour. The other argument is that the employments of women will double the burden of a woman as social conservatism and patriarchal division of labour will force the women living in developing societies to do the house-hold chores along with their jobs. Thus the global flow of capital, technology and knowledge is also viewed as a double edged-sword.

On the one hand, the global investment, technology and the free-flow of knowledge has been helping the rich, educated and skilled women to enhance their skills and income; on the other, it has marginalised the poor women from the economic realm. As the vast majority of poor women lack the technical skills to work in the modern industry. The marginalisation of the unskilled and semi-skilled labour from labour market will affect the poor women badly as their counterparts, i.e. the male members also work as unskilled labour. The use of capital intensive techniques will reduce the demand of manual labour and it will force the poor strata to do the odd jobs for survival. The economic necessities may lead poor women to prostitution and other immoral economic activities.[27]

Women have entered the workforce in large numbers in the developing countries as the global investment has opened the doors of employment at the initial stage of the liberalisation, privatisation and globalisation. The critics of liberalisation and privatisation argue that the foreign investment and the setting-up of the industrial plants in the developing countries are conditioned by the concept of the maximisation of profit by the Multinational and Transnational Corporations. To allow the free entry of foreign corporations in the developing countries have been forced to bring changes in national industrial and labour policies and to give more incentives to big business houses rather than to small scale industries. The cheap labour, liberal environment and labour laws of the developing countries have been traced as the major reason for the global investment in the developing countries.

The use of the capital intensive techniques and acquiring of the big chunk of the agriculture and forest land under the policy of Special Economic Zones (SEZ) and Export Processing Zones (EPZ) in the developing nations have resulted in further marginalisation of tribal, rural and indigenous people along with unskilled labour from the market. The marginalisation of the unskilled and indigenous labour from land definitely had an impact on the status of women.

The number of unpaid women workers has increased because of privatisation of economy and withering away of the welfare policies by the state in the developing countries. The private contractors and owners of the private firms do not follow the labour laws and thus workers are forced to work for longer hours and under the inhuman conditions. It is necessary to mention that the vast majority of the workers who are employed in the unorganised sector of economy are constituted by women. The hire and fire policy adopted by industry in the liberalised and privatised economies has also forced the labour to dance to the tunes of the management as the unemployment level in the developing countries is very high as compared to the developed countries.[28]

Women dominate the workforce in Export Processing Zones (EPZs) in most developing countries. For instance, in Philippines the share of women workers in total EPZ workforce was 74 per cent in 1980, which remained the same till 1994. In Korea, it was 70 per cent in 1990, which declined to 60 per cent by 1993. In the Dominican Republic, it was 60 per cent in 1995. In Bangladesh and Sri Lanka, it has been above 70 per cent. Some argue that the high proportion of female employment implies that the creation of Special Economic Zones (SEZs) shows that the women labour is cheap and also easy to regulate in comparison to male labour.[29]

Studies have shown that increased employment opportunities have empowered women and made them more independent improving their relative status and bargaining power within their households. Madani in the Dominican Republic found that SEZ wages were the main source of income for 38 per cent of women working in these zones and that almost half of them were single, divorced or widows.[30] According to Dunn many of the women workers were bread winners for their household as well. ILO in 1998 reports that in Guatemala 45 per cent and in Honduras 22 per cent of women reported that they were only bread winners for their family. It has been established that the economic participation of women and their presence in the workforce in quantitative terms is important not only for lowering the disproportionate levels of poverty among women, but also for raising household income and encouraging economic development in countries as a whole.[31] SEZs have provided job opportunities to many women from rural and adjoining areas that have been instrumental in reducing poverty in these regions. But there are several reports indicating exploitation of women due to SEZs.

The vast majority of workers in SEZ firms are young women aged 16–25 years. It is found that women are paid less than men for similar jobs[32] and are subjected to sexual harassment and violence. Further, there is evidence that the type of employment generated in SEZ firms is generally poor. Female employment is concentrated in low-paid and low-productive jobs. As the nature of employment in SEZs involves higher technology inputs, women are thrown out of employment. It has been observed that the proportion of women in SEZs has declined over time in many countries.[33] As wages rise, more men are attracted to SEZ employment and as production requirements increase (such as supervisors or skilled workers), demand for male workers increases. Thus, SEZs are a mechanism of exploitation of women and not of their empowerment, though country-specific experiences may vary. International Labour Organisation (ILO) in 1998 concludes that SEZs do play an important role in employment generation in developing countries, but employment generation by itself does not ensure human development and poverty alleviation. Thus, the crucial question is whether employment in EPZs results in higher wages, better working conditions and higher levels of living.[34]

The general perception is that minimum wages paid in the zones are lower than those paid outside the zones. This is because labour laws are not extended to the zone firms but where these laws are applicable, they are not enforced strictly.

In 2000, the Beijing+5 Documents, while reviewing progress of women under the new world since 1995, noted that globalisation presents opportunities to some women but leads to the marginalisation of many and thus it advocated that gender mainstreaming to be done in order to achieve gender equality.

The report of United Nations Development Fund for Women observed that in the past two decades the process of globalisation has contributed to the widening of inequality within and among countries. The developing economies of Sub-Saharan Africa and countries in transition like Eastern Europe and the former Soviet Union are facing problems of financial crisis and political uncertainties at the same time. The poor countries want that some measures should be taken to make globalisation people centric. Policies and programmes must be reshaped under human and democratic norms; the global financial and capital agencies must realise their social responsibilities and should adopt a human centric approach instead of focusing on profit.[35]

The new international economic order has not only changed international rules of trade and tariffs but it has also changed the life cycle of people across the globe. It has been noticed that the people of the same nation have different experiences of globalisation in relation to their socio, economic, political, geographical and personal skill positions. The present form of liberalisation, privatisation and globalisation has come under tough criticism due to the lack of principles of social-justice and sustainable development. The emphasis of the critics of the globalisation is that the welfare measures and policy initiative of the state should protect the vulnerable sections of society from the negative impact of globalisation.

Economic development in relation to socio-political changes is also facing many challenges from many quarters across the globe as a result of socio-cultural variations of the different groups. The global media and global information technology have different impact on different socio-religious and political identities. Role of women and their freedom in any society is also subject to the socio-religious set-up. On the one hand, it seems that the traditional societies in the developing nations are in fine tune with the global culture and global technology and on the other hand suppression of women still continue in the name of cultural, heritage, family values etc.

Women constitute half of the world population as well as of Indian population. The development and empowerment of women is on the top agenda of the global governance as well as that of the Government of India. India's commitment to the international conventions on the rights of women and other important documents and declaration like Beijing Platform for Action, Beijing +5, Beijing +10, Beijing +20 show concern of Indian leadership towards gender equality. The advent of globalisation, liberalisation and privatisation has led to the new changes and challenges in the socio-economic and political set-up of the Indian society.

The decade of 1990s not only witnessed the opening of Indian economy to foreign direct investment, but it also witnessed many changes in the economic policy of the Indian Government. A New Economic Policy (NEP) was adopted by the Indian Government under which the state not only made the new laws to promote private industry by ending the license, permit and inspector regime, it also went further with the de-regularisation and disinvestment policies on the direction of World Bank and International Monetary Fund (IMF). However, the withdrawing of social welfare measures by the state and cutting of the financial deficit under the NEP and SAP have affected the weaker sections of Indian society in general and women in particular.

The economic impact of globalisation on women and the socio-political changes along with the empowerment of women in India have been debated widely by social scientists and policy-makers since 1990s. Impact of the global capital, culture, media, technology and the emergence of global women movements for women empowerment has been a matter of serious analysis for them.

The Western values and the NEP policy not only posed new challenges of competitiveness, privatisation and profitism, but also created many new avenues for employment and social exposure for Indian women. The global exposure and competitive market have posed new challenges of managing the house-hold affairs while sharing the burden of earning with their male companions outside, which has not only increased their responsibilities and working hours but also exposed them to exploitation and occupational hazards at the working places. Globalisation has provided them with more opportunities to work in solidarity at regional, national and international levels in order to demand their rights.[36]

The impact of globalisation is visible on women employment, development and empowerment across the globe which have both the positive and negative sides, if the educated and urbanite women are getting more opportunities to work in global industry than the unskilled and semi-skilled women who are working in the small scale industry and unorganised sector; underprivileged women are becoming the victims due to the marginalisation of small scale industry.

The urge for global investment by the developing countries has posed the new challenges to the labour in general and to the women labour in particular. The social security to the working class has been withdrawn. It becomes important to recall the provisions which are enacted by national and international agencies to protect the women labour from the exploitative structure of the global capitalism and patriarchal set-up of the global economy. The legal provision which have been enacted by the governments in developing countries like India and what kind of legal initiatives has been taken to handle the new socio-economic and cultural challenges which has been posed by the advent of globalisation in the developing countries.

The notion of labour in developing countries like India is dominated by dichotomy in terms of organised and unorganised sectors (formal and informal sectors) workers. A sizeable section of labourers in the unorganised sectors has no job security and their working conditions are not regularised along with the low wages. They work for long hours and still remain extremely poor with regard to basic rights as well as a dignified human existence. The position of women workers is extremely marginalised due to various social regimentations such as caste, poverty, illiteracy, lack of training, migrations and crime etc.[37]

The most serious problem of women labour in developing countries like India is that their work is not given the due credit. The absolute majority of them is engaged in non-paid work i.e. house-hold chores and allied domestic activities. In the extreme historical situations they are forced to work only in the inside of the walls and were not allowed to go in the open labour market for work. Women have never been considered as the full economic actor in India. In fact they even did not get their labour price directly as the work and product to which women made are sold by male members of the family. The control over the family income and resources has always remained in the hands of the male head of the family and it never passed to the women in the historical context.

Women's Right to Livelihood as a Right to Earn with Dignity

Right to livelihood means right to earn with dignity and respect. As per Lord Buddha's writing right to livelihood is connected with first defining what right livelihood is, i.e. a livelihood which is moral and not against the principles of natural justice like livelihood without killing living beings, livelihood earned through honesty as well as dignity.[38] The right to livelihood has been promoted at international level through United Nations Organisation (UNO), Universal Declaration on Human Rights (UDHR)[39], International Covenant on Economic, Social and Cultural Rights (ICESCR)[40], International Labour Organisation (ILO), ILO Discrimination No. 111 (Employment and Occupation Convention) 1958, ILO Recommendation No. 111 Discrimination (Employment and Occupation) 1958, ILO Convention No. 156 Workers with Family Responsibility 1981, ILO Employment Policy Convention (No. 122) 1964, ILO Private Employment Agencies Convention (181) 1997, ILO Human Resource Development Recommendation No. 150, ILO Human Resource Development Convention (No. 142) 1975, ILO Domestic Workers Convention

(No. 189) 2011, The United Nations Fourth World Conference on Women Platform for Action, Beijing, China-September 1995, ILO Equal Remuneration Convention (No. 100) 1951, ILO Recommendation No. 90: ILO The Minimum Wage Fixing Convention No. 131, 1970, ILO Convention No. 110-Plantation Convention, 1958, ILO Convention No. 183 Maternity Protection 2000, ILO R-191 Maternity Protection Recommendation 2000, ILO Maternity Protection Convention No. 103 (Revised), ILO R-095 Maternity Protection Recommendation 1952, ILO Maternity Protection (Agriculture) Recommendation, UN General Assembly Resolution of Declaration on the Elimination of Violence against Women.

Working Women and Constitutional Provisions

At national level, our Constitution protects the rights of working women and restores dignity to every individual with regard to right to livelihood.[41] The Constitution has described right to livelihood as integral facet to life. The state is under obligation under Article 39 (a), 39(d) and 42 to provide, promote and protect the right to livelihood or the right to exist. If the right to livelihood is not treated as part of constitutional right to life, the easiest ways of depriving a person of his right to life would be to deprive him of his means of livelihood.[42]

The Human Right to Livelihood includes the following universal, inalienable rights:

1. Equality before the law.
2. No discrimination on the basis of caste, colour, gender etc.
3. Right to freely choose work or occupation.
4. Right to social security and adequate standard of living.
5. Right to equal opportunities and equal access to productive resources like scientific benefit, technology, training, education etc.
6. The right against exploitation, torture, inhumane or degrading treatment, harassment etc.
7. Right to live life with dignity.

8. Right to basic protections at workplace: freedom from forced labour, freedom to form trade unions/associations; adequate and safe working conditions, equal pay for equal work.

Despite of plethora of rights as well as efforts of large segments of governmental and Non-governmental organisations (NGOs), working women population continue to be deprived of their basic human rights. In today's socio-economic and political environment people's livelihoods are threatened by various factors. These factors include natural disasters, destruction of natural resources, crime, migration, mass displacements, agricultural hardships, political conflicts etc. On such events women perennially suffer the most in form of exploitation, discrimination and violence.[43]

Over six decades after the independence, numerous efforts have been made through legislations, programmes and policies to ameliorate the condition of working women in India. So that women can be accorded equality, *vis-à-vis* their male counterparts.

Dropping Rate of Women Labour Force

As per the ILO studies women in South Asia are far less likely to be working than men to have a role or to be looking for one. While 80 per cent of men in the region are either employed or searching for a job, the number of women is as low as 32 per cent. These low rates are largely due to cultural attitudes, social norms and crime against women. As a result in some parts of South Asia including India, women's participation in labour market is dropping and it can be seen as major cause behind slow economic growth of the nation.

According to ILO's Global Employment Trend 2013 Report on India's labour force participation rate for women fell from 37 per cent in 2004-2005 to 29 per cent in 2009-2010. Out of 131 countries with available data, India ranks 11th from the bottom in female labour force participation. Despite of very rapid economic growth in India in recent years, it has been observed that trend of declining female labour participation is prevalent across all age groups, across all education levels and in both urban and rural areas. In terms of declining employment opportunities, occupational segregation appears to play an important role in holding women back. Women in India tend to be grouped in certain specific industries and occupations such as basic agriculture, textile, elementary services like nursing, teaching, handicraft etc. The gender stereotyping in job market and failure to allow women full access to the labour market is an underutilisation of human resources that holds back productivity as well as the economic growth.

The female employment in India grew by 9 million between 1994 and 2010, but the ILO estimates that it could have increased by almost double the figure if women had equal access to employment in the occupations as their male counterparts. Thus, it is astonishing that more women in India are enrolling in schools, colleges as well as universities but then, disturbing question is why the number of women who are either working or looking for role is decreasing?[44]

In the period when the Indian economy grew at its fastest, the participation of working women declined the most between 2004-05 and 2011-12. India's female labour participation rate (FPLR) declined merely by 7 per cent and pointed to 22.5 per cent according to the National Sample Survey Office (NSSO) (2012 figures) even as the economy expanded at an annual growth rate of 8.5 per cent. Urban India the driver of economic growth has lower rates of FPLR than rural India. The rapid gains in the educational attainments of women in urban areas over past few decades have not translated into economic empowerment. A key reason why educated women tend to stay away or drop-out from work is due to wage discrimination, lack of social security, safety and supporting infrastructure.[45]

Challenges and Problems Faced by Women Workers

Now it is quite clear that the position of women workers is at a disadvantaged layer. Women workers constitute a marginalised category within the class of workers in general there exists layers of subordination determined by structural factors such as the working liberty, working time and decision making power which is determined by the socio-economic and political set-up of the society. It is quite evident in the case of women workers in the unorganised sector. Recent national and international reports have made successful attempt in exploring the vast multitude problems and challenges faced by working women in India, which presents a dismal picture. The problems and challenges faced by working women are described in following way.

Gender Stereotyping of the Labour

The ILO studies have reported that due to the gender stereotypes, the occupational role of women is undermined. As a result of this type of practice, a large segment of women workers are being debarred from entering many jobs and occupations. This sexual division of labour has negative implications on the wages and the possibilities for moving upwards in the work force for women. For example in occupations related to health sector, women are concentrated as nurses, midwives, para health workers and a very few doctors and of course a very-very few as specialists as compared to men. Similarly in the education sector, the occupational segregation is very clear. Men generally work as administrators while women are prominently teachers. A lot of men are placed at highest positions in education sector like Vice Chancellors in universities while women folk are seen to undervalue in this sector too. Likewise in various other sectors namely textile industry, agriculture sector, construction industry, ceramics industry, film industry, garment industry etc. women receive lower wages and have limited job mobility very often the gender stereotyping of labour is used as a justification for dubbing women's work as low skilled. The consequences of this sex-typing of jobs is true bold: even women with requisite skills, education and training find it difficult to get into the called "male dominated jobs" and the ones in which the women are concentrated are categorised as low skilled untrained and receive lesser wages.

Cultural Barriers and Negative Patriarchal Attitudes

In the Indian socio-cultural set up there are widespread presumptions in relation to employment choices for women. Due to the sexual division at workplace some specific sectors are generally and typically marked for women. The socio-cultural order itself offers stereotyped "Feminine jobs" for girls and women such as teaching, nursing, tailoring, domestic services, child mending etc. The negative patriarchal attitude also prevents women from taking up employment. It is a common phenomenon that even educated and trained women are not allowed to earn by the family members and are forced not to cross the so-called "lakshman rekhas" of the house. Thus, the patriarchal ideology determines the pattern of sexual division of labour and under this system the prime responsibility of the household caring for all family members, cooking, cleaning, fetching water or fuel, caring for cattle etc. falls on women as a result of this dominant patriarchal constraints women are barred from entering the workplace of their own choice and capability.

Discrimination in Wages

The Constitution of India provides for "Equal wages for Equal work". Also a specific legislation namely, The Equal Remuneration Act is placed for protecting the rights of workers. But wage discrimination in the workplace is prevalent and this practice is very evidently reflected with respect to the women workers. Women in India are mainly concentrated in the unorganised sector and hence they do not have the benefits of several laws such as the Minimum Wages Act or the Factories Act. Women get lower pay despite longer working hours and the conditions of work are substandard. However, it is assumed that women are paid less because of low levels of skill, lack of job training, and time of care for family members and also due to maternity and finally the assumption that only men are considered as the primary earners. Hence, women are generally employed in lower categories jobs in comparison than men, which are lowest, paid. For instance women working in the construction industry work for same duration as men but are not even enrolled in the muster register. Similarly in agriculture sector women work intensively but are paid less. The women workers often have poor bargaining power and that is why they cannot pressurize the employers for their rights, which results in their economic exploitation.

Substandard and Poor Working Conditions

Various studies have revealed that environment at workplace is substandard. The working conditions such as space, lighting, ventilation, temperature, hygienic facilities, sanitation etc. are cramped. It is true that the above mentioned conditions are crucial for enhancing the productivity of workers and for providing a healthy living at the workplace. These facilities are also helpful in preventing work related injuries as well as diseases. Women workers are highly vulnerable to infections and other work related diseases due to their physiology and low social status. Many studies have reported exceptional illness and diseases among women workers in many industries especially in the unorganised sector.

Due to substandard conditions at workplace women workers suffer from respiratory disorders, asthma, T.B., strained muscles, skin-related allergies, urinary infections, reproductive related diseases, also abortions, sometimes slip disc, exhaustion, disabilities due to any workplace accident etc. All of these are work-place hazardous and the loss of the workers should be covered under the social security but workers are generally not provided any compensation for work related injuries loss of limb diseases etc.

Problem of Sexual Harassment

Sexual harassment at workplace is again a serious human rights violation against women. Whether a women is employed in an organised sector or in an unorganised sector, whether highly paid or low paid, illiterate or highly qualified, she faces sexual harassment at workplace.

Taking cognizance of the fact that discrimination against women is a matter of global concern, the need for including a specific statement regarding status of women under international law was seriously questioned at the San Francisco Conference (1945). Therefore, in order to weed it out, the Charter expressed the resolve of the people of the world to strive and uphold fundamental human rights, dignity and worth of human person and equal rights of men and women.[46]

The Committee on the Elimination of Discrimination against Women, setup under the Convention, has since explicitly addressed the problem. The General Recommendation of 1989 of the committee recognised sexual harassment as a form of violence against women. Three years later, the General Recommendation of 1992 characterised gender-based violence as a type of sex discrimination and therefore a bench of CEADAW. The

Recommendation defines sexual harassment as unwelcome sexually determined behaviour and takes note that equality in employment can be seriously impaired when women are subjected to gender specific violence, such as sexual harassment in the workplace. It considers that sexual harassment is a form of gender-based violence. It is gender-based because it is directed against a woman because she is a woman or which affects women disproportionately. This includes acts which inflict physical, mental or sexual harm or suffering, threats of such acts and coercion. The work of the committee leads to the development of Declaration on the Elimination of Violence against Women.[47]

Recently following the Vishakha Guidelines[48] proposed by the Apex court, the Prevention of Sexual Harassment at Work Place has been adopted in 2013. Sexual Harassment at workplace is a common abuse (physical as well of mental) for majority of working women in India. Women are highly vulnerable to sexual harassment at workplace and many a times find themselves caught between the glass ceiling of gender discrimination and abuse and the landmines of sexual harassment below.

Lack of Economic Security

Most of the women workers lack economic security. Their work goes unaccounted, unrecognised and unpaid. Though the unorganised sector is labour intensive but it is also less rewarding for women workers. The plight of women workers in this sector is miserable as economic exploitation in this sector is maximum. Women work for extremely low wages, long working hours, unsatisfactory working conditions with total lack of job security. They can be dismissed from work even without any prior notice, thereby shattering them economically. Almost it has been seen "that workers are not protected by any government labour legislation especially in the unorganised sector. According to ILO Report of 2009, about 45 per cent of the women workers are shunned or replaced by their employers in a short span of 2-3 year of employment. At any stage of employment there always exists a fear of insecure livelihood. There are apparently no adequate economic and social protection measures, strengthened support systems for their families, equal access to the economic resources to fight and eliminate increasing as well as disproportionate poverty among women.

At international level to provide economic security to working women, the ILO conventions have codified universally applicable labour standards and have led many countries to accept these standards for providing force to women's improvement in economic sphere. The ILO in the year 1998 adopted the "Declaration on the Fundamental Principles and Rights at Work which further provide economic security to workers through right to organise, collective bargaining and elimination of discrimination and promotion of workplace ethics.[49]

Health Related Issues

Working women bear triple burden in respect to work i.e. their role in domestic work (household chores) reproductive role and finally the productive role at workplaces. This strenuously working of women and playing the entire above said triple role in life affects the health of the working women. Already women are placed at a lower standard in terms of health as compared to men due to social and cultural attitudes Discrimination occurs at the initial stage of a females life for example most of the girl child are discriminated in nutrition by the families themselves. At the same time women are poorly accessed to medical drives and other health benefits.

It is a common phenomenon that a large mass of working women suffer frequent headaches, stress, depression, high/low blood pressure, back pain cervical, circulation disorders, mental as well as emotional disorders due to hardened lifestyles and inadequate support system. The jobs which require concentration and more attention like embroidery, jewelry making etc. cause more exertion which further leads to increased mental and physical stress. Lack of basic facilities like proper toilets, rest rooms, dining spaces, light, ventilation etc. at the workplace cause a lot of physical discomfort as well as mental stress. These substandard and unhygienic conditions of work lead to urinary tract infection and other diseases particularly among pregnant women. Women working in some industries like construction, brick kilns, electronics, and textile industry suffer from genealogical problems, miscarriages, premature deliveries etc. and are always at risk to give birth with defects or with low weight.[50]

Health security is a prime concern for the workers especially in the unorganised sector. Various studies have revealed that reduced public health expenditure can have detrimental effect on the workers and their families. Illnesses which require hospitalisation could be catastrophic for poor women workers. Right to health and an adequate standard of living is a basic human right. But in recent years due to step rise in the cost of treatment, the health care sector has made the right to health a distant dream to achieve for majority of Indians.

Lack of Social Security

Social security of women can be linked with issues of gender inequality, discrimination, poverty, violence and crime etc. which are very much prevalent in our social and cultural system. The lack of social security acts as a barrier for many women to step out and join the workforce. The prevailing social attitudes and cultural norms and patriarchal approach hinder women participation in the workforce. All these factors ultimately make women more vulnerable to economic downturns thereby negating economic growth of the nation on the other hand where women are earning the evidence show that they suffer gender inequality, discrimination, exploitation and violence. Studies reveal that women workers are given secondary status at workplace as well as in the families. Women workers go even without normal social security measures the basic mental and emotional support system from the families. At workplace there is absence of social protection conducive working conditions job security etc., still the women workers are contributing to the national income?

A case study conducted on around two hundred working women (both of organised and unorganised sector) revealed that apart from social insecurity at the hands of family and the employers they face problems of the eve-teasing, assault etc. every day.[51] Women workers are hired first and also fired first, still they are the anonymous contributors to the national income which are invisible, unregistered to the glitzy, high tech environs of India. It is a paradox that working in India lack social, economic and legislative protections despite of plethora of laws and policies for women empowerment.

The various social issues including violence against women have brought into sharp focus the failure of the mainstream to alleviate their predicament. Despite of any social security benefits available in reality, the working women no doubt are contributing immensely to the national economy. The International labour organisation has termed them as the "ultimate entrepreneurs" for their ability to sustain livelihoods with very little capital as well as benefits.

Emotional Problems and Lack of Adequate Support System in Family Environment

Apart from inherited disadvantages like lack of social, economic and legal security, emotional problems disturb working women in different ways. Women lack the basic support from their families and also her participation in the workforce sometimes creates a hostile domestic environment in the relationships. A majority of working women suffer emotional problems which remain hidden. As per available research it was found that working women are not only harassed mentally and emotionally by the employers but also by immediate family members. There are various instances when character of working women is doubted. She is linked with other men at workplace, their dedication towards their profession and children is compared with their dedication towards family and the hard-core professional women are blamed to be over-professional and money minded etc. by their own family members. On the other hand, women workers at workplaces confront with other problems like sexual harassment, exploitation, discrimination in wages, long working hours assault on self-esteem and dignity etc. All these factors harm the health and constitute serious risk for the women worker's emotional stability. A large number of women workers suffer mood swings, depression, sadness, irritation, lack of concentration power which at the end negatively affects their work. As a result most of the women workers are branded as "unprofessional, unskilled and inadaptable."

Dual Burden of Work

Working women work additionally and are also burdened with major domestic duties. A considerable share of their time is consumed by socially productive and reproductive labour. This is called the double burden of work that distinguishes women from men. The reproductive role, child rearing role, and domestic duties are less visible and not recognised by the employers.

The Central Statistical Organisation of Government of India provided official visibility to this dual burden of work through a pilot study of utilisation of time by men and women in six states in 1998. The report classified the activities based on the System of National Accounts (SNA) into three following categories namely:

1. Those falling under the economic activities which are included in the SNA.
2. Those which are featured in SNA like domestic duties, caring of children, old, sick, but currently not included in the SNA.
3. Non-SNA activities like social and cultural activities, leisure and personal care etc.

The study found that women spend a disproportionate amount of time in the extended SNA. On the other hand, men spend a much greater time in non-SNA activities than women. As for non-SNA activities, the difference was not as striking as in the case of extended SNA.[52]

Even though the employment of women is accepted in most of the families but majorities of families do not provide any sort of support system to the dual responsibilities. Women are required to play dual set of roles as mothers, wives and as employees which results in adjustment problems. Hence, a kind of conflict arising from a lack of adjustment between two competing roles is faced by working women. The persisting social and cultural norms require a redefinition as they act like a barrier for women participation in the workforce.

Poor Implementation of Labour Laws, Policies and Programmes for Women Workers

The labour legislations for women in India are rooted in the Indian Constitution. The Indian Constitution recognises the rights of women through Article 14, 15(1), 15(3), 16, 39(a), 42, 44, 46, 51a(e), 348 (d) and (t),. Also a large number of women-related legislations have been enacted from time to time. The policies and programmes for women empowerment are being increasingly moduled through hike in gender budgeting. However gaps still remain in providing adequate safeguards to women in every sphere of life.

The findings of various studies at international and national level are not very encouraging. The rights of working women have been protected and safeguarded in various Acts but in reality these are being enforced merely on paper, due to poor implementation of the women specific legislation by the government. The condition of working women has not undergone much change. It is worst in the unorganised sector where population of working women is highest.

The law itself cannot offer any protection unless there is a sense of awareness of its existence. Moreover, there is one more tragic factor that has to be noted. The very laws which are meant for safeguarding the interests of working women are paradoxically turned against their interests by the unscrupulous employers. If the employers find it difficult to bypass this provision they get rid of the women workers and thus strike at the economic base of their livelihood. Hence all these factors need to be studied in depth while drafting policies and legal provision for the benefit of working women. Simultaneously, the existing laws, policies and programmes must be implemented and advertised with a passionate attitude so that welfare of women workers is possible in all spheres and all the existing loopholes are plugged out.

Other Obstacles in Way of Women Workers

There exist various other obstacles which hinder the progress and growth of women in world of work. Due to prevalence of gender discrimination women are given subsidiary statics at the workplace. Work environment for women is not made conducive but hostile. Women suffer wage discrimination; also the process of promotions in women employees is slow. There exists sexual division of labour, lack of social security long working hours, sexual harassment, absence of child care facilities, health facilities, non-conventional place of work, inadequate education and training, wage discrimination and poor implementation of gender-sensitive policies, schemes and legislations. All these problems deserve special emphasis and focus because such factors result in marginalised position of women workers. The overall picture that emerges is one of greater disadvantage for women worker. These obstacles ruin the possibility of women employees for upward mobility in the industry.

At the same time women workers suffer from high degree of casualty with dismal wage structure. They have hardly any protection or even access to the legislation process to protect them due to their dismal presence in legislative bodies. The activities of women add to household incomes in various forms but do not form part of the market economy. The quantitative contribution of poor women is not accounted for and the qualitative contribution is highly appreciated. Although more and more women are coming out in search of paid employment to support their families, the attitude towards women employees and their role in the family has not undergone much change. Women contribution is perceived as inferior, weak and second class employees as well as citizens.

Review of Literature

The status of working women varies enormously from one part of the world to another. A review of the studies of women at large and women workers in particular brings forth the point that studies on the status of working women still do not cover many aspects of the problems faced by working women whether employed in organised sector or in unorganised sector. Hence for better understanding of women's role in workplace, review of literature has been useful to an extent to build the current study.

Anupma Hazra[53] deals with the recent dynamics of the social security in India from the lens of Millennium Development Goals and focuses on the strategies adopted to address poverty, food security, primary education, women empowerment and primary health care. By linking India's strategies to deal with the endemic problems like poverty, illiteracy and the lack of primary health care, he suggests some comprehensive measures which can help in the better implementation of social security and sustainable growth of the social sector.

Monica Chawla[54] examines the prevailing laws for the promotion and protection of women rights in India. She elaborates on the marriage and divorce laws and offences affecting the dignity and body of women. The laws related to the economic rights of women like labour laws, Maintenance, Adoption, Guardianship and Succession are duly focused upon.

M.R. Biju[55] examines the influence of liberalisation, privatisation and globalisation on the employment and working conditions of women in the developing societies. By focusing on the rhetoric of liberalisation and privatisation and their real impact on the weaker sections in general and women in particular, he holds that women have been left far behind men in the unequal world. The study expresses the need for their upliftment and empowerment to ensure a sustainable and progressive world.

Tinku Paul Bhatnagar[56] examines the importance of gender equality in the development of a country. Tinku focuses on the importance of women contribution to the welfare of the family and society. He holds that despite the role played by women in running the human generations they are yet deprived of their full maternal rights.

A.N. Das[57] in his book discusses the linkage of women rights and human rights which emerged during the decades of 1980s and 1990s at the international level. He elaborates on the women movements around the world their networks and coalitions, which give greater visibility to the problem that a woman, face every day and to the centrality of women's experiences in economic, social, political and environmental issues. He vividly links the human rights framework with women rights of health, reproduction etc.

T. Lavanya[58] comprehensively examines the provisions and policy framework of the Indian Government which it adopted for the development and empowerment of women. While analysing the historical perspective of women development in India, she holds the Eleventh Five Year Plan as the first major attempt of Indian Government for addressing the issue of women development and empowerment. She appreciates the intervention and long-term strategies of government to end the violence and discrimination against women in the globalised India.

Indrani Mazumdar[59] analysised the impact of globalisation on women workers in India. She demystifies the phenomena of globalisation, offering an overview of its prime drives, processes and forces. Four sectoral studies of women are provided; two on factory women in garment exports and electronics, the third on home based workers in a range of manufacturing processes and industries and the fourth on middle class women working in information technology and services.

Monica Chawla[60] deals with the status of women and efforts made at the international level to remove all kinds of discrimination against women. She examines various constitutional provisions, the criminal law and the labour and industrial laws which benefit and protect women workers. She also explains the special laws enacted for the welfare of women. She criticised the Indian state for keeping the religious personal laws regarding marriage and divorce of women despite well-developed legal mechanism for the protection of women's rights in India.

Nomita Aggarwal[61] discusses various national and international provisions for the protection of socio-economic and political rights of women in India. She elaborates on the constitutional provisions relating to the rights of women, Penal Laws, Labour Laws and the 73rd and 74th constitutional amendments in the first section of this book. In the second section she discusses the international provisions for human rights and women rights along with the current issues of domestic violence and legal aid in India.

Neera Desai and Usha Thakkar[62] discuss the changing perceptions of the status and role of women at the threshold of the new millennium. They vividly define the emergence of women issues regarding health, employment and media projection of women. At the end of their study Neera and Usha have examined both the negative and positive aspects of liberalisation, privatisation and globalisation of Indian economy to women rights.

Shri Kudchedkar and Subiha AL-Issa[63] deal with the twin issues of violence against women and women against violence. They have argued that although violence against women has attracted so much attention in recent years. In this work they argued that all the claims of gender sensitivity and human rights to establish the social justice have proved fruitless when one sees mass violence against the weaker sections of society.

Pam Rajput and Hem Lata Sawrup[64] deals with the most critical concerns of globalisation, which were initiated in the last decade of the twentieth century for the development and empowerment of women. They focus on the global policies and initiatives of International Monetary Fund and World Bank and the conditions imposed by the structural adjustment programme on the developing countries and their impact on women.

In his article Vinoj Abraham[65] presents the recent trends of labour market and fluctuations in the labour participation of women which is probably due to short-term shifts in activities responding to favourable economic conditions. It argues that fluctuations in the labour market hit women hard. He explains that such fluctuations need to be placed in the context of a structural change in labour participation. It is found that the decline of women's share in the labour force as well as labour participation rate of women is linked with the social set-up of Indian society. The study holds that upward social mobility of women in Indian patriarchal society in the wake of growing incomes is probably symbolised by their withdrawal from paid labour and their confinement to unpaid domestic activities. Even under such adverse conditions employment growth of women is not stagnant. Those who do enter and remain in the labour market are women from the most vulnerable households, as marginalised informal paid labour, thus feminising the most precarious forms of labour in the country.

In their paper Yamini Mishra and Navanita Sinha[66] highlight the importance of gender responsive budgeting while analysing the manner in which the Government of India has planned out this process appears to be a classic case of putting the cart before the horse. This article analyses the two prime strategies adopted by the Government of India for institutionalising gender responsive budgeting, namely, the "Gender Budget Statement" and Gender Budgeting Cells to highlight what has gone wrong, and what needs to be fixed. The authors also draw on experiences from other countries, to argue that gender responsive budgeting in India needs a completely different rhythm if it has to translate into better outcomes for women in India. With the formulation of the Twelfth Plan under way, the moment is opportune to push for groundbreaking changes in the policy discourse on gender responsive budgeting.

In his paper Himanshu[67] examines the trends of employment and unemployment as thrown up by successive National Sample Surveys from the mid-1970s onwards. By analysing the employment trends, he suggests that the euphoria about high employment growth during 1999-2004 was not justified nor does the concern about jobless growth in the subsequent years capture the changes in employment structure. The study suggests that long-term analysis of employment trends reveal that changes in the employment pattern and workforce structure have been sluggish and do not confirm to the standard employment-output relationship. The analysis also flags certain issues which have bearings on the comparability of employment data before and after 1993-94. Large fluctuations seen after 1993-94 appear to be a result of the movement in and out of labour force of a substantial section of the population which is vulnerable and in the informal sector in a phase of rising overall rates of economic growth. The paper concludes with a brief discussion of the results of the recently released 2009-10 survey of NSSO.

In her article Nalini Nayak[68] examines the conditions and percentage of woman workforce in the unorganised sector of Indian economy. This study shows that 92 per cent of the total workforce employed in the unorganised segment, with the entire farm sector falling under the informal category, while only one-fifth of the non-farm workers are found in the organised segment. By giving illustrative figures she suggests that in the non-farm sectors, as we move up the income ladder, the share of the informal sector gradually declines. However, as far as the agriculture sector is concerned, irrespective of economic class, the share of the unorganised workforce remains flat. Further she reveals that the lack of social security in the unorganised sector of economy has not only impacted the working conditions but also worsened the lives of the poor people in their old age.

In her article Nirmala Banerjee[69] presents the pattern of economic development during the Nehruvian era. Through her work she provides important information on the failure of the modernisation project in getting rid of gender discrimination within the household and at the workplace. Through a historical analysis of government policies on women development and empowerment she explores how the issue of women development and empowerment has been negated by the Indian leader after the independence. Although Jawharlal Nehru himself presiding over the committee on women's status in the 1930s, but after the independence Nehru and the Planning Commission under his leadership proceeded to discard the radical economic measures, the committee had recommended establishing parity between men and women.

In their article Ghosh and Mukhopadhyay[70] analyse the available data on employment in India and point out that there has been severe reduction in the number of female workers in the last few years. While highlighting their displacement in the Indian Labour force they have built three hypotheses around the reduction of women workforce in India. First, the economic change might have caused the technological and occupational structure of the economy to undergo a transformation biased in favour of males. Secondly, the Indian economic scene, featured by growing unemployment and sluggish growth of income per head, has failed to provide sufficient opportunity or incentive to attract many of the potential workers; most of them are again female. Thirdly, the sex ratio might have undergone a change.

Rajeshwari Deshpande[71], elaborates upon the lack of social security for workers in the unorganised sector and comprehensively explains the provisions made for social security under the proposed bill for assuring the same. While analysing the position of women workers in the unorganised sector, she argues that the workers will lose their traditional rights if certain modifications in the proposed bill are not made.

In his book Davies[72] seeks to make her readers to see the relevance and importance of legal norms in historical context in the sphere of industrial relations. This is an accessible but thought-provoking introduction to labour law. She covers the ideological, theoretical debates on the labour welfare along with the analysis prevailing socio-economic and political situation in the United Kingdom. What Davies has done, in a remarkably clear-sighted fashion, is to identify where most debate over the form and content of labour law is now focused. She used the academic literature on labour law and makes considerable use of human rights arguments for the economic analysis of labour laws. Both of these approaches not only provide valuable insights into the underlying policy of the law but they can be rather off-putting for students who do not know the international human rights instruments, or who have no background in economics. This book introduces these wider perspectives on labour law and then applies them to a selection of topics, including anti-discrimination law, dismissal, working time, pay, consultation and collective bargaining, trade union membership and industrial action. The contributors[73] of this volume are well known international feminist sociologists who explored different situated contexts of women's citizenship in different cultures and countries. While analysing the shifting and contested nature of women's citizenship this book highlights the crucial importance of analysing all citizenships in an intersectional way, in which the gendered nature of women's citizenship is mutually constituted in the concrete reality of everyday life experience with other intersected social power axes, such as class, race, ability, sexuality and stage in the life cycle. The book highlights the construction of citizenship while emphasis the inclusionary as well exclusionary practices of participation of citizens in their day to day life and the policy making process at the political level in the state.

This volume highlights the decreasing of the economic borders and extending of the political and legal rights, it argued that active citizenship has potential to expand the gender equality. At the same time, the authors argue that the rise of neo-liberalism, withering away of the welfare state, decline of public sector, privatisation and the rising gap between the rich and poor has curtailed the rights of the certain categories of people.

Lucy's[74] work entitled "Working Time and Holidays" deals with the Working Time Directive (WTD) which was adopted by the members of states of European Union in 1993. In this book she dealt with the provisions which are made under the WTD for the security of workforce in the countries of European Union. She elaborated on the provisions of the health safety in routine and in the night work specially. While highlighting the decision of the European Court of Justice, Lucy elaborated the gap between the legal provisions and weak implementation of the provisions of the WTD in Europe. She elaborated on the frequent questions which are asked by the employers to the legal advisors on the question of weekly working hours and the week end, which can result into the reduction of working hours of the workers by the employers.

Lucy covered the provisions of the maximum working week, rest and breaks, annual leave, night work, young worker, unfair dismissal and detriment and enforcement comprehensively. The question of annual leave and maternity leave, annual leave and sickness, annual leave and part-time worker, annual leave and casual workers, annual leave and annualised hours/pre-determined shifts patterns, annual leave and payment in lieu of notice and annual leave and career breaks and sabbaticals critically evaluated by her with case laws.

Gross[75] and other experts on the labour laws made an academic attempt to link the labour laws with human rights. In his book Gross in the first chapter "A long Overdue Beginning" narrated the historical development of labour laws in the USA. He started with the National Labour Act, 1935 and linked the provisions of the Act with the provisions of Universal Declaration of Human Rights, Covenant on Civil and Political Rights and Covenant on Economic, Social and Cultural Rights, and some other relevant provisions of the international human rights laws. The other authors elaborated on gap between the international laws and U.S. Labour law and the question of health care in the ILO policies and programmes and the provisions of labour laws in USA. The question of collective bargaining and community support for workers is also elaborated in the light of human rights perspective.

Shagun and Nidhi Rawat[76] deals with two broad categories of labour laws, first the collective Labour Laws, which derives the relationship between employee, employer and union. Second is the individual labour law, which relates to the employee's rights and obligations at the workplace. They linked the development of labour laws and socio-economic development of the society with the industrial revolution. Their work comprehensively covers the laws like Labour Law Act, 1988, Apprentices Act, Employment Act, Payment of Gratuity Act, 1972, Minimum Wages Act and laws relating to industrial relations like Trade Union Act, Factories Act, 1948, Industrial Dispute Act, 1947 and Factories Act, 1948 etc.

Hiraway[77] along with the renowned economists highlights the importance and role of the unpaid work in the development of the community and nation across the globe. This work is based on Time-use Data in Developing Policies for development in the 21st century and international programmes, policies on women development and empowerment. The statistics on the unpaid work of the women questioned the global claims of gender equality, gender justice and gender development index along with principles of sustainable development. The contributors collectively argue that the unpaid work, across the world, is an area that has generally been ignored by the economists as well as by the development actors. This book establishes the necessity of measuring and incorporating unpaid work in analysing the critical concern of an economy. After assessing the position of the unpaid work of women in the South Asia Pacific, Africa and Latin America the book shows why time use data is essential for understanding critical socio-economic concerns.

Dr. Gupta[78] elaborates on the actual position of working women and the legal provision which provides special benefits to the women. Through her field survey of the Agra and Aligarh industries she collected the first hand information on the problems to which working women are facing as an industrial labour. She also attempted to understand the problems to which women are facing at home and their impact on their professional life as well as the impact of the problems of the workplace at their home. She comprehensively elaborated on the special laws, policy measures and the initiatives taken by the Indian Government to increase women labour force. She starts with the constitutional provisions and elaborated on the special legal provisions which are enacted to protect the rights of working women in India. Dr. Gupta also elaborated on the case laws which are related with the rights of working women and very vividly presented the judicial responses to the problems of the working women. The book also highlights the provision of the international laws declarations and the ILO perspective on the rights of working women and the gaps between the national and international perspective on the issue.

Janet and Stebbins[79] linked the problem of working women with the gender discrimination in a historical perspective. Although the study is covering the problems of working women across the world in the theoretical gender perspective, but their empirical focus is the labour laws and working women in USA. It covers the theoretical paradigms of international perspective on gender equality, the promise of modernisation, the impact of globalisation and the factors that promote gender equality. This book vividly depicts the differentials in Men's and Women's occupation and earning, exploitation of the earning penalties to women, education, experiences and human capital theory. The evidences of discrimination, gender typing and overcrowding with their implication of the USA internal labour market are comprehensively elaborated. A well attempt is made to present the legal remedies and social policies along with the legal facts and statistical data to show the gender discrimination and question of the gap between the legal provision and social policies in the labour market of USA in this book.

In this book Christa[80] first elaborate on the creation of new opportunities and comparative advantage of the free flow of capital, technology and free-flow of goods. She vividly narrated the opportunities which are particularly provided to the women with the initial launch of liberalisation, privatisation and globalistion first. Then she analysised the future of inequality, which can be created under the US dominant capital world trade, under which within a few minutes the economy of any country can be shattered. She presented the impact of the rising of economic gap between the rich and poor countries and its impact on the women life particularly in the poor countries. Christa draws her attention towards the impact of global technology on the employment of women and presented the impact of globalisation on the employment of women living in East Germany, Upper Lusatia, Bangladesh, Filippines, Brazil, Poland and Kuwait.

Research Questions

- What kind of problems women face at the workplace due to the gender discrimination?
- How women's respond to the discrimination to which they face at the workplace?
- What are the major hurdles to which working women are facing?
- What are the legal provisions which are enacted to protect the labour rights of women in India?
- What are the national and International standards and legal provisions for the protection and promotion of the rights of working women?
- Is there any institutional mechanism for the protection and promotion of the rights of working women at national and international levels?
- How the judiciary is responding to the issues related to the rights of working women?
- How much the labour laws are affected to protect the rights of working women in India?
- Whether women are given credit for their economic contribution to family and society?

Objectives of the Study

The objective of this study is to explicate the overall picture of the working women from the socio-political, legal and economic perspective. The main objectives of this study are:

- To study the importance of work participation of women in the economic activities of the nation.
- To understand the work participation of women in India in historical perspective.
- To explore and evaluate the impact of policy initiatives and legislative measures of the Indian government to protect the rights of working women.
- To study the factor which influence the work participation of women in India?
- To study the various legal provisions and policies which have been enacted to promote and protect the rights of working women in India.
- To study the International perspective on the women labour and work participation of women.
- To have a comparative understanding of national and international perspective on the women work participation and labour laws.
- To study the *de-jure* and *de-facto* enjoyment of special legal provision by working women in India.
- To study the patterns of work participation of women in India.
- To analysis the gap between the legal provisions and their implementation in India.

Relevance of the Study

The labour laws proved as a bone for the welfare, promotion and protection of the rights of the working women in India. Special attempts have been made to protect the rights of working women both in organised and unorganised sectors in the whole world. This study will be an attempt to understand the constitutional, legislative measures and policy initiatives taken for the protection and promotion of the rights of working women both in organised and unorganised sectors in India. This study will analyse the special laws and provisions which have been enacted at national and international level to promote the work participation of women.

Although a number of research studies are already available on the rights of working women in India, however, these studies are failed to establish a link between the women labour and labour laws. Simultaneously these studies are based on a single industry or either on some case studies, or a city or state. The present study will focus on the history of women labour and development of protective laws for working women in India along with the rise of the women movement at national and international levels. Moreover, this study will provide a comprehensive analysis of the national and international efforts which has been taken by the various national and international agencies for the promotion and protection of the rights of working women. It will provide an understanding of the work participation of women in the India and the problems to which working women are facing in the inside and outside of the workplace. Special emphasis will be given to analyse the policy initiatives and legislative measures of the state to increase the work participation of women in the liberalised, privatised and globalised economy.

Relevance of the study also emanates from the fact that the 21st century is called as the age of human rights and the women empowerment is on the core of the human rights. The work participation of this is a way to the economic liberty and freedom of women for the purpose a number of legal and policy initiatives have been taken at the national and international level to enhance the work participation of women. However, the various researches, census and the reports of NSSO holds that the work participation of women is decreasing despite of the rise in the education level of women this study will help us to understand the various factors which are responsible for the low work participation of women in India.

Methodology

Present study is an analytical study and is based on analytical, historical and comparative methods. As the whole study is theoretical and no field-work is conducted under the study so it is also a secondary study. Study materials will be collected from the variety of secondary sources including analysis of the publications of various governmental and non-governmental agencies at national and international levels related to women workforce. Besides the analysis of constitutional and statuary framework, governmental policies and programmes on the role of women in Indian economy. The analysis of the major decision and verdicts of the Courts on the protection of the rights of working women will be done. For this purpose books, journals, magazines, newspapers, government documents and the internet website will be used to collect the relevant research material.

Chapter Scheme

The study has been divided into 5 chapters in all.

Chapter 1 entitled introduction: Thinking about Women Labour and Labour Laws and it refers to the defining of labour, labour laws, labour market and gender division of labour. It includes the review of existing literature, research questions, and objectives of the study, methodology, relevance of the study and a brief introduction of the study.

Chapter 2 entitled "Work Participation of Women in India: A Historical Analysis", it is an attempt to analyse the work participation and economic rights of women in India. This chapter focuses upon the socio-religious; political and cultural factors which have imposed restriction on the work participation of women and non-recognising the economic importance of the women work in the ancient, medieval and modern India.

Chapter 3 entitled "Labour Laws and Women Labour: A National and International Perspective" present the national and international provision enacted to protect the rights of working women. A special emphasis is given to analyse the judicial verdicts on the rights of the working women in India.

Chapter 4 entitled "Working Women in India: A Present Scenario", it deals with analysis and pattern of work participation of women in India especially after 1980s. The policy initiatives of Indian Government for the development and empowerment of women after the Independence are duly focused upon in this chapter. A comprehensive analysis of the government initiatives to increase the work participation of women and its impact on the women labour force especially after the globalisation is critically evaluated in this chapter.

Chapter 5 is conclusion. The major findings of the study have been discussed and suggestions have been made for the better protection and promotion of the rights of the working women in India.

Notes

1. "The Status of Working Women in India", *euroasiapub.org/wp-content/uploads/2016/09/21ESSOct-2727-1.pdf,* Accessed: September 10, 2016, 10.00 am.
2 *"Chapter1IntroductionShodhganga"*, shodhganga.inflibnet.ac.in/bitstream/10603/48824/8/08_chapter1.pdf, *Accessed: September 10, 2016, 10.30 am.*
3. "Labour Legislation", *http://www.1911encyclopedia.org/Labour_Legislation,* Accessed: September 10, 2017, 10.00 am.
4. "What is labor? definition and meaning-Business Dictionary.com" *www.businessdictionary.com/definition/labor.htm,* Accessed: June 10, 2018, 10.00 am.
5. "Britannica Concise Encyclopedia, 3, Vol. VI, 2005", *https://en.wikipedia.org/wiki/Encyclopædia_Britannica,* Accessed: 6-15-2018, 10:51 am.
6. "Historical Development of Indian Labour Laws", *http://shodhganga.inflibnet.ac.in/bitstream/10603/57426/7/07_chapter%202.pdf,* Accessed: September 11, 2016, 09.30 am.
7. "O. Kahn-Freunds, Legal Framework, in A. Flanders and H. A. Clegg H.A. Clegg (eds.), The Systems of Industrial Relation in Great Britain: Its History, Law and Institutions (1954)", *journals.sagepub.com/doi/abs/10.1177/096466391037633,* Accessed: 12-3-2018, 10:00 am.
8. "Hornby Vs Close (1867) LR 2 QB 153", *ww.jstor.org/stable/1115083,* Accessed: June 11, 2018, 9.30 am.
9. "Taff Vale case I British law case [1900–1901]", *https://www.britannica.com/event/Taff-Vale-case,* Accessed: June 11, 2018, 10.00 am.
10. "Trade Union Act, 1871-ILO", *https://www.ilo.org/dyn/natlex/docs/ELECTRONIC/98373/117044/.../IRL98373.pdf,* Accessed: June 10, 2018, 10.30 am.
11. "Trade Disputes Act 1906-Wikipedia", *https://en.wikipedia.org/wiki/Trade_Disputes_Act_190,* Accessed: June 10, 2018, 11.00 am.

12. A.C.L. Davies, *Perspectives on Labour Law* (2nd edition), Cambridge University Press, Cambridge, United Kingdom, 2009, p. 5.
13. "Royal Commission on Trade Unions and Employers' Associations...", *https://en.wikipedia.org/.../Royal_Commission_on_Trade_Unions_and_Employers%2*.Accessed: June 11, 2018, 9:24 am.
14. Davies and Freedland, *Labour Legislation, Labour Legislation and Public Policy*, Clarendon Press, 1993, p. 42.
15. "Report of Royal Commission on Trade Union and Employers' Associations".
16. *Employment Act*, Section 11.
17. "Department of Employment, and Industrial Relations in the 1990: *Proposal for Further Reform of Industrial Relations and Trade Union Law* (1991)", *https://www.eurofound.europa.eu/.../changes-in-national-collective-bargaining-system*, Accessed: June 11, 2018, 9:34 am.
18. "Definition of 'Labour Market'—The Economic Times", *economictimes.indiatimes.com › Definitions › Economy, Budget*, Accessed: September 11, 2018, 10.00 am.
19. "The Beijing Platform for Action: inspiration then and now" UN Women...beijing20.unwomen.org/en/about, also see: Gender budgeting-Wikipedia *https://en.wikipedia.org/wiki/Gender_budgeting* Accessed: June 11, 2018, 9:40 am
20. *Ibid.*
21. "About Labour Law After Labour-UCLA Institute for Research on Labour", *www.irle.ucla.edu/events/2014/documents/OUPtypesetdraft.pdf*, Accessed: September 11, 2016, 11.00 am.
22. "Labour Law after Labour-Osgood Digital Commons-York University", *digitalcommons.osgoode.yorku.ca/cgi/viewcontent.cgi?article=1053&context=clpe*, Accessed: September 11, 2016, 11.30 am.
23. Madhudan Pandit, *Human Rights and Social Justice*, Swastik Publications, Delhi, 2011, pp. 91-93.
24. Asha Kapur Mehta, "Globalisation and Women", Raj Mohini (ed.), *Globalisation Culture and Women's Development*, Rawat Publications, Jaipur, 1999, pp. 54-61.
25. D. Padmavathi, "Empowerment of Women Through Micro Finance", Rameswari Pandya (ed.), *Women Welfare and Empowerment in India Vision for 21st Century*, New Century Publications, New Delhi, 2008, pp. 331-333.
26. "International Labor Organisation facts, information, pictures...", *https://www.encyclopedia.com/social-sciences...government/.../international-labor*, Accessed: June 11, 2018, 10:00 am.
27. Christa Wiichterich, *The Globalised Woman: Reports from a future of Inequality, Spinifex Press Australia*, Zed Books, London & New York, 2000, pp. 111-113.

28. Jane Harrigan and Paul Mosley, "Evaluating the Impact of World Bank Structural Adjustment Leading: 1980-87", *The Journal of Development Studies,* vol. II, no. 3, April, 1991, pp. 63-94.
29. T. Kusago and Z. Tzannatos, *Export Processing Zones: A Review in Need of Update,* World Bank Discussion Paper No. 9802, World Bank, Washington, DC, January, 1998, pp. 673-722.
30. D.Madani, *A Review of the Role and Impact of Export Processing Zones,* World Bank Policy Research Paper no. 2238, World Bank, Washington DC, 1999, pp. 542-592, also see: N. Heyzer, *Daughters in Industry: Work, Skills and Consciousness of Women Workers in Asia,* Asian and Pacific Development Centre, Kuala Lumpur, 1988, pp. 192-197.
31. "WEF, Women's Employment: Measuring the Global Gender Gap", World Economic Forum, http://www.weforum.org/pdf/ Global_Competitiveness_Report/ *Report/gender_gap.pdf,* Accessed:18-6-2016, 10:15 am.
32. Hooshang Amirahmadi and Wu Weiping, "Export Processing Zones in Asia". *Asian Survey,* vol. XXXV, no. 9, 1995, pp. 828-49, also see: D. Bhattacharya and Mustafizur Rahman, "Female Employment under Export-Propelled Industrialisation: Prospects for Internalizing Global Opportunities in the Apparel Sector in Bangladesh", *Occasional paper 10,* The United Nations Research Institute for Social Development (UNRISD), Geneva, 1999, pp. 87-92., P.Lang and S. Young "Foreign Direct Investment and Technology Transfer: A Case Study of Foreign Direct Investment in North East China", *Transnational Corporations,* vol. V, no.1, 1996, pp. 57–83.
33. T. Kusago and Z. Tzannatos, *Export Processing Zones: A Review in Need of Update,* World Bank Discussion, Paper No. 9802, World Bank Washington DC, January 1998, pp. 673-722.
34. "Impact of Special Economic Zones on Employment, Poverty-ICRIER", *icrier.org/pdf/Working_Paper_194.pd, Accessed: 23-10-2016,* 10:00 am.
35. Gurappa Naidu, "Globalisation and its Impact on Indian Society", The *Indian Journal of Political Science,* vol. XXXXXXVII, no.1, JAN.-MAR., 2006, pp. 65-76, also see: Chandan Sengupta "Conceptualising Globalisation: Issues and Implications", *Economic and Political Weekly,* vol. XXXVI, no. 33, 18-24 August., 2001, pp. 3137-3143, Sanjeev Kumar Sharma, "Demystifying the Globalisation Myth", *The Indian Journal of Political Science,* vol. XXXXXXV, no. 4, Oct.-Dec., 2004, pp. 659-661.
36. *Ibid.,* pp. 93-95.
37. ILO-WEP, "Informal Sector and Urban Employment: A Review of Activities in Urban Informal Sector", International Labour Office, Geneva, 1990.

38. Yin Shen, *The Way to Buddhahood*, Wisdom Publications, Somerville, 2006, p. 23.
39. See Articles 22-28 of *UDHR*.
40. See Articles 34, 37, 38 of *ICESCR*.
41. Articles 14, 15(1), 15(3), 16, 39(a), 39(d), 42, 51A(e) of *Indian Constitution*.
42. Chauhan, O.P and Dadwal Lalit, *Human Rights: Promotion and Protection*, Anmol Publishers, New Delhi, 2004, p. 45.
43. It is this incaused violation of right to livelihood that an organisation called PWESCR, (Programme on Women's Economic, Social Cultural Rights) in partnership with several other organisations globally has initiated an international network on women's right to livelihood, *www.pwescr.com*. Accessed:15-12-2018.
44. "The Status of Working Women in India", *euroasiapub.org/wp-content/uploads/2016/09/21ESSOct-2727-1.pdf*," Accessed: December 16, 2018, 10.00 am.
45. June 2013, "Special Issue of Finance and Development", *A Journal* of *IMF, International Monetary Fund*.
46. *United Nations Charter, Preamble*
47. United Nations Committee on the Elimination of Discrimination Against Women: General Recommendation No. 19 on Violence against Women (Eleventh Session, New York January 1992), Document No. CEDAW/1992/L-1/Add. 1
48. "Vishakha vs. State of Rajasthan", AIR SC 1986.
49. ILO Conventions, No. 87, 98, 100, 105, and 111.
50. R. Panday and S. Patel, *Women in the Unorganised Sector in India*, New Century Publications, New Delhi, 2010, pp. 55-57.
51. Hemlata, G., "Hazards faced by working women in era of globalisation, People's Democracy", Vol. XXX, No.17, *Weekly Organ of Communist Party of India* (M), 2003.
52. "Use Surveys in National Statistical System in India 24-Ministry of..."*wcd.nic.in/Schemes/research/TUS%20Report.pdf*, Accessed: 12-12-2016, 10.30 am.
53. Anupma Hazra, *India's Social Sector and Millennium Development Goals*, Rawat Publications, Jaipur, 2013.
54. Monica Chawla, *Women and Protective Laws*, Regal Publications, New Delhi, 2013.
55. M.R. Biju, *Globalisation, Democracy and Gender Justice*, New Century Publication, New Delhi, 2012.
56. Tinku Paul Bhatnagar, *Women Employment and Empowerment*, New Century Publications, New Delhi, 2011.
57. A.N. Das, *Global Campaign for Women's Human Rights*, MD Publications Pvt. Ltd., New Delhi, 2010.
58. T. Lavanya, *Women Empowerment through Entrepreneurship*, New Century Publications, New Delhi, 2010.

59. Indrani Mazumdar, *Women Workers and Globalisation: Emergent Contradictions in India,* Centre for Women's Development Studies, New Delhi, 2007.
60. Monica Chawla, *Gender Justice: Women and Law,* Deep & Deep Publications Pvt. Ltd., New Delhi, 2006.
61. Nomita Aggarwal, *Women and Law in India,* New Century Publications, New Delhi, 2002
62. Neera Desai and Usha Thakkar, *Women in Indian Society,* National Book Trust, New Delhi, 2001.
63. Shri Kudchedkar and Subiha AL-Issa, *Violence against Women: Women Against Violence,* Pencraft International, New Delhi, 1998.
64. Pam Rajput & Hem Lata Sawrup, *Women and Globalisation,* Ashish Publishing House, New Delhi, 1994.
65. Vinoj Abraham, "Missing Labour or Consistent De-Feminisation?" *Economic and Political Weekly,* vol. XLVIII, no. 31, August, 2013.
66. Yamini Mishra and Navanita Sinha, "Gender Responsive Budgeting in India", *Economic and Political Weekly,* vol. XLVII, no. 17, April, 2012.
67. Himanshu, "Employment Trends in India: A Re-examination", *Economic and Political Weekly,* vol. XLVI, no. 37, September, 2011.
68. Nalini Nayak, "Unorganised Sector Workforce in India", *Economic and Political Weekly,* vol. XLI no. 21, May, 2006.
69. Nirmala Banerjee, "Whatever Happened to the Dreams of Modernity—The Nehruvian Era and Women's Position?" *Economic and Political Weekly,* vol. XXXIII, no. 17, April, 1998.
70. Bahnisikha Ghosh and Sudhin K. Mukhopadhyay, "Displacement of the Female in the Indian Labour Force", *Economic and Political Weekly,* vol. XIX No. 47, November, 1984.
71. Rajeshwari Deshpande, "Social Security for the Unorganised Sector", *Economic and Political Weekly,* vol. XL, no. 22, May, 2005.
72. A.C.L. Davies, *Perspectives on Labour Law,* Cambridge University Press, Cambridge, United Kingdom, Second Edition, 2009
73. Margaret Abraham, (ed.), *Contours of Citizenship: Women, Diversity and Practices of Citizenship,* Ashgate Publishing Limited, Surrey, England, 2010.
74. Lucy Mclynn, *Working Time and Holidays: A Practical Legal Guide,* Oxford University Press, New York, 2009
75. James A. Gross, (ed.), *Workers' Rights as Human Rights,* Cornell University Press, United States of America, 2003.
76. Shagun Ahuja and Nidhi Rawat, *Labour Laws: Recruitment, Wages and Industrial Relations,* Regal Publications, New Delhi, 2015.
77. Indira Hiraway, (ed.) *Mainstreaming Unpaid Work: Time-use Data in Developing Policies,* Oxford University Press, New Delhi, 2017.
78. Dr. Meenakshi Gupta, *Women Rights under Labour Laws,* Regal Publication, New Delhi, 2016.

79. Janet Zollinger Giele and Leslie F. Stebbins, *Women and Equality in the Workplace*, Oxford University Press, London, 2003.
80. Christa Wiichterich, *The Globalised Woman: Reports from a future of Inequality, Spinifex Press Australia,* Zed Books, London & New York, 2000.

Chapter 2

Work Participation of Women in India

A Historical Analysis

Women in the workforce earning wages or salary are part of a modern phenomenon, one that developed at the same time as the growth of paid employment for men, but women have been challenged by inequality in the workforce. Until modern times, legal and cultural practices, combined with the inertia of longstanding religious and educational conventions, restricted women's entry and participation in the workforce. Economic dependency upon men and consequently the poor socio-economic and political status of women have had the same impact, particularly as occupations have become professionalised over the 19th and 20th centuries.

Women's lack of access to higher education had effectively excluded them from the practice of well-paid and high status occupations. Entry of women into the higher professions like, law and medicine was delayed in most countries due to women being denied entry to universities and qualification for degrees; for example, Cambridge University only fully validated degrees for women late in 1947, and even then only after much opposition and acrimonious debate.[1]

Women were largely limited to low-paid and poor status occupations for most of the 19th and 20th centuries, or earned less pay than men for doing the same work. However, through the 20th century, public perceptions of paid work shifted as the workforce increasingly moved to office jobs that do not require heavy labour, and women increasingly acquired the higher education that led to better-compensated, longer-term careers rather than lower-skilled, shorter-term jobs. Despite this, women are still at a disadvantage compared to men because of motherhood. Women are viewed as the primary caregiver to children still to this day, so their pay is lowered when they have children because businesses do not expect them to stay long after the birth.[2]

The other most important indication of the work participation is upliftment of the status of the person who is involved in production. As economists regards the rising productivity as a sign of a healthy economy, for the two reasons. First, it is the source of improvements in everyone's standard of living. Standards of living improve when the real wage rate rises. This occurs whenever there is an increase in the demand of labour. As demand increases more rapidly than supply, employers will have to offer more money in order to attract more workers into labour market.

It is pertinent to mention that the economic development also occurs under a socio-political set-up and the fruit of the economic development may vary to the socio-political position of the social groups and individuals. Historically women had been under the patriarchal set-up from the ancient to modern period of the world history. Their struggle for equality is a continue phenomenon for the women movement across the world even after the post-industrial and post-modern world. India is not exception to the world history and women have been discriminated by the patriarchal set-up throughout the history of India even after the 70 years of independence women are facing the discrimination, violence in the every realm of life.

The work-participation of women is one of the important issues nowadays across the world. Men and women have been working together throughout the history to build the family and society. In the historical sense women been the complete partner from the house-hold task to allied domestic activities and agriculture. Although the issue of the work participation of women is directly linked with the economic rights but as argued above the history of economic development is linked with the socio-economic and political set-up of the society, the same is true in case of the economic rights and work participation of women.

In the Indian history women have been presented as the house maker mother, sister and wife and never been as an economic actor.

Although their work and creativity have been recognised as a greatest artistic work but economic aspect of their work has never been highlighted. They worked inside the wall and their production has been sold by the male members of the house. From weaving and knitting of the clothes for family and market women do all the chores which were essential to maintain the economy of the family but they never claimed their share in the income and property of the family. The most shocking is that even after the 30s years of Independence, the domestic and allied activities of the women were not included in the category of un-paid work by the Census of India.

The status and rights of women in Indian society have undergone many changes and have always remained a matter of great concern for the socio-religious and political elites of India. The role played by a woman in her personal and family spheres has a great impact on society. Her affection, love, care and dedication for the family not only groom the personality of her children and help her family to develop, but also help in the all-round development of society at large. A study of the rights and roles of women in any society must be examined in relation to social organisations of society, which in turn is based upon socio-economic and political set-up of that society. A comprehensive analysis of the development of women rights in India needs a systematic study of socio-economic and political set-up of Indian society. In this chapter an attempt has been made to gauge the degree and level of the rights of women at different stages and periods of social evolution which are ancient, medieval and modern.

Women in Ancient India

The religious texts and the available literature on ancient India have assigned women a subordinate identity as these texts define the role of Aryan men in detail but women are ignored as the other subaltern classes. The holy Indian scripture *Bhagwad Gita* places Women, *Vaisyas* and *Sudras* in one category. According to another text, the punishment for killing either a women or a *Sudra* is the same.[3] Woman was never recognised as an independent identity. The subordination of women to men is clearly depicted in the *Manu Smriti*. Manu stated that a woman should never be independent:

as a daughter she should be under the surveillance of her father, as a wife of her husband and as a widow of her son.[4]

Some other historical evidences suggest that during the Vedic period women had an equal status to men. They were allowed to study the *Vedas* and participate in philosophical discussions. Even some hymns of the *Rig Veda* were composed by women. After finishing their education, they could either enter married life or devote themselves to religious and metaphysical studies just like men.[5]

According to the Vedic rituals the bride should be a grown-up woman, mature in body and mind. She is called a *Kanya,* who chooses a husband for herself. Religious scriptures and epics not only consider the wife and husband of equal status but also lay emphasis on her dignity and respect in social and personal life.[6]

Social Status of Women

The creation of universe has been described by the Aryans as the union of *Prakrti* and *Purusha*. Woman is supposed to be *Prakrti* and man *Purusha*; the union of these two has created the home and made the world. According to ancient ideals, the wife is the other half of man and hence as long as he does not obtain her, he is incomplete. The epic literature also depicts that a man's other half is his wife; therefore, she is called *ardhangini.*

A wife in ancient India was also known as *Sahadharmini* as she was held to be one with her husband not only physically but also spiritually. During the Vedic period, women enjoyed all the religious rights and privileges which men possessed. Her presence and co-operation were regarded necessary in performance of religious rites and ceremonies. The *Rigveda* refers to Ghosha and Lapamudra as well-versed in the vedic *mantras*. Man could not become a spiritual whole unless he was accompanied by his wife. Thus in the age of the *Samhitas* and *Brahmanas,* the religious status of women was as high as of men.[7] In *Manu Samriti,* a women is always important to her husband, since without a wife, a man is not considered a complete entity of society. Without her by his side as his partner in the performance of religious rituals, he could not fulfil his religious obligations.

Though Manu did not have a high opinion of female intellect, he insisted that women should be honoured. Manu assigns them the highest position of respect and says that a mother should, in no case, be outlawed even if she has fallen from moral rectitude.[8] The *Mahabharata* also says that one who desires prosperity must honour and respect a woman and consider her as the goddess of fortune.[9]

Buddha emphasises the principle of reciprocity. Buddha expresses the view that the wife has duties towards her husband and *vice versa*. The equal burden of responsibility and duty is the hallmark of Buddha's vision about the role of women in family life.[10]

A Hindu Marriage in ancient India was to be indissoluble; it was supposed to continue even after death. The *Rig Veda* and *Atharva Veda* entertained very high ideals about the sanctity of marriage. The *Sutra* literature condemns the practice of divorce. The *Apastamba* says that if the marriage vow was transgressed, both husband and wife would certainly go to hell.[11] Manu also did not cherish the idea of divorce. There is only one clear reference to remarriage of women, but there is enough literature in the *Manu Smriti* to prove that by and large it is against remarriage. However, Manu and Yajnavalkya both lay down that a man may abandon his wife if a serious disease of her was not disclosed by her parents before marriage or if there is a loss of integrity on her part.

Women were not provided with the social security in case her husband abandoned her, she was not entitled to any compensation. We have the bitter example of the wife of King Rama, who abandoned his wife, just on the provocation of a washer man, who questioned about the chastity of the Rama's wife (Sita), even without giving any factual evidence. The great-great king Rama has abandoned his wife without giving any social security to her.[12] Simultaneously, Manu allowed a woman to abandon her husband if he was insane (*unmatta*), impotent (*kliba, abija*) or suffering from an incurable or contagious disease (*paparogi*). According to the *Manu Smriti*, there were five cases of legal sanction. A wife is allowed to take a second husband if her husband is missing (*nashta*), or dead (*mrta*), or becomes an ascetic (*pravrajita*), or is impotent (*kliba*) or is degraded from the Caste (*patita*).[13] Kautilya also spoke on divorce (*moksha*), which could be obtained only in case of mutual enmity and hatred between husband and wife. But he maintains that marriage of the *Arsha* and *Prajapatya* forms cannot be dissolved at all.[14]

Women folk pass through many difficulties while abandoning their husbands. The religious scriptures and social norms imposed many restrictions on women in case of the death of husband or abandonment by husband. She needs to wait for long time; she is deprived of the rights which the women of modern India enjoy. *Yajur Veda* says that a woman shall wait for five years for second marriage in the case if her husband left her without any reason and went to any undisclosed place or lost. *Narade Smriti* says "When the husband is lost or dead, or turned a recluse, or impotent, or fallen from caste, a woman can take a second husband. The Brahmin woman shall wait for eight years for her husband who is gone abroad; if she has no issue she shall wait for four years".[15]

The position of widows has changed considerably from the time of the *Rig Veda*, confusion over the remarriage of widow prevailed during the period as it did not define the norms of widow remarriage and her rights over the husband's property; however, the practice of *Nagoya* remained popular, with the choice of husband for remarriage. But marriage by the widow from outside of her late husband's home remained debarred.[16] One cannot put the *Atharv Veda* in line with *Rig Veda* as it has remained silent over the rights and remarriage of widow. The period of *Dharmasastras* can be coded as the age of confusion and the stage from where the violation of the rights of women started. The *Manu Smriti* and other great epics of the time like *Dharmasutra* are not clear about the rights of women, as they approve them at one place and disapprove the same at another place.[17]

The rules about remarriage in the *Arthshastra* closely follow those laid down in *Dharmasutras.* They permit remarriage of a woman whose husband is dead, has become an ascetic or has gone abroad, after a period of waiting which varies according to circumstances.[18]

The *Dharmashastras,* Manu and Yajnavalkya forbid the marriage of widows but Narada permits it; following it, even later like *Parasara Smriti* and *Agni* lay down that a woman can remarry even during the life time of her husband if he is lost, has become an ascetic, is impotent or is an outcaste. Such remarriage was called *Punarbhu*.

The post-Vedic period, particularly of *Dhamarshashtras,* witnessed deterioration in the statutes of woman: her economic, social and political rights were badly negated by the established social customs and political establishments of the time. The birth of a daughter was regarded as a source of misery and that of a son as an object of desire.

Manu says it is against the norms and values of society to give economic benefits to a *Kanya* (Daughter). Although he was against dowry and hold that the evil practice of dowry is an economic transition, which converts woman into a commodity.

According to Manu, a woman must be honoured and adorned by her father, brothers, husband and brothers-in-law. Where women are honoured the gods are pleased but where they are not honoured, no sacred rite yields any reward. The house in which women are not duly honoured is accursed and perishes completely.

Thus Manu lays emphasis on the worshipping of women. At the same time Manu was not in favour of women's independence. In his words 'Na Satri Swatyam Arhat'—Women deserve no independence.

As a girl, young woman or even as an aged woman (as a mother), nothing shall be done by her independently. In childhood she is subjected to her father, in youth to her husband and when her husband is dead, to her sons, women must never be independent. Manu viewed that women were ornaments of the house that were to be kept safe and looked after with utmost care and vigilance.

Manu imposes some duties on women:

- Woman should consider her marriage as a sacrament and should discharge the duties befitting her life.
- For a woman, her husband should be everything.
- As a wife she should ever remain obedient to her husband, must never do anything that might displease him, be faithful to his memory after his death and never think of any other man.

Manu gives the circumstances under which a women is likely to go astray, which are considered as the six causes of her ruin, drinking, associating with immoral people, separating from her husband, roaming around, sleeping late and dwelling with other men, in the company of such women no sacramental rites should be performed.

Manu has pictured the low status of women. As he has said woman must worship her husband as god and she has no freedom to move out of the four walls of her house; if she does so, she can be punished. According to *Manu Smriti,* woman as a daughter, wife and widow is totally dependent on the male and an ideal women is one who is an ideal wife. The social, legal and religious status of woman was distinctively lower than that of a man.[19]

Regarding the practice of *sati,* or self-immolation, there is no direct reference to it in Vedic literature. It is contended by some that the practice of burning of widows was prevalent even in the early Vedic and Post-Vedic age. But, as Altekar has maintained, the customs of *niyoga* and remarriage has become unpopular gradually from the beginning of the Christian era. A widow was considered as a burden and she did not receive any sympathy in society, if she continued to live in the family of her husband, she had to work as a drudge. If she lived separately, she was given a pittance as her maintenance.[20]

Economic Status of Women

The right to property or inheritance was a matter of confusion in ancient India. The religious scriptures of the time do not give any clear reference to the rights of daughter, sister, wife and widow over the property of her father or husband. No reference of individual owning of property or commercial activity by women in ancient India are available.

Women were provided with equal rights of property in their association with husband and were also provided with the right to share in property of her father with their brothers. But confusion could be created, when one thought about independent status or independent economic rights of women. The husband was required to take a solemn vow at the time of marriage that he would never transgress the rights and interest of his wife in economic matters. In Vedic India wife was generally regarded as the co-owner of the family property along with her husband. *Taittiriya Samhita* holds wife as the mistress of the household and *Jamini* refers to it for establishing the contention that women could actually own property. They used to receive wedding gifts called *Purinahya* which later came to be known as *Stridhana.* However, Vedic texts do not confirmed any legal rights of wife over her husband's property. The religious texts of Jainism hold the wife as a partner in all legal functions. In the matter of adoption, her powers were co-extensive with those of the husband whether he was alive or dead. She has full rights over her *stridhana* which was of five kinds. The confusion over the right to property of Hindu women is also found in Kautilya's *Arthashastra*. Although he made a clear reference on women rights over the property of her deceased husband, however, he denied the very rights of women over her dowry and husband property if she disapproves the husband selected by her father-in-law and choose husband of her choice.[21] A woman was subject to the control of her husband as regarded her *Stridhana*. Manu says that women should never hold property which is common to many, nor from their own property without their husband's permission.[22] Yajnavalkya recognised the rights of wife on husband's property. He held that irrespective of the *Stridhana* wife has legitimate claim and can have an equal share to her son in the division of property if the property is divided during the life-time of her husband. But Yajnavalkya was against the independent economic status of women and wrote that the wife can only claim the property of her husband if she carries out the command of her husband even after he has renounced the wife.[23]

Further developments ın the *Smriti* laws on *Stridhana* were made by Katyayana. He defines many type of *Stridhana* like given to women before the nuptial fire, given to her at the time of the bride procession and given by brothers, grandmother and grandfather.[24]

Manu and Katyayana wrote that widows and sonless women do not deserve any rights of property.[25] In the Vedic literature unmarried daughters have no right of inheritance. Daughters could normally get property only by way of gifts from their relations at or subsequent to their marriage. However, a brotherless daughter was recognised as the first heir. For all religious purpose, the Vedic father could, thus, regard a daughter to be as good as a son.[26] *Smritis* and *Putrika* also mention the rights of a daughter living in her father's house; she or her son is deemed to be a son of the father for all purposes, secular as well as spiritual. The only exception we come across is a solitary reference in the text of the *Rigvada* of a brotherless daughter sometimes coming back and living with her parents. Some references are available in the *Mahabharata* where the daughters inherited kingdoms. The great

Yudhishthira of *Mahabharata* epic was asked to place daughters of the deceased kings on their thrones. The Buddha and Jain Agama literature is practically silent on the rights of inheritance of a daughter. Yajnavalkya also gives a share to the brotherless daughter in her father's property.[27]

The analysis of the legal and religious scriptures of ancient India reveals that women were provided with very few rights in the economic sphere. Although women were considered to be the better half of her husband's and also as the chief managers of the house, but in the law of inheritance they had no right over the property of their husbands in case a woman became a widow and in case her husband abandoned her. Women's rights to property were in full control of the male members of their family; so their right to property was limited to the right to *Stridhana* only.

Political Status of Women

Only a casual reference is there on the role of women in the politics of ancient India as the established political order and the socio-religious customs did not accept the appearance of women in public life. The compulsion of male heir under the dynastic and monarchical set-up of the ancient Indian society limited the role of Indian women to that of the princess or the queen. The role of the woman was either limited to helping her male associate or for praying to God for the victory of her husband.

The political thinkers of ancient India like Narada, Kautilya and Sukra suggested the succession of the crown only to the male descendants. Hence ancient Indian history does not furnish any instances of female sovereigns and administrators.

The Vedic age, however, presents a glimpse of women in political and administrative spheres and later in the Epic Age Kautilya was strict against trusting women for the state duty. Yajnavalkya and Vasistha did not allow the women to appear as witnesses, only Manu granted women the right of giving evidence but that also in exceptional cases when male witnesses were not available.[28]

As a general rule succession to the throne was confined to males.[29] The Aryan society, being patriarchal, does not furnish many names of female rulers. However, the Kings and Princes were influenced by their mothers and queens. The first Vedic reference comes as a simile in a hymn to Asvinau: Queen Visapala accompanied the King in a chariot to the forefront and lost her leg; nevertheless, her sacrifice struggle helped the king to win the war. The second detailed reference is of Mudgalani, also known as Indrasena's wife Mudgala, helped her husband in hunting and fighting against the robbers. When her husband was put in a tight corner, she took up her husband's bow and arrows giving a fierce battle to the robbers, defeating them and rescuing the state property. This shows women were trained in use of weapons and at times proved their skills.[30]

In later Vedic literature, women were mostly confined to the household, however, in the royal household, *Mahishi* (Chief Queen) was considered as a limb of the state. She ranked among those who helped the king, along with the Purohita, the Rajanya, the Suta, the Gramini and Samgrahitri and together they sustained the kingship. From this, it becomes clear that the royal ladies, especially Mahishi, Vavata and Parivrikti, continued exercising their powers as King's councillors. Ratnins were in Hindu polity a council for advising the King and helping him in the composition of the *Sabha* (the assembly). At the king's death, on the succession of the new ruler to the throne, the authority of ratnins was most felt.[31]

In the Buddhist literature, it appears that religion was mingled with political rights. It is due to the mingling of religious and political life that a few Queens like Mahapraja Gautami, Kshema Bhadda, Kundalakesa etc. embracing the Buddhist order have their appearance in the sacred texts. Regarding the political status of women, the views of Lord Buddha remained very negative and he disliked the idea of women participating in politics.[32]

Women in Medieval India

The period of Medieval India (1206-1761 AD) has been depicted as a dark period of Indian history. India became a soft target to successive invaders, some of them assimilated into Hindu culture, but the Muslims, adhering to their rigidity could not interact with Hinduism and remained a separate entity. The question of cultural supremacy between the Hindus and the Muslims created the sense of belongingness. While articulating their identity and creating the socio-religious boundaries, both the Hindus and the Muslims tried to create a concept of purity and pollution with a non-assimilating view of each other community. The sense of nation purity and the nation making through the gender purity had been developed during this period.

The non-accommodative views of both the communities had a lot of effect on the status of women indirectly and directly along with the other social implications on Hindu society. The Mughal invaders created a sense of social insecurity as the invaders looted the women along with the property of the Hindus. The emotional set-backs which the Hindu families, particularly of north-India, faced due to the abduction and looting of their women folk by the Muslim invaders resulted in many problems. The evil practice of infanticide and *purda* (veil) was developed during the medieval period. The Muslim conquerors attempted to impose their coercive norms on the conquered Hindu population, which resulted into more rigidity and conservatism of the Hindu society.[33]

The status and rights of women in medieval India can be grouped into four categories along with the socio-religious, economic and political set-up of medieval India. Among these categories one is of the upper caste and upper class Hindus and the second that of the lower caste and lower class Hindus. The third group is of the elite women from royal families in Muslim community and the fourth of the Muslim women from the commoners and poor families.

Social Status of Women

The social status of women in medieval India was largely castigated along the socio-religious divisions of the Indian society. The good and evil aspect of medieval Indian society had to do a lot with the caste and class of the women, if they were provided with some privileges due to their caste and class they were also deprived of many other privileges due the their caste and class. Although the economic and political role played by the women from the Muslim royalty had changed the perception of women in the Indian society. But no new development occurred during this period as the role of women was restrained in comparison with the much larger than role in ancient India.

The ladies of royalty enjoyed an exalted position in the Mughal courts. These women were not only provided with the materialistic comforts but also the opportunities of mental and spiritual growth. Moreover, the avenues of business and commerce were also open to their excellence. Some of the women from the royalty were even trained in warfare and political administration.[34] The women under the Hindu rulers were deprived of the rights which the elite women enjoyed during the Vedic and ancient period. In comparison to the women of Muslim royalty, the women from the elite Hindu families were more deprived of the social and economic rights, which were available even to the women from the low castes of Hindu society.

The respect of women as mothers continued and they enjoyed respect both among the Hindus and the Muslims in medieval India as it was in ancient India. In all the sections of Hindu society, mothers and other elderly ladies were given utmost respect and their commands were invariably carried out.

The Rajputs particularly showed great regard to their mothers and never dared to go against their wishes. There are many instances which show that the Rajput rulers did not do anything without consulting their mothers. For example Rana Sangram Singh of Mewar always took his meals after paying respect to his mother. The Muslims also showed great respect to their mothers.[35]

Marriage and Divorce

The conservatism and the social insecurity which was created after the establishment of the Mughal Empire resulted in restraints and encroachments upon women rights at large. One such heinous crime against the girl child and violation of the human rights of women was the child marriage. During the medieval ages child marriage became a popular feature of the Hindu society, although it had no religious sanction and had no mention in the Vedic age.

The parents who were afraid of alien rulers married their daughters at a very early age. Girls were generally married before they reached the age of nine or ten years. Both Hindus and Muslims fallen a prey to this evil practice. Among the Hindus sometimes daughters were married even before they had learned to walk and talk.[36]

Widow Remarriage was virtually non-existent among the Hindus. A Hindu widow had either to lead the life of celibacy for the rest of her life or to be burnt on the funeral pyre of dead husband.[37] Widow marriage was permitted amongst the Muslims but the widows were given the status of a second wife.[38]

The Hindus by and large practiced monogamy (one wife). However, a small section of Hindu population consisting of princes and wealthy persons married more than one woman. The Hindus of middle class married a second time only if their first wife proved to be barren or died. This was also done with the consent of the Brahamans. However, the Muslims who were permitted by *Quran* to have four wives at a time generally practiced monogamy. Only rich Muslims took to polygamy having (more than two wives) and maintained three or four wives at a time.

Divorce was rather uncommon among the Hindus, even though it was quite a regular feature amongst the Shias than among the Sunnis. In matters of divorce, the husband enjoyed absolute and unquestioned power.

The wives were denied such a right.[39] Irrespective of the above sufferings of women, there were many kinds of uncoded and unreported cases where women were not provided with any legal support and no defined legal text has been found in the history of medieval India, which prescribed the punishment to the male members of the family against exploitation of their female counterparts. The other reason was the silencing of the voice of women under the garb of family honour and women's dignity etc.

The matter of social prestige and the lack of voice and support to the women resulted in the violation of human rights of women at large. The evil practices of infanticide, *Sati* and *Jauhar* were connected with religion and family honour.

Particularly the Rajputs killed their daughters due to the scarcity of suitable matches or due to wars with the tribes and outsiders etc. In case of the defeat of a Rajput king, the whole women folk of the royalty were supposed to perform a *Jauhar*. In many cases, the male members of the family themselves pushed all the women of the family into fire in case of their defeat in war.[40]

Parda

Parda was the symbol of the lower status of women which was religiously preserved by the Muslim women across all the sections of the Muslim society. Although the practice of *Parda* was not common among the Hindus, their women used it as a protective measure to save their honour and hide their beauty from the foreign invaders. The practice of *Parda* among the Hindu women started particularly after the advent of the Turks in India. It also appears as a tendency to imitate the ruling class; abundant references to the observance of *Parda* are found in the accounts of contemporary foreign travellers.[41] *Parda* was mainly confined to the rich and well-to-do classes.[42]

Sati

Another grave tragedy in the lives of Hindu women was the death of their husbands. Unlike the Muslims, widow-remarriage was not permitted among the Hindus during the Mughal period except among some lower castes. A widow had to burn herself with the dead body of her husband otherwise she had to lead a life of misery and was treated with contempt by the other members of the family.

Widowhood was considered a great sin of the early life of a woman. The life of a widow was full of miseries; she was not only deprived of all the luxuries which she enjoyed with her husband, but also taunted by the Hindu society as a burden on the earth. In these circumstances, the widows were forced to perform the *sati*[43] and in case a widow refused to perform the *sati* and exempted from *sati* due to some reason, she was forced to live a pitiable life, was not allowed to grow her hair long or to put on ornaments or good dresses.[44]

The practice of performing *Sati* voluntarily was an ancient practice, but gradually it became a forced custom and women were forced to commit *sati* after the death of their husbands even against their wishes. It was mostly performed by the women of the Brahmin, Kshatriya and Bania community. The evils of *Sati* even continued during the period of Mughal emperors, although they issued many verdicts against it and even many women refused to burn themselves along with the dead body of their husbands.[45]

Akbar issued an order that a woman should not be forced to perform *sati*. Jahangir issued an order against the *Sati* under which he banned the performance of *Sati* by the young widow and made the permission of the king compulsory before performing of *sati*, especially in case of young widows. Aurangzeb also issued an order under which the widows who had children were banned to perform *sati*. The efforts of the Mughal emperors could not bear much fruit as they lacked a comprehensive strategy and strong will. Simultaneously, the religious differences between the rulers and ruled also became a major hurdle in the banning of *sati* during the medieval period.[46]

Dowry

The marriage of the girls sometimes becomes difficult because of the custom of dowry (Dahej). It is given at the time of marriage of the girl by her parents. It consisted of gifts given by the parents to the bride: like jewels, ornaments, furniture, elephants, horses, maids and other articles of luxury. It was an old custom and gradually it became rigorous. Dowry system was prevalent more among the commoners than the elite. The nature of dowry differed with the economic status of the parents. In opposition to the dowry was selling of girls to the grooms and it was prevalent mostly among the lower classes in the region now comprising of the states of Uttar Pradesh and Bihar. Under the system the aged and moneyed grooms could marry young girls by giving money to girl's parents. There was also a curious custom of giving away a younger sister of the bride to the bridegroom as a part of dowry.[47]

Education of Women

Women education was a distant dream both for the Hindu and the Muslims during the medieval India. The education of the girls was restrained to the learning of elementary reading and the reading of the *Koran* and the Hindu women even did not have this right.[48] But the women from the royal families were allowed to have literary activities in their harems and tutors were allowed to give tuitions in the harems of the rich Nobles. Reading and writing was an important activity of the ladies of royalty. They were occupied with reading, writing and composing verses. Due attention was paid to their education. Often the girls of the palaces gathered to receive education of the primary standard.[49]

Emperors and the royal families were very keen to make arrangements for the education of their women. During the reign of Akbar special arrangements were made to impart regular education to the ladies of imperial harem. Akbar paid great attention to the education of his daughters and other women of the royalty. They were taught to read and write and were even trained in other ways by matrons. He established a girl's school in Fatehpur *Sikri*.[50] Shahjahan and Aurangzab also took care of the education of their daughters and provided them with women tutors. The curriculum of women education included the study of Persian, Arabic, Theology, History etc. Some of the ladies learnt the *Quran* by heart while others took interest in reading books like *Gulistan* and *Bostan* written by Sheikh Sadi Shirazi.

In the Mughal harem, the first lady who engaged herself actively in literary pursuits was Gulbadan Begum, the daughter of Babar. She wrote *Humayun Nama*, on the request of Akbar, giving an account of social and political activities of the time. She was a lover of books and thus had a library of her own. The second daughter of Babar, Gulrukh Begum, also had a taste for poetry and wrote a number of verses.[51]

Jahanara Begum, the eldest daughter of Shahjahan, wrote many *Risalas* (Pamphlets). She wrote "Munis-ul-Arwah" a biography of Muslim saint Muinuddin Chishti and his descendants. Mir Muhammad Ali Mahir, entitled 'Murid Khan' wrote a *Masavi* (a long poem) in praise of Jahanara Begum in which he praised her generosity and patronage of literature.[52] Zebunnisa Begum, the eldest daughter of Auranzab was a great Persian poet. She was also skilled in the art of calligraphy and could write *Shikast, nastaliq* and *naskh* perfectly.[53] There are some works which are ascribed to Zebunnisa herself *Zibul-Munshaat* is a collection of her letters. Another work attributed to her is *Diwan-i-Makhfi*.[54] It is to be noted that the education was limited to the women of Muslims royalty and the women from other common Muslim and Hindu families were deprived of this right.

Simultaneously, the education of common women was not a popular concept and the opportunities were very few. As there were no regular and separate schools for girls, it is argued that boys and girls in the early years studied together, but it also seems doubtful due to the prevailing social evils.[55] The condition of the girl child from the Hindu families seems to be more pathetic as they were deprived of learning the sacred language, Sanskrit, along with the *dalits* and other lower strata of Hindu Society.[56]

Economic Status of Women

During the Medieval period, a Muslim woman had the right to property of her father as her brother had. Even after her marriage, she did not lose that right. In this respect, a Muslim woman was better placed than her Hindu counterpart. If she wanted, she could give this property to anyone she liked. Even her husband did not possess any right on her property. A Muslim woman also had the right to nullify her marriage, if she was married by her parents at a minor age. She had equal rights with her male counterpart to dissolve the marriage after attaining the age of legal maturity. The Hindu child brides and grooms, however, were deprived of this right.[57]

Allowances and Maintenance

During the Mughal period, the ladies in Mughal harem were given regular allowances and maintenance grants to meet their personal expenses. On occasions, they also received presents from the Emperor for the purchase of perfumes and other sundry articles. Usually one half of the amount of allowance in that case, was paid from the royal exchequer and the other half was given to them in the form of assignment of land the revenue from which usually yielded more than the required amount. Sometimes, the *jagirs* assigned to them used to be fairly large.[58] The practice of giving huge grants continued even during the reign of Jahangir and Aurangzeb, the last Mughal emperor also maintained the custom. Women were also the sole custodian of the presents which they received on special occasions like birthdays, wedding-ceremonies and gifts from her husband, relatives and friends etc.[59]

Trade, Commerce and Muslim Women

Some royal women from Muslims families took great interest in trade and commerce. But, there is no mention anywhere if Hindu and Muslim women from the middle and lower classes participated in trade and commerce during the medieval India.[60]

Employment

The labour force in the Caliphate was employed from diverse ethnic and religious backgrounds. While both men and women were employed in a wide range of commercial activities and diverse occupations in the primary sector (as farmers for example), secondary sector (as construction workers, dyers, spinners, etc.) and tertiary sector (as investors, doctors, nurses, presidents of guilds, brokers, peddlers, lenders, scholars etc.)

Muslim women also held a monopoly over certain branches of the textile industry, the largest and most specialised and market-oriented industry, of the time, and engaged in occupations such as spinning, dying and embroidery. Poor women, especially in the villages, worked in this sector and earned handsome money.[61]

Economically, the Hindu women were completely dependent on their men folk. They were not entitled to any share in the property even though they possessed a lot of property in the shape of ornaments and jewelry etc. However, the economic condition of the Muslim women was much better. They were entitled to a definite share in the inheritance and were free to dispose of their property.

Political Status of Women

Some of the royal women enjoyed high prestige and played an important role in politics. During the Sultanate period, the first instance of a royal lady interfering with the politics was of Shah Turkan, the wife of Iltutmish and mother of Ruknuddin Firoz. She was a very ambitious lady and took the Sultanate in her hands immediately after the death of her husband; she manipulated the politics and put her son Kukunuddin Firoz on the throne. Although Iltutmish had declared his daughter Razia as his successor, she did not bother about Razia and the wishes of her husband and declared her son as the king with the help of some nobles.

She started concentrating all the powers in her hands as she found her son pleasure loving and not a fit person to rule. To fulfil her ambitions she put to death many inmates of the harem and even conspirated to kill Razia but she failed and finally got killed by Razia.[62]

Issue of Farmans, Sanads, Nishans and Parwanas

The right of issuing imperial *farmans* was the exclusive privilege of the Emperor. The only exception to the rule is found in case of Nurjahan who shared this privilege with Jahangir and exercised her right of issuing *farmans,* though very rarely. In addition to *farmans,* there were other important official documents, like *Hasbul-Hukm,* which were issued by the prime minister and *Nishans* which were issued by the princes of the royal blood.

It was in very exceptional cases that official documents such as *Hukums, Sanads, Nishans* and *parwans* were issued by a Queen or a princess. This exceptional privilege was allowed only to those who held the highest rank in the imperial harem such as Hamida Banu Begam, Mary-uz-zamani[63], Nurjahan and Jahanara.[64] It was the privilege of the queens to seal the imperial *Farmans.* During the period of Shahjahan, after the death of his beloved queen Mumtaz Mahal, the seal was given to Begam Saheb Jahanara.[65]

In addition to the Royal seal which was used for matters concerning the empire, a separate seal was used for all matters connected with the female issues. Thus, the Muslim women have played a very important role in politics.

Women in Modern India

The history of modern India starts with the advent of the Europeans, particularly the British and East India Company rule over some provinces at the early stage. The arrival of the British is also taken as the starting point of the new age in Indian thinking as the connection with the British Empire provided them an exposure to the outside world and to rational and scientific education. The debate over the place and role of a woman in Indian society has been initiated with demand for change of the old social norms and conservatism by the new educated elite class of India along with the efforts of the British Bureaucracy and Christian missionaries.

The rights of women became matter of great concern for the social reformers of India and the very dawn of India's renaissance started with the advocacy of women education and liberation.[66]

The effort to restore a woman to the rights as a person may be traced across the social and political events which are attached with the destiny of the great land of India from the 18th century onwards. Thus one may follow the stages of development in the status of women through the pre-independence and post-independence periods.

The pre-Independence period may be taken as extending from the latter half of the 18th century to the middle of the 20th century. During this period many movements had taken place in every sphere of life in India and women as part of Indian society could not remain untouched by these movements.

These movements were basically concerned with aspirations of liberation of women as a human being and liberation of the nation. The quest for liberty, equality and freedom drew inspiration from the ideological renaissance blowing in from the Western values, with its emphasis on reason, rationality and humanism. The spreading of new ideas not only resulted in the questioning of irrational values and conservatism of Indian society but it also resulted in the questioning of the legitimacy of colonial rule imbued with the desirability of self-government.

Secondly, the introduction of market economy, modern educational system and the new values of equality, rationality, secularism and respect for individual generated a new social environment pressing for a change in the old feudal structure of Indian society.

The initiatives which were led by British Bureaucracy and the Christian missionaries against the social evils were further followed by the Indian reformers. The support of the India's educated elite to the British bureaucracy against the social evils like *Sati*, Infanticide, Child Marriage and Women education proved to be the backbone of the British initiatives. However, the vested interests of the British Christian Missionaries and the indigenous reformers, who were advocating the supremacy of Indian culture, mysticism and Indian values over the West and the liberation of Indian women through the values of this land of great heritage led to a clash of interests, which further led to the different reform movements with different leanings, ideologies, techniques and methods.

The lack of secular approach to the upliftment of women led to the criticism and the questioning of the efforts of the socio-religious institutions and government efforts which were initiated during the colonial India for the upliftment of women. However, the efforts which were either made by the Indian social reformers or by the British bureaucracy have had a deep impact on the Indian society, which largely benefited Indian women.

Infanticide and Social Reforms in Colonial India

Infanticide was practiced in most parts of Northern India particularly in the Jat and Rajput heartlands, i.e., of north-western parts of Uttar Pradesh, Rajasthan, Madhya Pradesh, Modern Haryana and Punjab of the present day India. The people of these regions preferred a son in place of a daughter due to socio-religious and economic reasons.

Female infanticide was in 1780, brought to light by Janathan Duncan, the then Resident Commissioner at Banares who was later appointed as Governor of Bombay. He was the first English bureaucrat to lead the campaign against infanticide. It deserves a mention that infanticide was first detected by Emperor Jahangir in the early part of the seventeenth century and he disapproved this custom.[67] The second person to raise his voice against this crime was Raja Jai Singh of Jaipur State of Rajasthan who acceded to the throne in 1755.[68]

The English tried to dissuade the people from this heinous crime and they even obtained undertaking to stop infanticide from some of the Rajas and chiefs.[69] Two regulations were also passed by the Government, to suppress infanticide, i.e. Regulation XXI of 1795 and Regulation III of 1804. However, these resolutions could not be proved effective and the crime against the girl child continued. Determined to stop this crime, the British Government passed an official declaration prohibiting infanticide through an Act in 1870. According to this Act, it was compulsory for parents to get the birth of their children both boys and girls registered.[70]

Child Marriage

Child marriage was as rampant as infanticide, it was a continuing phenomenon for many centuries and it was imbedded to the fabrics of the all sections of Indian society. Child marriage became a matter of great concern not only to the Indian social reformers but also to the British bureaucracy, as it was a greater social evil than any other social evils which affected the society at large. First it resulted in the physical, mental and moral degradation of a child bride and then furthers in a society an increase in the number of sick mothers and the sick child brides and high rate of mother and child deaths.[71]

The Brahmo Samaj, the Arya Samaj and all other such socio-religious reform movements worked against this social evil. It was felt that a law should be passed to prevent child marriage. Ishwar Chandra Vidyasagar did pioneering work on the issue of child marriage and his efforts met with success when in 1860 Indian Penal Code included the child marriage as a punishable offence. Early marriage, however, remained unchecked despite the earnest efforts of the reformers who continued to oppose it.[72] The movement against child marriage took a long period and could get some success only when the Government of India passed the Child Marriage Act, popularly known as the Sarda Act of 1929.

The Sarda Act too could not become very effective as people living in villages were not aware of it. The lack of adequate resources and attitude of the government machinery in the enforcement of Sarda Act remained one of the major problems in the proper implementation of this Act.[73]

Sati

Sati was another social evil which became prevalent in the upper caste Hindus, particularly among the Brahmin, Bania and Rajput Castes. The voice against the *Sati* was first raised by the British officers and it was followed by enlightened Indians like Dwarkanath Tagore and Raja Ram Mohan Roy. Ram Mohan Roy had seen his brother's wife committing *Sati* in 1811 and he fought since then for its abolition.[74] Raja Ram Mohan Roy continued his campaign against *Sati* with the zeal of a national reformer. Undoubtedly, the ground for this social reform had been first prepared by Ram Mohan Roy. The first major step against the *sati* was taken by Lord William Bentinck, the then Governor-General of India (1829-1832), who decided to abolish the evil practice of *sati* by passing a law against it. Lord William Bentinck got the *sati* abolished legally in 1829 and it was declared "illegal and punishable by criminal courts" by regulation XVII. It provided that anybody who abetted a widow to commit *Sati* was to be punished for culpable homicide.[75] The law was first applied to Bengal, but the Madras Government also passed a similar regulation on 2 February, 1830.[76]

Widow Remarriage

After the abolition of *Sati*, another social evil which attracted the attention of a majority of the social reformers was the miserable plight of Hindu widows and restrictions on their remarriage. When *Sati* was abolished, a widow was permitted to exist, but her life was miserable. She was treated badly by her in-laws. To end this social evil, social reformers like Raja Ram Mohan Roy and Ishwar Chandra Vidyasagar in Bengal, Malabari, Narmad, Ranaday and K. Natarajan in Bombay and Dayananda Saraswati took an initiative to improve the condition of widows advocating the right of a widow to remarry.[77] This was in the first quarter of the 19th century when remarriage became the centre of their reform activities concerning women. In October 1855, Vidyasager came out in print with the argument that it had the sanction of the Shastras and a petition was signed by more than 900 Bengalis along with Vidyasagar, and it was sent to the British government, demanding that remarriage be given legal sanction. But Bengali Hindus particularly the priestly class was against such reform and protested against Vidyasagar. The bitter opposition of the Bengali Hindus was negated by the British bureaucracy and a Bill for widow remarriage was introduced in the Governor-General's council by J.P. Grant in 1856 and this Bill became an Act.

Polygamy

Polygamy was the result of extreme sexuality and it reduced the woman's status to a sexual commodity. Simultaneously polygamy deteriorated the position of women at large and converted the moral institution of marriage into a sexual one. The position of women under the polygamy system can be judged from the orders of the Raja of Darbhanga which he issued in 1805 to prohibit polygamy. In his order, the Raja prohibited the people of his state from taking more than five wives. It means that a man could enjoy luxury of having five wives even after the prohibitionary orders of the King.[78] Muslims were also allowed to have four wives with religious sanction.[79]

Maharaja of Burdwan and Rani Shurnomoyee of Cassim Bazar presented petitions in 1856 to the Bengal Government to pass a legislation banning polygamy. In the petitions they narrated the pitiable plight of women who were victims of this system. Ishwar Chandra Vidyasagar also raised his voice against this custom and drafted a Bill. However, nothing substantial could be done to curb this evil. In 1938, three private Bills on the subject came before the Central Legislature. One of the Bills allowed the taking of a second wife with the permission of the District Judge under exceptional circumstances. The other two Bills were for the total prohibition of a second marriage unless the first marriage was dissolved. None of these Bills were passed.

The Baroda state Government was first to pass an Act in 1942, declaring the second marriage illegal if the first spouse was alive or if the first marriage had not been dissolved. Bombay followed the Baroda and in 1946 passed the Prevention of Hindu Bigamous Marriage Act, but this could not become effective as the intending parties could go to the neighbouring areas and contract second marriages.[80] The Hindu Marriage Act, 1955, was passed after independence when bigamy was declared an offence.

Purda System

Purda was a practice which made the women to suffer due to many reasons one of which was seclusion and segregation of women from society. It was very common in north India. The evil custom of *Purda* was started with the arrival of Muslims and soon became stronger as the upper castes and upper classes from the Hindus also started adopting this system. Amongst the Muslim, a woman was not supposed to appear before a man to whom she was to be married. The women who observed *purda* went out in covered palanquins. Those who could not afford this luxury had to go in *burqa* which is a sheet covering them from top to bottom.

Almost all the socio-religious reform movements of the Hindus and Sikhs like Brahmo Samaj, Arya Samaj and Singh Sabha had worked to create public opinion against this evil practice. A large number of articles were written by reformers in various magazines of such movements. To name of the few, *Punjabi Bhain, Azad Bhain, Istri Sudhar* etc. The mass condemnation of such irrational socio-religious customs and practices certainly gained momentum under the leadership of Mahatma Gandhi. Under his influence appeals were signed by men and women of Bihar demanding the total abolition of *Purdah*.[81]

Dowry

The custom of giving dowry in the marriage of a daughter was generally unknown in ancient India but it started in the medieval India and this evil practice continued till today, however, it has increased to an unbelievable level.[82]

Unsuccessful attempts have, however, been made to end the evil of dowry. The Anti-Dowry League was started in the first session of the Madras Students' Convention. All unmarried members had to pledge that they would not accept dowry. Similar leagues were started in northern India (1914).

There was no Government enactment to check this growing evil under the British Raj. The Government of India passed an Anti-Dowry Act in 1961 to check this evil. This act, however, could not become affective as the evil practice of dowry is not only continuing, but the dowry deaths are also a matter of routine in our day to day life.[83]

Education and Women

The new thinking and the competitiveness which was created by the Christian Missionaries for emancipation of women led many social reformers to advocate the same under their reform movements. It forced them to make a strong arrangement for the education of their women, which was a necessary effort to control influence of Christianity and Western values over their women folk.

The opening of the separate schools for girls by the Christian Missionaries was immediately followed by similar efforts of the Indian reformers. The opening of Hindu College in 1816 in Calcutta to promote women education was a major step in that direction. The Christian Missionaries under the guidance of Miss Cooke made arrangements for the education of women in 1812. She opened thirty schools and made efforts to attract the girls from the upper caste Hindu families, her schools also enjoyed the patronage of Hindu gentlemen and staffed by Brahmin Pundits, however, she failed to attract girls from the higher castes.[84] One of the most important schools for girls was Hindu Balika Vidyalaya opened in 1849 in Calcutta by J.E. Drinkwater Bethune, legal member of the Governor-General's Council and President of the Council of Education.[85]

The matter of women's education remained an important issue for the British Government also. Lord Dalhousie, Governor-General of India from 1848 to 1856 declared that no single change was likely to produce more important and beneficial consequences than female education. Sir Charles Wood, President of the Board of Central Education from 1853 to 1855, issued an education dispatch in 1854 that detailed a shift in Government Policy, from providing higher education for the elites to support for mass education in the vernacular. This new focus on a total system of education was aimed to include both sexes. With the opening of Bethune School in 1849, the efforts of British government for the education of Indian women had been initiated.

The Education Commission of 1882 further recommended the expansion of girls education with the result that the post of Inspectors of Girls Schools were created and a few training schools for women teachers were also established. By the end of the nineteenth century, there were 12 colleges, 467 secondary schools and 5,628 primary, schools for girls with a total enrolment of 4,44,470 students. Miss Mary Carpenter, who visited India twice between 1866 and 1869, was able to secure a grant of £12,000 per annum, for five years on matching basis, for the establishment of normal schools. It was in 1868 that the Madras, Bombay and Uttar Pradesh Governments recommended to the Government of India, to open normal schools, a step necessary for the promotion of female education.[86]

The breakthrough came with the establishment of government schools, such as Bethune's and schools sponsored by reformist religious institutions. First the Brahmo Samaj, then the Prarthana Samaj, the Arya Samaj and the Theosophical Society all supported women education. Annie Besant focused on specific problems and by 1901 had written an article for the Indian Ladies Magazine on the "Education of Women".[87]

In North India women education was encouraged by the Arya Samaj under the teachings of Swami Dayanand Saraswati. By the end of the nineteenth century, progressive Arya Samajists recognised the importance of involving women in their reform efforts. The Jullundhar Samaj opened the Arya Kanya Pathshala (Girls School) in 1890 with a lady principal in charge.

In 1854, there were approximately 626 girls' schools. In 1872, Carpenter Keshub Sen, and another English woman, Annette Akroyd, set up a normal school. Later Akroyd broke with Keshub and worked with another group of Brahmos to establish the Hindu Mahila Vidyalaya (Hindu Girl's School). By 1878 this school had merged with the older Bethune school to become Bethune College, an affiliated college of Calcutta University. By 1900 the Sharada Sadan had trained eighty women who were able to earn their own living through teaching or nursing.[88]

Modern India witnessed many campaigns and movements launched by the social reformers, educated elites, socio-religious organisations and British bureaucracy. These resulted not only in the legislative provisions to protect the women against structural violence of Indian society but also resulted in the social awakening of Indian people.

Economic Status of Women

Under the new political set-up and the written laws a debate over the rights of women to property had also become a matter of serious concern for the colonial bureaucracy as well as for the Indians. The most important was the entrance of Indian women in the commercial sector under the organised economy. In ancient period women had property rights like *Stridhana*. But the colonial judiciary changed this concept and lay down that inherited property is not *Stridhana*. A new legal principle was gradually introduced through court decisions that whether the property is inherited by a woman through her male relatives (Father, Son, Husband) or through her female relatives (Mother, Mother's Mother, Daughter), it is not her *stridhana* and that it would devolve on the heirs of her husband or father. The women lost the right to will or gift away their *stridhana* and it acquired the character of a limited estate. Any transaction by a widow in respect of the property inherited by her had to be justified on two grounds: legal necessity or religious or charitable purpose. Upon the widow's death, the property reverted back to the husband's male relatives. The introduction of this concept of 'reversionary' which is basically a legal principal under the English law, bestowed upon the male relatives the right to challenge all property dealings by Hindu widows. To provide concrete examples of this trend, some decisions of the newly evolving legal machinery of British India are discussed below. These judgments have several commonalities. The litigations against the widows were initiated by the husband's heirs. In significant number of cases, following local customs, the lower courts upheld the women's rights over the property. The lower court decisions, however, were reversed by the higher judiciary and then became binding principles of law. Some cases which determined the economic status of women under the new colonial set-up are discussed below. These decisions were from property disputes within the Bengal presidency but under the considerable scheme of the hierarchy of courts, they became the binding principles of law for other presidencies.

In another landmark case around this time, the Privy Council held that the property inherited by the widow from her husband cannot be her *stridhana*. The Privy Council reversed the judgment of the lower court and proclaimed:

> Under the law of the Benares school, notwithstanding the ambiguous passage in the Mitakshara, no part of her husband's estate whether movable or immovable to which a Hindu women succeeds by inheritance, forms part of her *stridhana*."

The legal precedents set by the Privy Council became the binding blocks of the rule of law and it proved as a lethal blow to the property rights of Hindu widows, as the decisions of the various High Courts in the subsequent decade reveal.

The period between 1850 and 1930 witnessed the elimination of a wide range of customs which diverged from the Anglo-Hindu law as the level of proof required was very high. The local customs had very bleak chances to survive. Derrett comments that in this manner the Anglo-Hindu law with its *Dharmashastra* background was spread more widely than it had been ever before. The customs which were the only customs of the agricultural classes in the Punjab and matrilineal practices of the Malabar region were also interpreted on the lines of Anglo-Hindu Law. The tendency of both the British courts and of the urban Hindu middle class was to ignore the diversities and to impose Hinduism legally upon the local communities.[89]

Until the twentieth century women did not have the right of disposal over their separate property. The husband could transact all property dealings on her behalf; therefore, married women did not have a legal existence. As soon as a woman got married, she lost her legal identity. Her identity merged with that of her husband.

The decade 1920-30 witnessed some developments of far-reaching importance. The most important question that was raised during this period was women's property right to provide a degree of economic security to a near female relation. And the partial success was achieved in the form of Hindu Law Inheritance (Amendment Bill) of 1929 which recognised son's daughter, daughter's daughter, sister and sister's daughter as heirs "if it is not contrary to special local custom sharing the force of law." The women's right to property got further momentum when the Hindu Women's Right to Property Act of 1937 was passed under which a widow had the same interest in the property as her husband had.[90]

More importantly, the colonial set-up provided women an entry into the modern economic sector and also in the organised sector of the economy. Women were trained and employed in the new professions like teaching and medicines, factories, mines, and plantations.

Medicine was one of the new careers opened to Indian women in late Nineteenth century and demand for women medical professionals grew very fast: there were 68,000, medical women professionals, 30,000 women employed in educational and scientific fields and 6000 women in law and business. But the largest employer of women was the manufacturing sector, both in established mills and factories and in minor manufacturing units such as vegetable oil production and tailoring. Domestic workers numbered 7,37,000. In 1928 about 2,50,000 women worked in factories, about 58,000 of them in cotton mills and 55,000 in jute mills. Another 2,50,000 women worked in tea gardens, where they were 27 per cent of the workforce.[91]

During the last quarter of the nineteenth century factory legislation, designed to improve working conditions for women, receive attention from many quarters. A seven member government committee was established to analyse the condition of working women by the British government in the last quarter of 1870s. This commission recommended the first factory Act and by 1881, this Act became legislation, despite all local hostility.[92] Another progressive step for the working women came in 1891, when the Factory Act of 1881 was amended and new Factory Act 1891 was enacted and this Act limited the working hours of women to an eleven hour day and also prohibited women from working at night.[93]

Political Status of Women

The politicisation of the women and the demand for the political rights by the women came with the politicisation of the masses and other weaker sections of the Indian society. Broadly, the demand for the political rights of the Indian women during the colonial rule can be divided into two streams. One was by the mainstream politicians and social reformers, who recognised the equal rights of women along with the other weaker sections of the Indian society and second is by the educated elite women and women organisation which directly concentrated on women rights and demanded the same rights for the Indian women as were available to women in West at that time.

The saga of Indian struggle and sacrifices to get the liberation from the colonial yoke would be incomplete if the role, struggle and sacrifices of the Indian women are not mentioned. Women not only participated in the freedom movement but also proved to be the winning power against the atrocities of the British forces, when the men were brutally tortured and laid down in the field of freedom struggle. Then women took the challenge of standing peacefully against the might of imperial power.

The peaceful protest of Mahatma Gandhi not only trained a large number of women in *Satyagraha* and *Ahimsa* but also made them so committed that their participation became a necessity for the success of every struggle against British might. *Swadeshi* Movement could not have succeeded without the help of women. They joined the *Satyagraha* struggle in large numbers under the leadership of Gandhi. Indian women in South Africa had set the example by exhibiting the strength of the Passive Resistance Movement. They took training in *Satyagraha* from Mahatma Gandhi.

The year of 1914 witnessed the beginning of the First World War. During this period women had started taking interest in civil and political matters concerning India. Annie Besant and Sarojini Naidu started to take interest in the political affairs of the country. The period of Home League agitation (1914-1915) started by "Annie

Besant prepared a ground for the Gandhian Freedom Movement in which women have played a prominent part."[94]

The participation and support of women which the national leaders received during the Baroda Satyagraha of 1923-24 and the Bardoli Satyagraha of 1928 are memorable. Women commitment for the 'no tax campaign' which was launched under the leadership of Sardar Patel was so high that they did not bother about the confiscation of their land and cattle by the government.

Dandi March is a saga of women heroic participation in the freedom of their mother land. When the male *satyagrahis* and their leaders were arrested and succumbed to the might of British forces, the women folk was out in the streets to answer the wrongs of British Empire, to complete the work of their men folk which was left due to their arrests by the British forces. The protest led by Smt. Swaroop Rani against the salt law in Allahabad can be considered as a historic one as the women did not bow against the most hideous act of *lathi* charge and other atrocities.[95]

The Demand for Women's Franchise

The demand for right to vote by the Indian women during the freedom struggle is evident in the fact that the Indian women were fully conscious of their rights and despite being good partners of their male counterparts in the struggle for Independence and the recognition of their identity in the political sphere. Indian women did not lose any chance to demand their rights from the colonial rulers. It is to note that the efforts to demand equal rights for franchise for the Indian women similar to the women in the West was due to the initiatives of the educated women of India, even though the Indian leadership did not support it wholeheartedly.

The first initiative for the political rights and right to franchise for the Indian women was taken by Women's Indian Association (WIA). It was in 1917 when the first delegation of Indian women led by WIA met the Montague-Chelmsford Committee on Constitutional Reforms. Montagu-Chelmsford Committee suggested increasing the representation of Indians in the legislative council and widening the electorate, however, it did not make any reference to the women franchise in India.

The hopes of Indian women were further dashed by the Southborough Committee which was appointed by the British government to investigate the suggestions made by the Montagu-Chelmsford Committee. Without wasting any time, the 40 branches of WIA showed the numerical support for their demands. The committee was presented with a petition signed by 800 educated women and statements supporting women's suffrage from the All-India Women's delegation. The Southborough Committee's report, however, stated that extension of the right to vote to women would be premature in a society which continued to enforce *Purda* and prohibition against female education.[96]

The decision of Southborough Committee was met with strong protests from women across India and created an environment favourable to recognition of the equal rights of women by all the political parties across the country. Provincial Congress Committees passed a resolution in favour of women's suffrage, while both the Home Rule League and the Muslim League recognised that women should be given the right to vote on the same basis as men. A special deputation, compromising Sarojini Naidu, Annie Besant, Mrs. Herabai Tata, and Mithan Tata, went to London in 1919 to give evidence before the Joint Parliamentary Committee on the Government of India Bill. They were able to get the support of British women's organisations, particularly from the Women's Freedom League and the women's International League, who began to lobby on their behalf; the politicisation had its impact and the Joint Select Committee recommended that sex disqualification be removed. However, the initiative for this would have to come from the individual legislative councils, a provision which would allow the more conservative areas to retain an all-male electorate.

Madras led the way and granted women the right to vote in 1920 and Bombay followed suit in 1921. Bihar retained the sex disability for the council of the state and the legislative council until 1929. Muthulakshmi Reddy, the first women legislator, was appointed to Madras legislative council in 1927, Kamaladevi Chattopachyay and Mrs. Hannen Angela contested the election for the council.[97] They were enthusiastically supported by the WIA, not because of their political views, for which the association was not responsible, but because of the necessity of the presence of women in the council.

The WIA list of women in public life (1927) included five members of legislative councils (all nominated), 32 members of municipal committees (six elected), four members of Taluk Boards (all nominated), 32 Honourary Magistrates, Justices of the Peace (all nominated), and four members of the university senate (all elected). Women were proud of their achievements, and there were no complaints because so many women had been nominated.[98]

Post-Independence Period

A saga of new dreams for the Indian women has started with the dawn of Independence. A time of fulfilling the promises which the Indian leadership made and the potential of the women development were now in those hands with whom the Indian women had stood for years in the socio-political and economic fields against the might of British Empire. The first emphasis was to design a Constitution under which not only the broader goals of the freedom struggle were to be fulfilled but also the smooth growth of the very Indian society should come in a harmonistic way.

Promulgation of the Constitution of India on January 26, 1950 was a defining moment in the history of human rights in India. The Preamble, Fundamental Rights and Directive Principles of the State combined together provided the basic human rights for the people of India. Democratic socialism spelt out in the Preamble and the Directive Principles meant to provide the context in which the fulfillment of Fundamental Rights had to be achieved. While Fundamental Rights stressed on the existing rights, Directive Principles provided the dynamic movement towards the goal of providing human rights for all. To enable the citizens to enjoy human rights, many pieces of social legislation have been enacted over the last 60 years. In addition to these, the Supreme Court of India through judicial interpretation has widened the horizons of human rights in India.

All provisions of the Indian Constitution are applicable in equal measure to men and women, and can, therefore, be invoked by women for the assertion of their rights in Article 14 of the Constitution of India enunciates the general principle of right of equality and prohibits the state from denying to any person, "equality before the law".

The word 'status' refers to women's position and rights in different fields of Hindu law, namely property, succession, matrimonial relief, guardianship, will making power and choice in adoption, which has now been the natural outcome of Article 14 and other allied provisions of the Indian Constitution. In the past, a woman was frequently deprived of this status but new laws granted her better position in domestic as well as property matters. The underlying principle of Article 14 of the Constitution of India is reflected in the statement: "Like should be treated alike". Therefore, amongst equals, law should be equal, and should be equally administered. Article 14 of the constitution, firstly, confers on women the equality of status and, secondly, protects them against any violation of this principle. Article 14 recognises "women" as a class and declares this "class" to be different from men as a class. By this, the legislature was empowered to pass the Hindu Succession Act, 1956 and remove the traditional disadvantages attached to women.

Favourable Discrimination

Section 354 of the India Penal Code which makes assault or use of criminal force with intent to outrage the modesty of women (and does not include "woman", within the provision of the section), is not valid as being a violation of the equal protection of law.[99]

Article 15 (3) simultaneously provides that nothing in this Article shall prevent the state from making any special provision for women and children.

For example, in pursuance of this, the Parliament has enacted the 73rd and 74th Constitutional (Amendment) Act, providing 33 per cent reservation of seats in Gram Panchayats, Block Samitis and at the level of Zila Parishads.

Article 16: Equality of opportunity in matter of public employment Clause (1) of Article 16 provides equality of opportunity in matters to employment or appointment to any office under the state. Discrimination on the basis of sex has been specifically prohibited under the constitution so as to bring women at par with men. Sex shall not be the sole ground of intelligibility for any post.

Article 21 of the Constitution states "No person shall be deprived of his life or personal liberty except according to the procedure established by law"

Article 21 proved to be the back bone for the protection and promotion of women rights. For example, the Court in a series of cases held that right to life enshrined in Article 21 meaning something more than survival or animal existence.[100] It would include the right to live with human dignity. This Article has been interpreted over the years to provide speedy trial, especially in cases of rape[101], free legal aid[102], health care[103], education[104], protection of insane persons. In this case, the court held the imprisonment of a person is unconstitutional after that person declared insane.[105]

Article 21A: Right to Free and Compulsory Education, although the right to free education is provided to the children of both the sexes, looking into the socio-economic set up of the Indian society it can be said that the girl child will be more benefited from this Act in comparison to the boy child.[106]

Furthermore, Article 23 of the Constitution of India provides for prohibition of trafficking in human beings and forced labour.

The state in pursuance of the above provision has enacted the Suppression of Immoral Traffic in Women and Girls Act, 1956, which has been recently amended, is known as the PITA. Bounded Labour System (Abolition) Act, 1976, the Indecent Representation of Women (Prohibition) Act, 1986 are the milestones in ensuring the dignity of Indian women.

Directive Principles of State Policy

Although the Directive Principles of State Policy are not enforceable by the Courts, they are the fundamental principles for guidance to the various organs of the State. However, in recent times judiciary has broadened the concept of directive principles and given a wider definition to them.

Article 39, provides: (a) that the citizens, men and women, equally have the right to an adequate means of livelihood; (b) that there is equal pay for equal work for both men and women; (c) that the health and strength of workers, men and women are not abused and that citizens are not forced by economic necessity to enter a vocation unsuited to their age and strength. The principle underlying this provision is "equal wages for equal work", irrespective of "sex".

In furtherance of these principles, suitable provisions have been included in various labour laws passed from time to time e.g. the Equal Remuneration Act, 1976, the Factories Act 1948, the Mines Act, 1952 and several other statutes. In this regard various international labour conventions and recommendations of the international labour organisations have been kept in view. For example, The Equal Remuneration Convention 1951 was followed by the Equal Remuneration Act, 1976. Article 42 and 43 specially addresses the States' responsibility to make provisions for securing just and human conditions of work and maternity relief." Article 43: "The state shall endeavour to secure, by suitable legislation or economic organisation or in any other way, to all workers, agricultural, industrial or otherwise, work, a living wage and conditions of work ensuring a decent standard of life."

The cumulative effect of these Articles is that "the state is under an obligation to provide the suitable legislation to ensure just and human conditions in various industries and maternity benefits to women".

Article 51-A: stipulates the Fundamental Duties to be followed by citizens. Among others, it states: "it shall be the duty of every citizen of India to renounce practices derogatory to the dignity of women".

Other Legislations Protecting Women

Besides the Constitutional provisions, The Indian Penal Code, 1860, the Code of Criminal Procedure, 1973 and the Indian Evidence Act, 1872 along with other 54 major legislations are there to protect and promote women rights.

Penal laws: Looking at the social conditions and norms prevailing in Indian society, the penal code has offered special provisions for the protection of a woman who might become a victim of offences relating to her sexual identity. These special provisions relating to women are not exceptions but are to guard against special offences as a woman faces many problems in her public and private life because of her womanhood and her social position.

There are some special provisions for women in the criminal procedure code regarding search, seizure, arrest and imprisonment etc.

Some sections which give special protection to women or deal with the offences which either specially refer to women or protect women are enumerated in the chart below:

Table-A (1): Protection under the Indian Penal Code

S. No.	*Name of offence*	*Section*	*Minimum punishment*	*Maximum punishment*
1.	Obscene acts and Song in public place	294	-	3 months or fine or both
2.	Dowry Death	304-B	7 years	Life imprisonment
3.	Causing miscarriage without women's consent	313	-	Life imprisonment or ten years and fine
4.	Death caused by act done with intent to cause miscarriage	314	-	imprisonment for 10 years, or fine.
5.	Voluntarily causing hurt	323	-	One year and also fine up to Rs. 1000/- or both
6.	Grievous hurt or wife beating	325	-	7 years and also fine
7.	Assault or criminal force to women with intent to outrage her modesty	354	1 year	5 years or fine or both
8.	Kidnapping, abducting or inducing women to compel her marriage	366	-	10 years and also fine
9.	Procuration of minor girls	366-A	-	10 years and also fine
10.	Importation of girls from foreign country	366-B	-	10 years and also fine
11.	Selling minor for purpose of prostitution	372	-	10 years and also fine
12.	Buying minor for purpose of prostitution	373	-	10 years and also fine
13.	Rape	376	7 years	Life imprisonment and also fine
14.	Punishment for causing death of resulting in persistent vegetative state of victim	376-A	20 years	Life imprisonment
15.	Sexual intercourse by husband upon his wife during separation.	376-B	2 years	7 years and also fine
16.	Sexual intercourse by a person in authority.	376-C	5 years	10 years and also fine
17.	Gang rape	376-D	20 years	Life imprisonment
18.	Cohabitation caused by a man deceitfully inducing a belief of lawful marriage	493	-	10 years and also fine
19.	Marrying again during life of husband or wife	494	-	7 years and also fine
20.	Bigamy with concealment of former marriage	495	-	10 years and also fine

(Contd.)

Table-A (1): *(Contd.)*

S. No.	*Name of offence*	*Section*	*Minimum punishment*	*Maximum punishment*
21.	Marriage ceremony fraudulently gone through without lawful marriage	496	-	7 years and also fine
22.	Adultery	497	-	5 years or fine or both
23.	Enticing or taking away or detaining with criminal intent a married women	498	-	2 years or fine or both
24.	Subjecting a women to cruelty	498-A	-	3 years and also fine
25.	Word, gesture or act intended to insult the modesty of a woman.	509	-	3 years, or fine or both

Source: Khera, Ramesh (2019), *Criminal Major Acts* (Diglot), Delhi: Allied Book Company.

Provisions under the Criminal Procedure Code

Like the Indian Penal Code, the criminal procedure code has also recommended some provisions in favour of women. Section 47 (2) provides that if any person or police officer has reason to believe that the person to be arrested has entered into or is residing in the house, he can enter into the house and arrest him. But section 47 (2) provides that if such place is in the actual occupancy of a female (not being the person to be arrested) and who, according to custom, does not appear in public, the police officer shall, before entering into the apartment, give notice to the woman that she is at liberty to withdraw and shall afford her a reasonable opportunity to withdraw. Section 51 (2) provides that where a female is arrested by the police officer, she can be searched only by another female with strict regard to decency. Section 53 (2) provides that if a female is arrested and medical examination is necessary so as to get evidence of commission of crime, such examination shall be made only by or under the supervision of a female registered medical practitioner. Such examination for obtaining evidence is not violative of Article 20 (3) of the Constitution of India which grants protection against self-incrimination.

Section 64 provides that when the summons cannot be served to the person summoned, it can be served to an adult male member of the family residing with him. However, it cannot be served to the witnesses to attend the place or *thane* as required by the investigating police officer, but clause (2) provides an exemption from such requisition for women and male person under the age of fifteen years.

The Criminal Law (Second Amendment) Act of 1983 has introduced a sub-section of 174 of the code. This provides that the post mortem in all cases is necessary where a married woman has died within seven years of her marriage and a relative of such a woman has made a request in this regard.

Section 415 of the code empowers the High Court to postpone the execution of death sentence in case the convicted woman is pregnant. Section 437 provides an exception to this rule that a woman may be released on bail even if the offence charged is punishable with death or imprisonment for life. It is a special provision in favour of women.

The Indian Penal Code takes care of the girl child for that purpose, feticides (section 315), infanticide, seduction (section 366) procuration of minor girls (section 366-A), importation of girls from a foreign country (section 366-B), selling minor girls for prostitution (section 372), buying minor girls for the purpose of prostitution (section 373) and cohabitation caused by a man deceitfully inducing a belief of lawful marriage are punishable offences. Thus, Indian Penal Code allows for special provisions and lays down guidelines for meeting out special treatment to women in varied situations.[107]

Marital Rights

Hindu women under Hindu law have acquired new status and position in society. The Hindu Marriage Act was passed in 1955 and it has brought the following changes: "Hindu cannot have more than one wife. A marriage performed in violation of age requirements is still valid; it is neither void nor voidable under section 13 (2) (IV). The marriage was to be solemnised before the age of 15 years and the woman has repudiated the marriage after attaining that age but before attaining the age of 18 years." Section 13 of the Hindu Marriage Act provides grounds for divorce, which are available to both the parties. Adultery and cruelty are both sufficient grounds for obtaining a divorce.[108] Daughters have equal right as sons to their parent's property. They have a share in the ancestral property under section 6 of the Hindu Succession Act, when unmarried; they have right to shelter in the parental home, right to maintenance according to the income and status of their family and the right to have their marriage expenses paid out of the assets of the joint family.

A married woman has exclusive right over her individual property. Unless she gifts it in part or whole to anyone, she is the sole owner of her assets whether earned, inherited or gifted to her. Regardless of her income, the wife is entitled to maintenance, support and shelter from her husband, or if her husband is living in a joint family it has to be suitable according to the share of her husband in the joint property of the family.[109]

A mother is entitled to maintenance from her children. She is also a class 1 heir of her husband property. All property owned by her may be disposed of by her solely, she can gift it to any one as per her will because she is a full owner of her property under section 14 (1) of the Hindu Succession Act, 1956. In case she dies intestate, her children inherit equally, regardless of their sex under section 15 (1) and 16 of the Hindu Succession Act, 1956.

The Hindu Succession Act came into force on June 17, 1956, with a view to conferring absolute ownership on Hindu a woman in the property which was in her possession when the Act came into force. The limited estate of Hindu females is enlarged and the reversionary rights have now been abolished to a great extent. The theme section (1) of the Act provides women with some proprietary status.

The Dowry Prohibition Act, 1961

The dowry prohibition Act was first legislated in 1961; the Act was amended in 1984 to make the offence of "dowry" cognizable. The Act provides for a minimum punishment of imprisonment up to 6 months for the offence by way of demanding, giving and taking dowry. The maximum punishment for these offences has been increased to two years imprisonment and punishment by way of fine for these offences has also been increased substantially.[110] The amendment to other laws has also been made to strengthen the process of prosecution against dowry offence. Section 498-A has been introduced in the Indian penal code to deal with dowry.[111] The Criminal Law (Second Amendment) Act,

1983 has amended the code of criminal procedure, to secure post-mortem in case of suicide or death of a woman under suspicious circumstances within seven years of her marriage.

The punishment for committing such dowry deaths shall be imprisonment for not less than 7 years; it may also extend to imprisonment for life. It is to mention that Indian penal code was amended in 1986 specially to make the proper provision to deal with the dowry deaths under section 304-B.[112]

Labour Laws and Women

Economic empowerment of women is central to considerations of personal independence and self-esteem. To this end employment and entrepreneur opportunities would go in a long way in making a woman, self-reliant. To end discrimination against women in the field of employment and to realise their right to work, women should be given the right to employment opportunities, the free choice of profession, job security, equal remuneration, the right to compensation in respect of domestic work, the right to protection of health and safe conditions, especially in safeguarding the function of reproduction and special protection, in times of pregnancy, from work that may be harmful.

The working women have been provided with various benefits, concessions, protection and safeguards under different labour legislations in order to provide security against various risks peculiar to their nature. The women workers not only enjoy better rights but they also have better remedies in factories, mines, plantations and other industries.

Equal Remuneration Act, 1976

The Equal Remuneration Act, 1976 provides for the prevention of discrimination on the ground of sex against women and also in the matter of employment and for matters connected therewith or incidental thereto. The Act also prohibits discrimination while recruiting men and women workers for the same or similar nature of work except where the employment of women in such work is restricted or prohibited by or under any law for the time being.[113] The Act places duty on the employer to pay equal remuneration to men and women workers employed by him in an establishment or employment for performing same or similar nature of work. It also forbids discrimination against women workers either at the time of recruitment or in any condition of service subsequent to recruitment such as promotion, training or transfer. This protection does not extend to places where the employment of women is prohibited or restricted by any other law in force.[114]

Maternity Benefits Act, 1961

Performance of the biological role of child bearing necessarily involves withdrawal of a woman from the workforce for some period. During this period she is not only forced to stop her work but also needs extra income for her medical expenses. In order to enable the women worker to subsist during this period and to preserve her health, the law makes a provision for maternity benefits so that the women can play her productive and as well as reproductive role efficiently.

One of the earliest conventions adopted by ILO was on the Maternity Protection Convention, 1919. All the member countries of ILO were directed to pass suitable legislation to extend certain benefits to women during pregnancy and after childbirth.[115] The Royal Commission on Labour was appointed in the year 1929 to study the conditions in the country. In the report submitted by the commission, it was strongly recommended that the women workers should be provided leave with wages before and after confinement. However, the Government of India did not act on the recommendations.

It was the government of the state of Bombay that enacted the first maternity benefits legislation in the year of 1929. The Act provided for a leave of seven weeks and an allowance of 50 paisa per day during the leave period, for any women worker who was due to deliver. To be eligible to receive this benefit, the women should have worked in that factory or establishment for at least a period of six months.

Soon some other states followed the example of Bombay state and enacted similar laws with some minor variations. It was in the year 1961 when the Central Government, with a view to bring some uniformity in the provisions of various maternity benefits, enacted the Maternity Benefits Act, 1961.

Initially, the Act was provided to Industries at large but in 1988 its provisions were extended to all shops and establishments in which ten or more persons were employed on any day in the preceding twelve months.[116]

The Act provides for payment of cash maternity benefits for certain periods before or after confinement, grant of leave and other medical facilities. This benefit is available in case of confinement, miscarriage, sickness arising out of pregnancy and premature birth of the child. In 1995, the Act was amended to extend the benefits to women undergoing tubectomy, Medical Termination of Pregnancy (MTP) and for any illness arising out of tubectomy or MTP.

The maximum period for which any woman is entitled to maternity benefits is 12 weeks i.e., six weeks up to and including the day of her delivery and 6 weeks immediately following that day. The Act provides for payment of maternity benefits to the women employees at the rate of average daily wage for the period of their actual absence immediately preceding and including the day of their delivery and for 6 weeks immediately following that day.

Factories Act, 1948

Factories Act, 1948 is an important legislation as it contains certain provisions regarding the nature of work to be given to women workers and hours of work for them, etc. The Act prohibits the employment of women from 7 pm to 6 am. No exemption can be granted from provisions related to daily hours.

This Act states that no woman shall be required or allowed to work except between the hours of 6 am to 7 pm. This Act mentions that these limits may be varied by the State Government but no variation shall be authorised for exemption of women between 5 am to 10 pm; there shall be no change of shifts except after a weekly holiday or any other holiday.

The Factories Act, 1948 does not allow women workers to handle excessively heavy weights. Both the Factories Act and the Mines Act, 1952 authorised the State Governments to fix the maximum weights which can be lifted, carried by men, women and children. The Act prohibits the employment of women in any part of a factory for pressing cotton in which cotton opener is at work.[117]

The Mines Act, 1952 and Plantation Labour Act, 1951

In these Acts, apart from the usual sections regarding the licensing of mines, inspection, penalties etc., the following provisions are specially meant for women. No woman and child are to work under ground. They must be given work only on surface. No night work is allowed for women. Under Mines Act, the Central Government is authorised to make rules requiring the mines to maintain crèches if a certain number of women workers are employed in the preceding 12 months.[118]

Beedi and Cigar Workers (Conditions of Employment) Act, 1966

This Act also contains some special provisions for women workers. The important provisions are for a crèche for the infants and babies of women workers and restriction on night work of women.[119]

Political Status of Women

Empowerment of women is the key issue in the women movement. Empowerment contains the word 'power' which is exercised in economic, social and political relationship between individuals and groups. Power may be overdefined as control over resources and control over ideology. As per this view women are considered to be relatively powerless because they do not have control over resources. Hence it leads to no decision making power for women, yet numerous decision are made which affect women everyday.

After independence, the task before the government was to create a situation for actual and meaningful participation of women in political and economic decision making. The political identity and the equal role of the women have been recognised by the Constitution of India. Special provisions are also made not only under the Constitution but also by the political actors and political parties to encourage women's role in political affairs. Article 325 and 326 of the Constitution of India guarantees political equality, equal right to participation in political activities and right to vote respectively. While the latter has been exercised and enjoyed by a large number of women, the former i.e., right to equal political participation is still a distant dream. The participation of women in the politics and their number in elected bodies of the state has shown the reverse.

The percentage of winning candidates has been below ten per cent in the Parliament, in all the past elections. No variation whatsoever has occurred in half-a-century. During the same period, Indian women have achieved commendable progress in literacy, education, and employment. They have achieved rights equal to that of men for parental assets. The above statistics suggests that it is not the law and constitution which control and regulate the Indian politics but there are other factors which dominate the politics and political participation of women in India.

With a view to tackle the problem of apathy, indifference and non-participation of the women in rural development programmes, the Government of India appointed B.R. Mehta Committee (1957), which wanted that women should not only become beneficiaries of development, but also contribute to the development process.[120]

The next major landmark regarding the role of women was the Committee on the Status of Women in India (CSWI, 1975), which highlighted that the majority of the Indian women are facing a situation of subordination and deprivation, which has increased the gender inequality in society.[121] The Committee revealed that although women are participating in increasing numbers in economic and political activities and in the process of change, they are not necessarily the actual beneficiaries, nor are they able to control the process of change to meet their needs or aspirations. They are increasingly becoming victims along with other weaker sections. In the units of local governance, rural women rarely get elected directly. Instead they are nominated or co-opted. Often, they are ignorant of the purpose and procedure of the Panchayat institution and are also discouraged by their family members from participating effectively. With the publication of CSWI Report 1975, a demand for the representation of women in the Panchayats by reservation rather than by nomination was voiced and reiterated. This was followed by the Ashok Mehta Committee Report (1977), which laid emphasis on the need to reorganise and strengthen women's constructive decision-making and managerial roles.[122]

The National Perspective Plan for Women (1988) recommended that thirty per cent of the executive head positions from the villages should be reserved for women.[123] Thus, the debate on political representation concerning women, from 1957 to 1989, has been on how to encourage women to participate actively and in large numbers in the Panchayats at various levels.

The United Nations Organisation gave special attention to the empowerment of women. Its Decade of Women's Development (1975-1985) generated a lot of interest throughout the world. India also took special interest towards the problems of women. At this juncture, a number of women organisations came into being and started fighting for women's cause. They took a positive approach that they should be perceived as dignified human beings instead of being treated as objects of pity.[124] However, there was no meaningful effort to provide satisfactory representation for women in the legislative, executive and other similar bodies.

It was in this background that in September 1991, the Congress Government under the leadership of P.V. Narasimha Rao introduced the 73rd (Panchayats) and 74th (Nagar Palikas) constitutional amendment Bills in the Parliament. They were referred to a joint select committee; the Lok Sabha passed the Bills on 22nd December, 1992 and the Rajya Sabha, the following day. Following the ratification by more than half of the State Assemblies, the President gave his assent on 20th April 1993, and the Acts were brought into force by a government notification on 24th April 1993 as the 1992 Constitution (Seventy Third and Seventy Fourth) Amendments. These amendments provide for one-third reservation of seats and offices of chairperson to women in the local self-government institutions throughout the country.

The reservation of 33 per cent seats for women in the local self-government could not help the women to represent their interest as a collective political voice against the established ethos of patriarchy. The studies conducted into the different states on the role of women in the local self-governments, hold some common features across the majority of the states. These features are: (1) They display a lower level of political awareness, (ii) they owe their primary loyalty to their families, (iii) their role of an elected representative is merely an extension of their role as a house wife, (iv) they enter the political arena for protecting the constituency of their male relatives and are prepared to vacate the same, once de-reserved (v) Illiteracy is considered as a major cause for women to be used as sheer proxies. (vi) It is also observed that the male members in the family often dominate the women *panchas*, they train women to speak at meetings, or actually do the necessary paper work when women are illiterate.[125] The more shocking is the women representation in national politics and in the political parties. Although the political parties are claiming to be gender sensitive and want to recruit more and more women members to their parties, even after the passing of 70 years of independence no political party can cross the data of 5 per cent for women membership into their party in India. The scenario is grimmer if one looks at the key posts. Hence if one wants to have a fair knowledge of women and politics in India, one definitely needs to study women participation in party politics.

Analysis of the electoral processes in India reveals that mobilisation of women by political parties has been opportunistic with short-term goal of winning the elections and not for long term goals of bringing about a social change for women. Further, they have approached women for their quantitative votes as a supportive group of citizens for general purposes rather than acknowledging their special interest and perspective for an improved quality of life. The election manifestos of parties indicate that women constitute a backward section of society to whom special privileges should be granted to bring them at par with men.

The more surprising is the dual role of political parties on the women reservation bill, i.e., the reservation of 33 per cent seats in the Parliament and state legislatives. On the one hand, all the political parties, irrespective of their ideological lines, are claiming to be the supporters of the women reservation bill, on the other hand the male chauvinism across the party lines have been opposing the Bill on one or the other excuse, since 1996.[126]

Notwithstanding the horrific position granted to women in the pre- and post-Aryan period and in the Vedic times, that too in a substantive and mandatory manner, made binding on society by the tenets of religion and observance, women of later periods spanning between the middle and modern ages have been denied their rightful place of honour owing to a variety of reasons both religious and mundane. Indian society, a vortex of innumerable castes and communal combinations, has paid scant regards to the education and welfare of women culminating in child marriage, *sati*, ban on widow remarriage, and divorce, to name a few atrocities committed on them. It is a pity that the rulers never tried to defy the orthodox religious beliefs by initiating reforms, which would have enhanced the prestige and status of women. Even the few women who hobnobbed with Mahatma Gandhi and the frontline leaders of the freedom movement were from rich and educated milieu and did not represent the backward and downtrodden womenfolk of India subjected to all kinds of exploitation and torture.

The concept of labour laws has been linked with the socio-economic and political set-up of every society and it has developed into the workers' rights only after the industrialisation and spreading democracy across the world. However, the focus of the industrialised economies is to increase the work participation of the citizens to increase the quantity as well as the quality of their products in the competitive globalised economies. The special concession and facilities to the working women like maternity benefits, crèche facilities, child care leave, flexible working hours and work from home etc. are the progressive steps to enhance the work participation of women who are half of the population.

Although historically the economic role of women has been ignored in India, but after the establishment of the British Empire and revival of the Indian renaissance a focus on the women education and to end the evil social practices has been initiated by the Indian leadership as well as by the British bureaucracy. Although the right to property and inheritance became abysmal as the colonial judicial system interpreted the law of inheritance while referring to the religious scriptures and ignored the local customs while deciding the daughter and widow right to property. However, the spreading of modern-education and scientific temper and the emergence of Trade-Union movement during the national freedom struggle has not only resulted into the development of labour laws during the colonial India, but it has a long-term impact on the political formation of independent India.

The constitution of free India although did not provided any special provisions to the working women, but it made certain provisions in the fundamental rights and directive principles of the state policy to protect the women rights along with the other weaker sections of the Indian society. India leadership also proved its commitment to enhance the socio-economic and political status of women by signing the International Conventions and participating in international policy initiatives taken for the development and empowerment of women.

As it is mentioned at the beginning of this chapter that the recognition of the economic role and the work-participation is a depending variable and decided by the socio-economic and political set-up of the society. Historically, the importance of economic role and work-participation of women in India has been ignored by the vested interests of the Indian society. Even the initial five years plan has focused on the development of women as healthy mother and house maker not as an individual woman. It is pertinent to mention that till 1970s the domestic work and allied activities of the women did not appeared in the index of the Indian census. It mean that even after the 30 years of independence the absolute work of the women which is also unpaid could not get any attention from Indian Government and its leadership.

Notes

1. "The effects of women in the workforce Essay Example for Free", *https://studymoose.com/?the-effects-of-women-in-the-workforce-essay*. Accessed:13-6-2018, 8:58 am.
2. "Women in the workforce-WikiVividly", *https://wikividly.com/wiki/Women_in_the_workforce*, Accessed: 13-6-2018, 9:08 am.
3. Savita Vishnoi, *Economic Status of Women in Ancient India*, Kusumanjali Prakashan, Meerut, 1993, pp. 71-75, also see, Sukumari Bhattacharji, "Economic Rights of Women in Ancient India", *Economic and Political Weekly*, vol. XXVII, no. 9, March, 1991, p. 507.
4. R.S. Sharma, *Material Culture & Social Formulations in Ancient India*, Macmillan India Ltd, Madras, 1983, pp. 89-134.
5. V.S. Singh, *Indian History*, Allahabad Law Agency, Faridabad, 1986, p. 65.
6. Vijay Kaushik & Bela Rani Sharma, *India Women through Ages*, Sarup and Sons, New Delhi, 2005, p. 29.
7. *Ibid*. p. 118.
8. Jayshree Dubey and Anuradha Sharma, "Women and Hinduism", Anil Dutta Mishra (ed.), *Women and Religion: An Encyclopedia on Women in Different Religions of the World*, vol.1, Regal Publications, New Delhi, 2011, p. 44.
9. R.S. Sharma, *Material Culture & Social Formations in Ancient India*, Macmillan India Ltd, Madras, 1983, p. 89.
10. Anuradha Sharma and Jayshree Dubey, "Women and Buddhism", Anil Dutta Mishra (ed.), *Women and Religion: An Encyclopedia on Women in Different Religions of the World*, vol. 2, Regal Publication, New Delhi, 2011, p. 45.

11. Singh, n. 5, p. 65.
12. P. Thomas, *Indian Women Through Ages*, Asia Publication, Bombay, 1964, pp. 176-197.
13. M. Sophie Tharakan & Micnael Tharakan, "Status of Women in India: A Historical Perspective", *Social Scientist*, vol. IV, no.1, November-December 1975, pp. 119-120.
14. Thomas, n. 12, pp. 141-149.
15. Anjali Kant, *Women and Law*, APH Publication, New Delhi, 2003, pp. 25-26.
16. Dubey & Sharma, n. 8, pp. 54-55.
17. Sangeeta Sharma, *Women's Liberation*, Rawat Publications, Delhi, 2010, p. 57.
18. Kaushik & Sharma, n. 6, pp. 36-40.
19. Vishnoi, n. 3, pp. 6-7.
20. A.S. Altekar, *The Position of Women in Hindu Civilisation*, Mohit Banarsidass Publishers Private Limited, New Delhi, 1978, p. 117.
21. J.C. Jain, *Life in Ancient India as Depicted in Jain Canons*, Vikas Publishing House, New Delhi, 1947, p. 163, also see, Kaushik & Sharma, n. 6, pp. 36-40.
22. Vishnoi, n. 3, pp. 46-47.
23. Clarisse Bader, *Women in Ancient India: Moral and Literary Studies*, Anmol Publications, Delhi, 2000, pp. 60-68.
24. *Ibid.*
25. Vishnoi, n. 3, pp. 63, 65.
26. Kiran Devendra, *Status and Position of Women in India*, Vikas Publishing House Pvt. Ltd., New Delhi, 1985, pp. 2-3.
27. Shakuntala Rao Shastri, *Women in Vedic Age*, Bharatiya Vidya Bhavan, Delhi, 1954, pp. 54-55, also see, Sadhana Thakur, *et al.*, *Women and Jainism*, Anil Dutta Mishra, *Women and Religion: An Encyclopedia on Women in Different Religions of the World*, vol. 3, Regal Publications, New Delhi, 2011, pp. 20-21.
28. Vishnoi, n. 3, p. 13.
29. M.C. Joshi, *Princes and Polity in Ancient India*, Kusumanjali Prakashan, Meerut, 1986, pp. 39–40.
30. Tripal Sharma, *Women in Ancient India (From 320 AD to 1200 AD)*, ESS Publication, New Delhi, 1987, p. 10.
31. H.M. Chadwick, *The Heroic Age*, Cambridge University Press, Cambridge, 1912, p. 370.
32. *Ibid.*
33. Padmalaya Mahapatra and Bijoyini Mohanty, *Elite Women of India*, APH Publishing Corporation, New Delhi, 2002, p. 57.
34. Mriducchanda Palit, "Power behind the Throne: Women in Early Mughal Politics", Mandakranta Bose (ed.), *Women and Power*, Deep & Deep Publications, New Delhi, 1985, p. 202.

35. Neelam Upadhyay & Rekha Panday, *Women in India: Past and Present*, APH Publishing, New Delhi, 1990, p. 18.
36. S. C. Raychoudhary, *History of Mughal India*, Oxford University Press, New Delhi, 1986, p. 251, also see: N.V. Jagannatha Rao and Godavari D. Patil, "Changing Role and Status of the Indian Women", J.P. Singh (ed.), *The Indian Women: Myth and Reality*, Gyan Publishing House, New Delhi, 1996, p. 213.
37. *Ibid.*, p. 251.
38. Upadhyay & Panday, *n.* 35, pp. 17-18, also see: Rao and Patil, *n.* 36, p. 212.
39. Rekha Misra, *Women in Mugal India*, Munsiram Manoharlal Publisher, Delhi, 1967, pp. 131-132.
40. *Ibid.*
41. P.N. Chopra, *Society and Culture in Mughal Age*, Oxford University Press, New Delhi, 1955, p. 104.
42. Irfan Habib, *Agrarian System in Mughal India*, Asia Publishing House, London, 1963, p. 155.
43. Mishra, n. 39, p. 132.
44. Withington, *Early Travels*, Oxford University Press, Delhi, 1975 p. 219.
45. Thomas, n. 12, pp. 262–265, also see: Dubey and Sharma, n. 8, pp. 53-54.
46. Vijay Kaushik and Bela Rani Sharma, *Indian Women Through Ages*, Sarup & Sons, New Delhi, 2005, pp. 178-185, also see: B. Suguna, *Women's Movements*, Discovery Publishing House, New Delhi, 2009, p. 14.
47. Misra, n. 39, p. 131.
48. Kant, n. 19, p. 53.
49. Meenakshi Poonia & Virender S. Poonia, *Women and Human Rights in India*, Sonali Publications, New Delhi, 2011, p. 37.
50. Misra, n. 39, p. 87.
51. P.N. Ojha, *Some Aspects of Northern Indian Social Life*, Gyan Publishing House, Delhi, 1975, p. 132.
52. Misra, n. 39, p. 90.
53. Yusuf Husain, *Glimpses of Medieval India Culture*, vol. 30, Asia Publishing House, Delhi, 1956, pp. 192-193.
54. Yusuf Husain, *Educational System in Medieval India*, Gyan Publishing House, Delhi, 1956, p. 121.
55. J.N. Sarkar, *Studies in Mughal India*, Atlantic Publishers & Distributors Ltd., Bombay, 1925, pp. 79-90.
56. *Ibid.*, p. 155
57. Irfan Habib, *Agrarian System in Mughal India*, Oxford University Press, Delhi, 1970, p. 155.
58. Thomas, n. 12, pp. 254-256.
59. S. Das, *The Status of Indian Women*, ESS Publications, New Delhi, 1979, pp. 66-69.

60. Misra, n. 39, p. 59.
61. *Ibid.*, p. 135.
62. I.H. Querashi, *Administration of the Sultans of Delhi*, Atlantic Publishers, New Delhi, 1990, p. 65.
63. V. Janapathy, *Indian Women: Through the Ages*, Gyan Publishing House, New Delhi, 2002, p. 152.
64. Misra, n. 39, p. 67.
65. Ibn Hasan, *Central Structure of the Mughal Empire* (2nd edition), Asia Publication, New Delhi, 1970, p. 102.
66. Kant, n. 15, pp. 56-57.
67. Manmohan Kaur, *Women in India's Freedom Struggle*, Sterling Publishers Private Limited, Delhi, 1968, p. 9.
68. Altekar, n. 20, p. 4.
69. Kaur, n. 67, p. 9.
70. Devendra, n. 26, p. 4.
71. Devendra Kumar Chaudhary, *Arya Samaj in Punjab 1877-1901*, M. Phil Dissertation (Unpublished), Punjabi University, Patiala, 1979, pp. 121-122.
72. Government of India, "Towards Equality", *Report of the Committee on the Status of Women in India*, Ministry of Human Resource and Development, New Delhi, 1974, p. 81.
73. Charles H. Heimsath, *Indian Nationalism and Hindu Social Reform*, Princeton University Press, Princeton, 1964, p. 147, also see: Thomas, n. 12, p. 338.
74. Annu Menon Muzamdar, *Social Welfare in India*, Asia Publishing House, Bombay, 1964, p. 107.
75. Kiran Devendra, *Changing Status of Women in India*, Vikas Publishing House Pvt. Ltd., New Delhi, 1994, p. 9.
76. Thomas, n. 12, p. 30.
77. Pratima Asthana, *Women's Movement in India*, Vikas Publishing Pvt. Ltd., New Delhi, 1974, p. 22, also see: V. Rajendra Raju, *Role of Women in India's Freedom Struggle*, Discovery Publishing House, New Delhi, 1994, p. 11.
78. Devendra, n. 75, pp. 11-18.
79. Kaur, n. 67, p. 19.
80. Devendra, n. 26, p. 18
81. G.S. Dutt, *A Woman of India*, Vikas Publishing House Pvt. Ltd., New Delhi, 1977, p. 74.
82. Y.S. Parmar, *Polyandary in the Himalayas*, Vikas Publishing House Pvt. Ltd., New Delhi, 1973, p. 33.
83. Sita Ram Singh, *Nationalism and Social Reform in India*, Vikas Publishing House, Delhi, 1968, p. 237.
84. R.Vishalakshmi Neduncheziar, "Education of Girls and Women in Tamil Nadu", R.Vishalakshmi (ed.), *Status of Women Souvenir* 1973, Task-force Sub-Committee on Education, Madrass, 1985, pp. 62-65.

85. J.C. Bagal, *Women's Education in Eastern India: The First Phase,* World Press Private Ltd., Calcutta, 1956, pp. 77-95.
86. Y.B. Mathur, *Women's Education in India, 1813-1966,* Asia Publishing, Bombay, 1973, p. 25.
87. Arthur H. Nelhercot, *The Last Four Lives of Annie Besant,* University of Chicago Press, Chicago, 1963, pp. 17-55.
88. Kenneth, W. Iones, *Arya Dharm: Hindu Consciousness in Nineteenth Century, Punjab,* Manohar Publication, Delhi, 1976, pp. 104-05.
89. "Bhugwandeen Doobeyan VS. Myna Baee (1867) 11 Moore's Indian Appeals, Vekayyanma Garuvs Venkataramanayyamma Bahadur... on 18...," *IndianKanoon.org/doc/*86124, Accessed: 22-4-2017, 10:00 am.
90. Anjali Kant, n. 15, pp. 70-71.
91. "Modern Era", *www.indohistory.com,* Accessed: 12-12-2016,10:00 am.
92. "The First Factories Act—Indian History", www.*indhistory.com/factory-act.html,* Accessed: 12-12-2017, 10:00 am.
93. "The Factory Act" *www.indhistory.com/factory-act.html,* Accessed: 12-12-2017, 10:00 am.
94. Vijay Agnew, *Elite Women in Indian Politics,* Vikas Publishing House Pvt. Ltd., New Delhi, 1979, pp. 34-35.
95. Suguna, n. 46, p. 40.
96. Thomas, n. 12, p. 334.
97. *Ibid.,* p. 103.
98. Vina Mazumda, *Symbols of Power: Studies on the Political Status of Women in India,* Allied Publishers Private Limited, Bombay, 1979, pp. 8-9.
99. "Gridhar Gopal v. State", AIR *1953,* Madh. Bharat 147.
100. "State of Maharastra v. Chandrabhan", AIR 1983 SC 803.
101. "Sheela Barse v. Union of India", AIR 1986 SC 773.
102. "Hussainara Khatoon v. State of Bihar", AIR 1979 SC 1369.
103. "Parmanand Katara v. Union of India & others", AIR 1989 SC 2039, *see also: "M/s Cosmopolitan Hospitals & others* v. *Smt. Vasantha P. Nair and Other",* 1992 (1) CPR 820.
104. "Miss Mohanijain v. State of Karnataka & others", AIR 1992 SC 1858.
105. "Veena v. State of Bihar", AIR 1983 SC 339.
106. Nomita Aggarwal, *Women and Law in India,* Women's Studies and Development Centre, University of Delhi, 2002, pp. 27-28.
107. Roma Mukherjee, *Legal Status and Remedies for Women in India,* Deep & Deep Publications, New Delhi, 1998, pp. 63-66.
108. P.D. Mathew and P.M. Bakshi, *Hindu Marriage Act,* Indian Social Institute, New Delhi, 1986, pp. 1-20, also see: Monica Chawla, *Gender Justice: Women and Law in India,* Deep & Deep Publications, New Delhi, 2013, p. 41.
109. Aggarwal, n. 106, pp. 1-21.
110. P.D. Mathew and Shalu Nigam, *Law Relating to Dowry Offences,* Indian Social Institute, New Delhi, 1986, pp. 1-50.

111. Aggarwal, n. 106, p. 32.
112. *Ibid.*, p. 54.
113. *Ibid.*, pp. 119-130.
114. "Equal Remuneration Act 1976", *ww.excelconsultancyservices.co.in/EqualRemuneration.htm,* Accessed, 09-4-2017, 11:20 am.
115. "International Labour Organisation, 1919" en.wikipedia.org/*wiki/international-labour-organisation-*, Accessed: 11-4-2016, 2:00 pm.
116. E. A. Anguestine, *Working Women and Maternity Benefits,* Indian Social Institute, New Delhi, 1989, pp. 1-10.
117. Monica Chawla, *Women and Protective Laws,* Regal Publication, New Delhi, 2006, p. 130.
118. *Ibid.*, p. 132.
119. "Beedi & Cigar Workers (Conditions of Employment) Act, 1966", *www.advocatekhoj.com/.../bareacts/beediandcigar/index.phd?... Beedi%2...*, Accessed: 19-10-2017, 11:00 am.
120. Iqubal Naryan, "Panchayati Raj Democracy and Development" Ramesh Arora (ed.), *Peoples Participation in Development Process,* State Institute of Public Administration, Jaipur, 1979, p. 39.
121. Naryan S. Kotvi, "The Myth of Gender Equity", *World Affairs,* vol. V, no. 3, July-September, 2001, pp. 35-37.
122. B.S. Bhargava and V. Venkatakirshnan, "Panchayat Raj Movement: An Analysis of Its Phases", G. Palanithurai (ed.), *Empowering People: Issues and Solutions,* Kaushik Publishers, New Delhi, 1996, p. 213.
123. Veena Mazumdar, "Reservation for Women", *Economic and Political Weekly,* vol. XXIV, no.50, 10 June, 1989, pp. 35-41.
124. J.K. Baral and Kumudini Patnaik, *Gender Politics,* Discovery Publishing House, New Delhi, 1990, pp. 6-7.
125. Sudha Pai, "Pradhanis in New Panchayat: Filed Notes from Meerut District", *Economic and Political Weekly,* vol. XXXIII, no. 18, May, 1998, pp. 1010-1011, also see: Mahi Pal, "Women in Panchayat", *Economic and Political Weekly,* vol. XXXIII, no. 4, January, 1998, p. 150, Bhaskar Manu, "Women Panchayat Members in Kerala", *Economic and Political Weekly,* vol. XXXII, no. 17, April, 1997, p. 15. George Mathew & Ramesh Nayak, "Panchayat at Work: What it Means for the Oppressed", *Economic and Political Weekly,* vol. XXXI, no. 27, July, 1996, p. 1765. Biduyat Mohanty, "Panchayati Raj, 73rd Constitutional Amendment and Women", *Economic and Political Weekly,* vol. XXXIX, no. 49, December, 1995, p. 3348.
126. Raichel Matthai, "Political Status of Indian Women: Progress Since Independence", *Mainstream,* vol. XLV, no. 1, December, 2006, pp. 38-39.

Chapter 3

Labour Laws and Women Labour

A National and International Perspective

From time immemorial women have been working–working everywhere at home, in fields, factories and many other workplaces. However, women as a distinct segment of workers emerged and got recognition only with the emergence of industrial production.[1]

Women's labour constitutes the foundation of the international economic competitiveness of most of the Asian countries. The forces of a swiftly growing global economy and privatisation expose women in Asia to diverse mechanisms of exploitation. There is no single pattern but rather an array of complex ways in which gender hierarchy, national capital, foreign capital, and the state negotiate and adapt to privatisation, at the expense of women workers. Women's labour plays a crucial role in the contemporary restructuring of Asia's industrialising economies. Women are becoming increasingly active in both the rural and the urban economy.

It is their labour that provides the ultimate basis of international competitiveness of most Asian countries. Women are a direct source of cheap labour, especially in export manufacturing industries, whether as formal, informal, or casual labour. Among the workers of the world, women are all too often the most vulnerable and the most exploited during the adjustment and/or restructuring processes dominated by privatisation.[2]

Globally, women lag far behind men in access to education and employment. Education is widely recognised as gateway to economic security and opportunity—particularly for girls and women. According to world figures in literacy of the 130 million 6-11 year old children not going to school, a majority of 60 per cent are girls. According to UNESCO Institute of Statistics, it is estimated that two-thirds of the world's 875 million illiterate adults are women.[3]

In addition, working women are often paid less than men for their work and are concentrated in insecure, unsafe and low-wage work. The major reason behind this phenomenon is the perception of women as housewives, caregivers, mothers and secondary sources of household income. Women are often responsible for children, household labour and unpaid community work, which limits their opportunities to decent salaried employment.

At the same time, salaried employment is very important for women's empowerment. This is since salaried employment makes women less economic dependent of male kin and the spouse, and offers women exit options i.e. in cases of domestic violence. Labour force participation is however, perceived to not be necessarily positive *per se*, since it can be a result of economic pressure, inequalities or poverty, and can place a double burden of work on women who are responsible for all domestic work in the household.[4]

At the national front contrary to the common perception, a large per cent of women in India work. The National data collection agencies accept the fact that there is a serious underestimation of women's contribution as workers. In urban India women have impressive number in the workforce for instance 30 per cent of workforce at software industry is female. Women are progressing in most of the fields including those which have traditionally been untouched like aeronautics, armed forces, air force and navy, etc. The Census of 2001 data showing six point increase in sex ratio (number of females per 1000 males) between the census years in 1991 and 2001. Similarly, progress has been made with respect to indicators like health and nutrition, female workforce participation, female life expectancy, female infant mortality and maternal infant mortality.[5] In rural India, agriculture and allied industrial sectors employ as much as 89.5 per cent of the total female labour.[6]

For centuries, women all-over the world have not only been denied full justice, social, economic and political but as a "weaker section" they have been used, abused, exploited and then discarded to lead immoral, street vagrant and destitute life till their death. The general though unfortunate impression have ever since been that women are sub-human societies, an attempt of contempt and ridicule, a commodity for barter, an expendable asset and a plaything for mere sexual enjoyment. The Indian society is a tradition bound society where women have been socially, economically, physically, psychologically and sexually exploited from time immemorial. The concept of equality between male and female was almost unknown to us before the enactment of Indian Constitution. Thus, to combat socio-legal aspects regarding the rights relating to women, now efforts are undertaken both nationally and internationally.[7]

Indian Constitution and Working Women[8]

Constitutional rights and duties enumerated in Part III and IV of the Constitution of India are pivotal to the demand for protection of laws of women workers. The principle of gender equality is enshrined in the Indian Constitution in its Preamble, Fundamental Rights, Fundamental Duties and Directive Principles. The Constitution not only grants equality to women, but also empowers the State to adopt measures of positive discrimination in favour of women. Within the framework of a democratic polity, our laws, growth policies, plans and programmes have aimed at women's progress in different spheres. India has also ratified various international conventions and human rights instruments committing to secure equal rights for women.

The Preamble to the Constitution

The Preamble to the Constitution contains various goals including "the equality of status and opportunity" to all the citizens. This particular goal has been incorporated to give equal rights to women and men in terms of the status as well as opportunity. It has been the basis for much legislation like the Modern Hindu laws which aims at giving equal status and rights to the women.

Fundamental Rights

Even though, all the fundamental rights contained in Part III, Articles 12 to 35 are applicable to all the citizens irrespective of sex, certain fundamental rights contain specific and positive provisions to protect the rights of women. The Indian Constitution in its Part III has the following provisions for making women at par with men:

Article 14 of the Constitution guarantees to all equal protection of laws and equality before the law. Both these expressions have also been used in Universal Declaration of Human Rights (UDHR).[9] The equality before law is guaranteed to all without regard to sex, race, colour or nationality.

Accordingly Article 15(1) prohibits gender discrimination and Clause 3 of Article 15 of Constitution of India grants that the State may make special provision for women; this is a protectionist strategy and not an equalisation measure. Women should be provided with affirmative action by the State in order to help them overcome the handicap which they suffered under the patriarchal regime. State positively discriminate in favour of women by making special laws to empower women's socio-economic rights in the file of Criminal law, Service law, Labour law, etc. resorting to Article 15(3). As all the fundamental rights are made women-centric, there is every possibility of getting equality for women, and the Courts too have upheld the validity of the Article 51-A (e) which is related to women. Article 51-A (e) states that "It shall be the duty of every citizen of India to promote harmony and the spirit of common brotherhood amongst all the people of India transcending religion, linguistic, regional or sectional diversities; to renounce practices derogatory to the dignity of women" protective discriminatory provisions on the basis of Constitutional mandate. Article 16 of Constitution of India also explicitly mentions equality of opportunities for all and prohibits the discrimination against women.

As per the Article 21 of the Constitution of India, no person shall be deprived of life or personal liberty except according to procedure established by law. According to Article 21A of the Constitution of India, the State shall provide free and compulsory education to all children of the age of six and fourteen years in such manner as the State may, by law, determine.

Here, it is worth mentioning that women were considered as ineligible to work in arduous and hazardous jobs, such as in mining, glass industry etc. Of late, it is internationally being questioned as to whether it is proper to impose such restrictions or whether it would be better for it to be left to women to decide whether they can work in such jobs or not. One feels that such an approach would be right, as it has become quite common to see women loco-pilots, metro rail crew, flight commandants, astronauts etc. areas which were hitherto considered out of reach for women. The significant of the presence and contribution of women in several other areas including professional areas like accountancy, medical and legal professions show that they are second to none.

Seventh Schedule: Labour laws and its regulation are listed in the Union List and the Concurrent List in the 7th Schedule of the Constitution of India. The Parliament of India is thereby empowered to make laws with respect to the matters enumerated in the Union List and both, the Parliament of India, and the Legislature of any State is empowered to make laws with respect to the matters enumerated in the Concurrent List. The entries with regard to labour and its regulation in the 7th Schedule of the Constitution of India are given below: Union List: Entry No. 55: Regulation of labour and safety in mines and oil fields. Entry No. 61: Industrial disputes concerning union employees. Entry No. 65 Union agencies and institutions for professional, technical or vocational training. Concurrent List: Entry No. 22: Trade unions; Industrial and labour disputes. Entry No. 23: Social security and social insurance; employment and unemployment. Entry No. 24: Welfare of labour including conditions of work, provident funds, employers' liability, workmen's compensation, invalidity and old age person and maternity benefit.

International front: Millions of women throughout the world live in condition of abject deprivation and attacks against their fundamental human rights for no other reasons than that they are women. For example, the Supreme Court of United States in the year 1873 affirmed this 'divine ordinance' in Bradwell v. Illinois where Myra Bradwell's application for license to practice law was denied solely because she was woman giving the reasoning that the paramount destiny and mission of woman was to fulfil the noble and benign office of wife and mother, this being the law of creator. To combat this, the international community has since ages tried to play a decisive role in protecting human rights of women.[10]

The advancement of women has been a focus of the work of the United Nations since its creation which is evident by the United Nations Charter that proclaims one of the purpose of the United

Nations to achieve international cooperation in promoting and encouraging respect for human rights and fundamental freedoms for the people without any discrimination to race, sex, language or religion. The Commission on the Status of Women (CSW) established in 1946 as a mechanism to promote report on and monitor issues relating to the political, economic, civil, social and educational rights of women. Among its activities, the CSW drafted several conventions and declarations, including the Declaration on the Elimination of Discrimination against Women in 1967 and women focused agencies such as The United Nations Development Fund for Women (UNIFEM) and United Nations International Research and Training Institute for the Advancement of Women (INSTRAW).[11] Other efforts include the three key conferences held during the U.N. sponsored International Women's Decade (1976-85)-Mexico City (1975); Copenhagen (1980) and Nairobi (1985) that paved the way of the international scheme in the national protection of rights of women. Another significant conference was the Fourth World Conference on Women, held in 1995 in Beijing that referred to 'Women's right as human rights'.

The International Labour Organisation (ILO) ever since its inception has highlighted the role of women as worker by emphasizing that women worker should be given special attention as they have special difficulties which drive from her function in the family and from social attitudes and customs, in the interregnum between the two world wars, the ILO drafted and adopted three conventions on maternity protection (1919), on the limitation of employment of women in night shifts (revised in 1934) and on the ban on employing women in Sub-terranean work (1935). During the past two decades the notion of 'empowerment' of women has significantly impacted the paradigms of development. In 2001, the United Nations Population Fund (UNFPA) had promised gender equality and empowerment of women by 2005 as one of the eight Millennium Development Goals (MDGs). World Bank, World Health Organisation, (UNFPA) accepts women as disadvantaged gender globally, more so in developing nations. The lack of education and economic independence are the biggest factors that affect women's health. The UNFPA has indicated the need of investment in women education and healthcare in order to empower them and drastically reduce the gender violence. A strategic intervention is required if MDGs are to be met.[12]

In the present chapter the key Indian labour legislations, policy initiatives with special reference to working women (mentioned below) in the light of judicial judgements have been analysed. Protection given to women labour at the international level wherein effort has been made to discussion in comparison to Indian Constitution, legislative measures and policy framework along with the Conventions, Recommendations and Resolutions adopted by UNO and ILO. Labour laws in India have been enacted to cover, non-discrimination of women, equal and minimum wages, conditions of work and social security measures which is well depicted in the following classification:

I. Non-Discrimination Laws

1. The Maternity Benefit Act, 1961
2. The Sexual Harassment of Women at Workplace (Prevention, Prohibition and Redressal) Act, 2013

II. Wage Payment related laws

1. The Minimum Wages Act, 1948
2. The Equal Remuneration Act, 1976

III. Law relating to Health and Welfare of working women

1. The Factories Act, 1948
2. The Plantation Labour Act, 1952
3. The Mines Act, 1952
4. The Beedi and Cigar workers (Conditions of Employment) Act, 1966
5. The Contract Labour (Regulation and Abolition) Act, 1970
6. Inter-State Migrant Workmen (Regulation of Employment and Condition of Service) Act, 1979
7. Building and Other Construction Workers' (Regulation of Employment and Conditions of Service) Act, 1996

IV. Social Security Laws

1. The Employees' State Insurance Act, 1948.
2. The Employees' Provident Funds and Miscellaneous Provisions Act, 1952.
3. The Payment of Gratuity Act, 1972.
4. The Workmen's Compensation Act, 1923.

I. Non-Discrimination Laws

1. The Maternity Benefit Act, 1966

"One thing that conspicuously distinguishes women from men is that only women become pregnant; and if you subject a woman to disadvantageous treatment on the basis of her pregnant status, you would be denying her equal treatment under the law."[13]

Women with infants and young children, often have to pick between their job and their responsibility towards their children, due to that lack of facilities at their workplaces, in order to accommodate both. This problem stems from the idea that a woman's primary or natural responsibility is keeping of the home and raising children. Though crèches have to be mandatorily provided, such provisions are only possible in the formal workplace. The informal sector, where a majority of the active female populace is employed rarely provides such facilities. Thus resulting in, child bearing and rearing becoming deterrents for women's employment. The provision of maternity protection is essential in furthering the idea of equal opportunity in employment. The idea of providing for such benefits is to prevent childbirth from working as a deterrent to women, and to ensure that women do not have to pick between their "reproductive and productive roles."[14] Therefore, it is essential that maternity benefits through legislative or any other mechanism be provided mandatorily to women at the workplace in order to encourage more women to actively be part of the workforce.

The ILO Maternity Protection Convention and Recommendations of 2000, maternity leave is a mother's right to a period of leave for the purpose of rest and recuperation from childbirth and its consequences thereof. The convention provides for cash and medical benefits [Article 6(3)] and also a right to breast feed her child after returning to work (Article 3).

The ILO Maternity Protection Convention (2000) extends the provisions of ILO Maternity Protection Convention (Revised) 1952[15], providing that maternity leave (which is defined as leave from work granted to a woman for a continuous period before and after giving birth) ought to be provided to all employed women for a period of at least 14 weeks (Article 4.1). This refers not only to those women employed in the formal sector, but also those women employed in the informal sector. It further provides that unless otherwise provided by the national government, at least 6 weeks of maternity leave must be taken after the birth of the child (Article 4.4). The ILO convention also makes a provision for leave to be provided even after the maternity leave period either before or after childbirth in the case of medical complications or illness, if an appropriate medical certificate is provided (Article 5). The ILO Maternity Protection Recommendations 1981 also endorse an extension of the maternity leave period to 18 weeks, and to provide for protection against dismissal for a certain period after return from maternity leave. The ILO Maternity Protection Convention in Article 8 awards the right to return to the same work or a position with the same pay, after maternity leave. It also makes it unlawful to dismiss such an employee, except on grounds unrelated to pregnancy or the consequences thereof, with the burden of proof being the employer's to relieve. Many EU countries and other first world countries in order to alleviate the position of these new mothers provide for cash benefits to reduce the burden of having lost income for the period of maternity leave.[16]

The Maternity Benefit Act is one of the first legislations in India that was enacted exclusively to secure the interests and right of working women.[17] Motherhood is a very special experience in woman's life. A woman needs to able to give quality time to her child without having to worry about her job and her source of income.

The Maternity Benefit Act, 1961 is a social legislation whereby every woman employed, whether directly or through an agency, is entitled to the payment of maternity benefits at the rate of the average daily wage.[18] The Act extends to factories, mines, plantations, shops and establishments, and establishments to which the provisions of this Act have been declared to be applicable. The Employees State Insurance Act, 1948 (ESI) also provides for maternity benefits to specific employment sectors.[19] Factories and establishments which are covered by the ESI Act, 1948, do not fall under the purview of Maternity Benefit Act, 1961, since the maternity benefits of the ESI Act will apply to those factories and establishments.[20]

The Act follows the employer's liability approach, which means that the employer solely bears the full amount of liability for providing maternity protection and the employees are not required to make any contribution for availing of maternity benefits.

Section 5(3)[21] provides that a woman shall be entitled to maternity benefit for a maximum period of twelve weeks of which not more than six weeks[22] shall precede the date of her expected delivery.[23] In addition to this, the Government of India also makes provision for child care leave.[24]

Section 5(4)[25] provides that a woman who legally adopts a child below the age of three months or a commissioning mother shall be entitled to maternity benefit for a period of twelve weeks from the date the child is handed over to adopting mother or commissioning mother[26] as the case may be. The decision of Madras High Court dated March 4, 2013[27] to grant maternity leave to a mother who had a child through surrogate[28] procedure is important turning point in women's right and makes a distinction to motherhood. In the present case, the learned counsel for the petitioner drew attention of the court to the Universal Declaration of Human Rights evolved by the United Nations and adopted by the General Assembly on 10.12.1948. He placed reliance upon Article 25(2) which reads as follows:

> "(2) Motherhood and childhood are entitled to special care and assistance. All children whether born in or out of wedlock, shall enjoy the same social protection."

He also referred to the Beijing Declaration and Platform for Action Fourth World Conference on Women, dated 15.09.1995, wherein the right of all women to control all aspects of their health, in particular their own fertility is basic to their empowerment was reaffirmed. Articles 17 and 33 reads as follows:

> "17. The explicit recognition and reaffirmation of the right of all women to control all aspects of their health, in particular their own fertility, is basic to their empowerment;
>
> 33. Ensure respect for international law, including humanitarian law, in order to protect women and girls in particular;"

He further referred to the Convention on the Rights of the Child by United Nations General Assembly by a resolution on 20.11.1989, wherein Article 6 reads as follows:

> "1. States Parties recognise that every child has the inherent right to life. 2. States Parties shall ensure to the maximum extent possible the survival and development of the child."

In the light of this, he submitted that the petitioner is undoubtedly the mother of a minor girl child and she is entitled to develop bondage with the child obtained through surrogate agreement and there is no moral issue involved in this matter. In the interest of the child, the petitioner is entitled to have the leave granted in her favour and in future also she is entitled to have the name included as her daughter in the FMI card as she is the legitimate daughter of the petitioner. In the result the writ petition was allowed and the respondent was directed by the court to grant leave to the petitioner in terms of Rules 3-A recognizing the child obtained through surrogate procedure.

In the case of *B. Shah* v. *Presiding Officer, Labor Court*[29], wherein the petitioner claimed that she was paid her maternity benefit wages by deducting the wage due to her on Sundays, the Supreme Court defined the term 'week' to include wages for 7 days including Sundays and not 6 days.[30] The Court applying the principles of Article 4 of Convention No. 103, i.e. the Maternity Protection Convention (Revised), 1952[31] held that in interpreting provisions of beneficial piece of legislations like this one in hand which is intended to achieve the objective of doing social justice to women workers employed in the plantations and which squarely fall within the purview of Article 42 of the Constitution, the beneficial rule of construction which would enable the women workers not only to subsist but also to make up her dissipated energy, nurse her child, preserve her efficiency as a worker and the level of her previous efficiency and output has to be adopted by the Court.

The judicial approach to discrimination on the basis of sex in India is tremendously influenced by protectionist approach to gender difference, which has operated to preclude any entitlement to equality.[32]

The Supreme Court has held that not just regular women employees but even women who are engaged on a casual basis or on muster roll on daily wage basis can avail of the benefits of this Act.[33] The Supreme Court held that the Delhi Municipal Corporation was an 'industry' under the Industrial Disputes Act, 1947 and that the workers on the muster roll were 'workmen'. The Court applying the non-discrimination provisions of the Convention on the Elimination of all forms of Discrimination Against Women, (CEDAW) to the women workers held that the benefits of the Act, was directly applicable to the women employees on the muster roll as much as regularised employees. The amount of the maternity benefit entitled to the women prior to her expected delivery must be given to the woman within 48 hours of her producing proof of her expected delivery. The employer is under a duty to make a payment of Rs. 3,500 to the woman as medical bonus if no pre-natal confinement and post-natal care is provided for by the employer free of charge.

Maternity Leave—In Other Parts of the World[34]

In the developed economies and the EU, no countries provide less than 12 weeks maternity leave. 46 per cent of these countries provide 14-17 weeks of leave, while 46 per cent provide 18 weeks or more. The situation is similar in the non-EU and CIS (Commonwealth of Independent States) countries. All countries in this region provide at least 14 weeks maternity leave. Concerning cash benefits, 78 per cent of the countries in developed economies and the European Union provide cash benefits equal to at least 2/3 of earnings during 14 weeks of maternity leave, which is in conformity with ILO Convention No. 183. Only 22 per cent of these countries provide unpaid maternity leave or maternity leave that is paid less than 2/3 of earnings.

Africa

In Africa, 18 per cent of the countries provide less than 12 weeks of maternity leave. The most extreme case is Tunisia, which only allows women to be on leave for a period of 30 days. 34 per cent of the African countries provide 12-13 weeks of leave, while 48 per cent provide 14-18 weeks. This means that no country in this region provide 18 weeks or more. In regard to payment, 39 per cent of the countries in Africa provide cash benefits for at least 2/3 of earnings for 14 weeks. This is about half of the corresponding number for the developed economies and the EU. However, almost all of these countries (37 per cent in the region) pay 100 per cent of earnings. Concerning unpaid maternity leave, 61 per cent of the countries in Africa provide no cash benefits or benefits less than 2/3 of earnings for 14 weeks.

Asia and the Pacific

Similarly to Africa, no country in Asia and the pacific provide maternity leave for 18 weeks or more. Concerning the current ILO standard, only 4 countries (17 per cent) in the region provide at least 14 weeks of leave. Most countries (65 per cent) provide 12-13 weeks of 21 maternity leave, while four countries (17 per cent) provide fewer than 12 weeks. These are Malaysia, Nepal, Papua New Guinea and the Philippines.

Concerning cash benefits, only 17 per cent of countries in Asia and the Pacific provide at least 2/3 of earnings for 14 weeks. This is the lowest number among the three regions compared in this chapter. Out of this 17 per cent, one example is Mongolia that provides 70 per cent of earnings for 120 days, and another is Vietnam that provides 100 per cent of earnings for four to six months. It should however be noted that a large number of countries in this region provide full earnings during maternity leave, but for less than 14 weeks. Examples are Afghanistan (90 days), India (26 weeks), and Nepal (52 days).

Sexual Harassment of Women at Workplace (Prevention, Prohibition and Regulation) Act, 2013

Sexual harassment is one of the most venomous problems that the society is facing today. In addition to pay equity as a key dimension of gender equity in the workplace, another important aspect is the atmosphere and the working conditions, such that a worker, male or female, is able to do his or her job without the annoyance or barrier of being treated as a sexual object. The term had not been coined till 1974 when a clerical employee at Cornell University and several of her colleagues began to name the problem.[35] During the late 1970s, Cathrine MacKinnon (1979) developed a legal analysis of the problem and the conceptualisation of two kinds of sexual harassment: one that implicitly or explicitly demanded a quid pro quo exchange of sexual favours as a condition of employment; the other that created a hostile atmosphere that interfered with employee's work.[36] It has taken different connotations and inspired varied viewpoints over the period of time. Sexual harassment can be broadly defined as 'an unwelcomed sexual advance that leads to the creation of a hostile and offensive work environment for a person'. The laws of different countries have attempted to define it in different ways.[37] However, analysing the phenomenon of sexual harassment through the narrow prism of 'unwanted sexual behaviour' would highly limit our understanding of the concept.

Sexual harassment in the form of eve-teasing, molestation, sexual assault and rape is a wrong against the honour, dignity and self-respect of a woman. She loses confidence in life and her career is put at stake. Sexual harassment at the workplace is a universal problem.[38] What to talk about an ordinary employer, U.S. President Bill Clinton was also sued for sexual harassment of a women, who was employed by the State of Arkansas when he was the Governor there. She claimed that he demanded sex, in what she says was a crude and gross abuse of power when he was her boss.[39] In India, there are so many examples of sexual harassment of women for instance Jessica Lal murder case. In this case Jessica Lal, a 34-year-old local actress and model, had been hired to work as a celebrity bartender at the Tamarind Court restaurant in Delhi. She was working along with fellow actor Shayan Munshi. About three hundred people had reportedly been at the restaurant that night, including Manu Sharma, the 24-year-old son of Venod Sharma, who was a Congress Party minister at the time, arrived at Tamarind Court along with three friends, at around 11:15 pm. The bar officially closed at midnight, but there were a few who attempted to buy a few more drinks after the fact. Sharma was the last. According to Ramani, the owner of the restaurant who overheard the conversation between Sharma and Lal, Sharma walked up to the bar again at around 2 a.m. to order another drink. After he was told that the bar was closed, he offered Jessica Lal 1,000 rupees. She, in return, told him "I wouldn't give you a sip even if you gave me a thousand bucks." The word "sip", in this case, could have been a double entendre, and when Lal refused Sharma's advances so sharply he felt more inclined to draw his revolver. He fired two shots, one at the ceiling and the other at Jessica Lal. She was hit near her temple and collapsed. An ambulance was called and she was rushed to the hospital, where she was pronounced dead a few hours later.

The initial trial began in August of 1999. By the end of the hearings, four of the main witnesses who said they were present on the night of the murder turned hostile by retracting their initial statements. After extensive hearings of dozens of witnesses, all nine suspects, including Manu Sharma were acquitted in the lower courts on February 21, 2006.[40]

In another case of *Rupan Deol Bajaj* v. *K.P.S. Gill*[41], a senior IAS officer, Rupan Bajaj was slapped on the posterior by the then Chief of Police, Punjab—Mr. K.P.S. Gill at a dinner party in July 1988. Rupan Bajaj filed a suit against him, despite the public opinion that she was blowing it out of proportion, along with the attempts by all the senior officials of the state to suppress the matter. The Supreme Court in January, 1998, fined Mr. K.P.S. Gill Rs. 2.5 lacs in lieu of three months rigorous imprisonment under sections 294 and 509 of the Indian Penal Code.

Supreme Court in Bajaj judgment has clarified certain issues as to what constitutes 'modesty' and how it is to be judged. It has relied on common notions of mankind as to judge what is affront to women's dignity. Also, this has been considered bearing in mind contemporary social standards. In the dynamics of today's society, the uncharitable approach towards women cannot be acceptable. Courts have effectively expanded the scope so as to safeguard women's rights. This case set a precedent for ground breaking verdict in the case of Vishaka and reinforced the principle that nobody is above the rule of law and justice would be done.[42]

The Indian judicial experience with sexual harassment started with the case of *Vishaka* v. *State of Rajasthan.*[43] The case dealt with the brutal gang rape of Bhanwari Devi, a social worker who was working to spread awareness to end child marriage. The court decided to use this opportunity to create a protective framework for the female workforce of this country, an area where there had been huge lacunae in Indian Law. Thus, comprehensive guidelines were issued by the Supreme Court to ensure that the female workforce of this country is protected from sexual violence and sexually charged gender-discrimination in the workplace.[44] In the instant case for the first time sexual harassment had been explicitly-legally defined as an unwelcome sexual gesture or behaviour whether directly or indirectly as:

1. Sexually coloured remarks
2. Physical contact and advances
3. Showing pornography
4. A demand or request for sexual favours
5. Any other unwelcome physical, verbal/non-verbal conduct being sexual in nature.

It was in this landmark case that the sexual harassment was identified as a separate illegal behaviour. The Court held that it violated the Constitutional rights under Article 14, 15, 19(1) (g) and 21 and laid down a set of guidelines to deal with sexual harassment at the workplace till the legislature enacted a suitable legislation. In *Apparel Export Promotion Council Ltd.* v. *A.K. Chopra*[45], is the first case in which the Supreme Court applied the law laid down in Vishaka's case and upheld the dismissal of a superior officer of the Delhi based Apparel Export Promotion Council who was found guilty of sexual harassment of a subordinate female employee at the place of work on the ground that it violated her fundamental right guaranteed by Article 21 of the Constitution.

In accordance with and pursuant to the *Vishaka* judgment, several educational institutions and other establishments set up complaints mechanisms and formulated guidelines to inquire into and prevent sexual harassment at the workplace.

In both cases, the Supreme Court observed, that "In cases involving Human Rights, the Courts must be alive to the International Conventions and Instruments as far as possible to give effect to the principles contained therein such as the Convention on the Elimination of All forms of Discrimination Against Women, 1979 [CEDAW][46] and the Beijing Declaration[47] directing all state parties to take appropriate measures to prevent such discrimination."

The guidelines and judgments have identified sexual harassment as a question of power exerted by the perpetrator on the victim. Therefore, sexual harassment in addition to being a violation of the right to safe working conditions is also a violation of the right to bodily integrity of the woman.

In *Chairman Railway Board and Others* v. *Mrs. Chandrima Das and Others*[48], wherein the employer was vicariously held liable to compensate the victim of gang rape who happened to be a stranger and a foreigner, committed by its employees within its premises having far reaching implications. Thus, if a woman employee or even a stranger is subject to acts of sexual harassment of grave nature wherein the offender is another employee, the prospect of the employer being held vicariously liable for the acts of his servant committed on or within his premises appears to be real and opening the eyes of employers.

In *Arati Durgaram Gavandi* v. *Tata Metaliks Ltd. Vengrula and Ors*[49], this case was related to Article 15 and 21 of Constitution. Petitioner supervisor was only woman employee in the company. She was subjected to sexual harassment by an officer in company. Petitioner made complaint to management upon which management did not act as per guidelines laid down by Supreme Court in Vishaka. It was held that after receipt of complaint of sexual harassment, management was duly bound to act as per guidelines laid down in Vishaka's case.

It reveals from a critical analysis of various reported cases that the higher judiciary of the country has played a dynamic role in upholding the human right of women enshrined in the Constitution of India and as declared in several international instruments on human rights. It has been bold enough to lay down law on this sensitive issue.[50]

Unlike some of the developed countries of the world like Australia, Canada, U.K. and U.S.A. there is no central or state legislation to curb the evil of sexual harassment in India until 2010, only guidelines of the Court were there, but, no legislative step was taken to stop this heinous crime against the women even after 65 years of independence.[51] Therefore, looking into the gravity of the issue several attempts have been made by the Central Government to comply with the directions and guidelines laid down by the judiciary by proposing Bills on sexual harassment right from the year 2000. 3 September 2012 became a red letter day when Lok Sabha passed Sexual Harassment of Women at Workplace (Prevention, Prohibition and Redressal) Bill, 2010 without any discussion.[52]

The Sexual Harassment of Women at Workplace (Prevention, Prohibition and Redressal) Act, 2013[53]

It was the case of *Medha Kotwal Lele and Ors.* v. *Union of India*[54] which led to the making of the Act. In this judgment, the Hon'ble Supreme Court highlighted the non-compliance and non-adherence to the Vishaka guidelines in workplaces in India and urged the need for legislative enactment in this direction. The main objective of the passing of Act was that with more and more women are joining mainstream economy, so as to ensure safe, secure and enabling environment to every women, irrespective of her age, or employment status, free from all forms of sexual harassment by fixing the responsibility on the employer is the objective of the Act.

In chapter I of the Act various definitions are provided including the definition of employer, employee and workplace etc. It is a duty of every employer to prevent the Sexual Harassment of women from his organisation. It also provides that the promise of preferential treatment or the threat related to the employment by the employer will also counted as Sexual Harassment of women.

The chapter II of the Act makes it mandatory for an employer to set up an 'Internal Complaints Committee' at each office or branch of an organisation employing at least 10 employees to hear and redress grievances pertaining to sexual harassment. Extensive provisions have been made in chapter III for the constitution and jurisdiction of Local Complaints Committee. The Act provides for the constitution of Local Complaints Committee for the redressal of complaints of sexual harassment at workplace. It is the duty of every District Officer to constitute in the concerned district a local Complaints Committee for dealing with the cases of sexual harassment of those establishments where the internal complaint Committee has not been constituted. The District Officer shall designate one nodal officer in every block, taluka and tehsil in rural or tribal area and ward or municipality in the urban area, to receive the complaints of Sexual harassment. Such nodal officer is under obligation to forward such complaints of sexual harassment to the concerned local committee within 7 days, so that the committee can take action against the harasser as soon as possible. In chapter IV of the Act the procedure of making the complaint of sexual harassment has been dealt. A woman aggrieved of sexual harassment can make a complaint to the Internal Complaints

Committee or Local Complaints Committee along with the supporting documents and the names and addresses of the witnesses. Chapter V empowers the Internal Complaints Committee or Local Complaints Committee during the pendency of the inquiry to recommend to the employer, at the request of the aggrieved employee, interim measures for the prevention of any further harassment of a woman. These are the basic things which should be taken into consideration at the time of determining the quantum of compensation. Though the monetary compensation cannot restore the dignity of a woman but it may help her only in coming out of distress and meet other expenses which may arise out of the incident of Sexual harassment. The Act prescribes obligation and duties of employer. Chapter VII of the Act provides the duties and powers of District Officer to monitor the timely submission of reports furnished by the Local Committee; or to take such measures as may be necessary for engaging non-governmental organisations for creation of awareness on sexual harassment and the rights of the women. Chapter VIII of the Act contains the miscellaneous provisions which provide that the Committee should prepare and submit the annual reports to the employer and the District Officer. It also provides that if an employer fails to constitute an Internal Complaint Committee or does not comply with the requirements prescribed under the Sexual Harassment Act, a monetary penalty of up to Rs. 50,000 may be imposed on him. A repetition of the same offence could result in the punishment being doubled and/or de-registration of the entity or revocation of any statutory business licenses. So it is mandatory to comply with the provisions of the Act.

Sexual Harassment in Developed Economies

Incidents of sexual harassment are increasing exponentially, especially in Asian countries, which have over half the world's population. In India, a woman is sexually harassed every 12 minutes.[55] In China, 80 per cent of working women experienced sexual harassment at some stage of their career.[56] In Germany, a survey indicated that 93 per cent of working women were victims of sexual harassment as of 1998.[57] Approximately 6 of 10 nurses in Australia have experienced sexual harassment.[58] In Hong Kong most complaints received by the Equal Opportunities Commission

(EOC) in some recent years were of sexual harassment.[59] In the United States over 50 per cent of employed women had been sexually harassed.[60] In Canada, 51 per cent of women reported having experienced sexual violence at least once[61] and in Singapore almost 50 per cent women have been victims of sexual harassment.[62]

Graver forms of sexual harassment such as rape, incest, violent assault have been criminalised in almost all countries. Efforts to address sexual harassment problems started with the enactment of anti-discrimination laws prohibiting sexual harassment at the workplace.[63] Here, it is pertinent to take note of legislations pertaining to sexual harassment in different countries:

Australia

Under Australian Law, a person who sexually harasses someone else is primarily responsible for his behaviour. However, in many cases, the company also be held vicariously liable for sexual harassment by the employees, agents and contractors, unless it can show the steps that it took to prevent the sexual harassment from occurring. Under the Act[64], the employer must take all reasonable steps to minimize the risk of discrimination and harassment occurring. The Sex and Age Discrimination Legislation Amendment Act, 2011 amended the Sex Discrimination Act, 1984 in May 2011 to expand the protections against sexual harassment. The victims can complaint to the Australian Human Rights Commission in case he/she has been sexually harassed. The Commission will then investigate the complaint and will try to resolve the complaint through a process of conciliation, during which it will help the two parties involve by acting as an impartial person. If the complaint is not resolved, then the victim can take the complaint to Court.

Britain

The Acts that are applicable in Britain if you are subjected to sexual harassment at work are the Sex Discrimination Act, 1975. The Sex Discrimination Act makes it unlawful for employers in Great Britain to subject someone to sexual harassment. The Act also makes it unlawful to harass a transsexual person because they intend to undergo or are undergoing, or have undergone gender reassignment. Sexual harassment itself is prohibited by the Sex Discrimination Act but, in many instances, it will be accompanied by other forms of unfavourable treatment such as not being recruited, criticism of work, lack of promotion, enforced transfer and ill health or dismissal. The Employment Equality (Sex Discrimination) Regulations 2005 amended the Sex Discrimination Act in 2005. The new law extends the protection of sex discrimination rules to cover sexual harassment.

Brazil

In 2001, the Brazilian Government enacted a criminal law[65] defining sexual harassment as an embarrassing conduct performed by a worker in a superior hierarchical position against someone hierarchically inferior at work, in order to obtain advantages or sexual favours. The law made sexual harassment a crime with imprisonment from one up to two years. This legislation has set Brazil apart from most countries where harassment is dealt with under civil law.

Germany

Under the Protection of Employees Act, Employers and managers shall be required to protect employees against sexual harassment at the workplace and also both male and female employees can file a complaint if they are sexually harassed. Employees affected shall have the right to complain to those responsible in the enterprise or the department if they feel that they have been sexually harassed. The employer has an obligation to investigate the complaint and take appropriate measures to prevent the harassment from continuing. If the employer fails to do so, or applies measures which are obviously inadequate, the employees who are harassed shall have the right to suspend their activity at the workplace concerned, without loss of wages or salary, for as long as this is necessary for their protection. In effect as of 18th August, 2006, the German General Equal Treatment Act (Alleghenies Gleichbehandlungsgesetz-AGG) came into force. Objective of the law is to provide comprehensive protection against discrimination on the basis of race and ethnic origin, gender, religion or belief, disability, age or sexual orientation. For the area of employment law, the Act regulates in Sec. 7 AGG the prohibition to discriminate employees on the basis of the protected criteria.[66]

Denmark

Sexual harassment is defined as, when any verbal, non-verbal or physical action is used to change a victim's sexual status against the will of the victim and resulting in the victim feeling inferior or hurting the victim's dignity. Man and woman are looked upon as equal, and any action trying to change the balance in status with the differences in sex as a tool, is also sexual harassment. In the workplace, jokes, remarks, etc., are only deemed discriminatory if the employer has stated so in their written policy. Women are viewed as being responsible for confronting harassment themselves, such as by slapping the harasser in the face. Law number 1385 of December 21, 2005 regulates this area.

Spain

The Spanish Labour Act provides certain guarantees against sexual harassment. These rights include protection against physical or verbal conduct that may constitute sexual harassment. Under a recent amendment, 54.2 g of the Labour Act considers sexual harassment at workplace as a breach of the employment contract and hence it is valid clause to dismiss the harasser.

France

Article 222-33 of the French Criminal Code describes sexual harassment as, "The fact of harassing anyone using orders, threats or constraint, in order to obtain favours of a sexual nature, by a person abusing the authority that functions confer on him..." This means the harasser can only be someone with authority on the harassed (basically, there can not be sexual harassment between co-workers of the same rank).

Since the initial enactment of anti-sexual harassment legislation in France in 1992, sexual harassment was not only prohibited under the French Labour Code but was also a punishable offense under the Penal Code. However, the definitions in the Labour Code and the Penal Code were both vague and not entirely in sync and the French Counsel Constitutional (Constitutional Council) ruled them unconstitutional on May 4, 2012 (Consul Constitutional, May 4, 2012, n2012-240).[67] The new articles in the Labour Code and the Penal Code now both read as follows: "Harassment is the fact of imposing on a person, in a repetitive fashion, statement or behaviour of a sexual connation which violate a person's dignity by virtue of their degrading or humiliating character or create as concerns such person an intimidating, hostile or offensive situation."

II. Wage Related Laws

1. The Minimum Wages Act

In India the initiative for determination of minimum wages started in 1920 when a proposal for setting up Boards for determination of minimum wages in each industry was mooted. [68] Subsequently, in 1943 on the recommendation of the Standing Labour Committee and Indian Labour Conference, a Labour Investigation Committee was appointed to investigate into the question of wages and other matters like housing, social conditions and employment. The Indian Labour Conference considered a draft bill in this regard in 1945. The Standing Labour Committee in 1946 recommended enacting a separate legislation for the unorganised sector including working hours, minimum wages and paid holidays. Accordingly, a Minimum Wages Bill was introduced in the Central Legislative Assembly to provide for fixation of minimum wages in certain employments which was passed in 1946 and came into force in 1948.[69]

The Minimum Wages Act derives its principles from Article 39 and 43[70] provided in Directive Principles of State Policy of Constitution of India. The Minimum Wages Act[71] in India is welfare legislation which applies to the workers in the unorganised sector who lack power to collectively bargain with their employer. Wages in the organised sector are determined through negotiations and settlements between employer and employee. In unorganised sector, where labour is vulnerable to exploitation due to illiteracy and lack of effective bargaining power, minimum rates of wages are fixed both of Central and State Governments in the Scheduled employments falling within their respective jurisdictions under the provisions of the Minimum Wages Act, 1948.[72]

According to Section 3(b)[73], The State Government is empowered to fix minimum rates of wages for different classes of employees—skilled, unskilled, clerical, supervisory, etc., employed in any scheduled employment and to review and revise the same from time to time, the interval between the two revisions not exceeding five years.

In *Workmen of Reptakos Brett and Co. Ltd.* vs. *The Management of Reptakos Brett and Co. Ltd.*[74], the Tripartite Committee of the Indian Labour Conference accepted five norms for the fixation of 'minimum wage'[75]:

1. In calculating the minimum wage, the standard working class family should be taken to comprise three consumption units for one earner, the earnings of women, children and adolescents being disregarded.
2. Minimum food requirements should be calculated on the basis of a net intake of 2700 calories as recommended by Dr. Akroyd for an average Indian adult of moderate activity.
3. Clothing requirements should be estimated on the basis of a per capita consumption of 18 yards per annum, which would give for the average worker's family of four a total of 72 yards.
4. In respect of housing, the norm should be the minimum rent charged by Government in any area for houses provided under the Subsidised Industrial Housing Scheme for low-income groups; and
5. Fuel, lighting and other miscellaneous items of expenditure should constitute 20 per cent of the total minimum wage.

According to Section 12[76], the employer is bound to pay to every employee engaged in scheduled employment under his wages, at a rate not less than the minimum rate of wages fixed for that class of employees in that employment, without making any deduction therefrom except those permitted under the Payment of Wages Act.

The fact that an employer might find it difficult to carry on the business on the basis of minimum wages is an irrelevant consideration.[77] On similar lines it was held in *Workmen of Reptakos Brett and Co. Ltd.* v. *The Management of Reptakos Brett and Co. Ltd.*[78], the employees are entitled to the minimum wages at all times and under all circumstances. An employer who cannot pay the minimum wage has no right to engage labour and no justification to run the industry.[79]

Similarly, according to Section 13(1)(1), in regard to any scheduled employment, minimum rates of wages in respect of which have been fixed under this Act, the appropriate Government may fix the number of working hours; provide for rest day with wages and for payment for work on a rest day at a rate not less than the overtime rate.

Concept of National Floor Level Minimum Wage (NFLMW)

In order to have a uniform wage structure and to reduce the disparity in minimum wages across the country, the concept of NFLMW[80] was mooted on the basis of the recommendations of the National Commission on Rural Labour (NCRL) in 1991. The NFLMW, however, has no statutory backing. The State Governments are persuaded to fix minimum wages such that in none of the scheduled employments, the minimum wage is less than NFLMW.

Variation in the Minimum Wage Across the Globe

The Rate: The calculation of minimum wages is a cumbersome exercise often beyond the capability of the small scale unorganised sector employer and most often beyond the awareness level of the employee. Simplicity and uniformity in the calculation of minimum wages will go a long way in the enforcement of minimum wages. Implementation of minimum wage is not uniform across the States as the Variable Dearness Allowance (VDA) is not clubbed with minimum wage like for instance agriculture is not covered under the VDA in most States.

Nearly 50 per cent of the workforce consisting mainly of women is outside the purview of this Act[81] even after nearly 66 years of enactment of the Act. Further women are working in piece rated jobs or as helpers in own account enterprises where they are either paid much below the minimum wages or no wages (National Commission on Rural and Self-Employed Women).[82]

Minimum wage levels vary markedly across countries. This is often shown by comparing Minimum wage to wages in the middle of the wage spectrum (the so-called "median wage"). According to this measure, minimum wage range from 40 per cent or lower in the Czech Republic, Mexico, United States, Estonia and Japan, to more than 60 per cent in Slovenia, France, Chile and Turkey. At more than 80 per cent of the median wage in the formal sector, the minimum wage in Colombia is much higher than in any member country of Organisation for Economic Co-operation and Development (OECD).[83] The most controversial aspect of the minimum wage is, of course, the rate at which it is set.[84]

The OECD recently tweeted, "It illustrates the after-tax value of the hourly minimum wage, in US dollars, in the OECD countries that have instituted one. Australia and Luxembourg lead the group with wages over $9 an hour each, and Latvia and Mexico are at the bottom with wages under $2. The US, where the federal minimum wage is $7.25 per hour, or $6.26 after taxes, ranks 11th.

Broken down by state, however, some variation is found among the 45 states that require a minimum wage, ranging from $9.05 per hour in Washington, DC, to $5.15 an hour in Georgia and Wyoming. *The Guardian* reported that 21 States raised their minimum wage in 2015, and multiple states have begun the process of raising their minimum wages to $10.10 an hour."[85]

United States of America: Fair Labour Standards Act, 1938

The Fair Labor Standards Act (FLSA) applies to "employees who are engaged in interstate commerce or in the production of goods for commerce, or who are employed by an enterprise engaged in commerce or in the production of goods for commerce" unless the employer can claim an exemption from coverage.

Generally, an employer with at least $5,00,000 of business or gross sales in a year satisfies the commerce requirements of the FLSA and therefore that employer's workers are subject to the FLSA's protections if no other exemption applies. Several exemptions exist that relieve an employer from having to meet the statutory minimum wage, overtime, and record-keeping requirements.[86]

United Kingdom: National Minimum Wage Act, 1998

The National Minimum Wage Act, 1998 created, for the first time in the UK, a minimum wage which applies across all parts of the country and almost all sectors of the economy.[87] According to this Act minimum wage must be paid to all 'workers'.[88] This term is defined in s. 54(3) of the Act to exclude those who are genuinely self-employed.

Initiatives by International Labour Organisation (ILO) Conferences[89]:

Convention No. 26, Eleventh Session (1928)

Eleventh Session held on 30th Convention No. 99, May, 1928, was convened at Geneva. Adoption of proposals with regard to Minimum Wage Fixing Machinery was the first item on the agenda of the Session.

Convention No. 99, Thirty Fourth Session (1951)

The Thirty Fourth Session was held on 6th June, 1951 and the Convention concerning the Minimum Wage Fixing Machinery in Agriculture was the eighth item on the agenda of the Session. The guidelines for creation/maintenance of adequate machinery whereby Minimum Wages can be fixed for agricultural workers were similar to those stated for Minimum Wage Fixing Machinery in the 11th session of the ILO.

Convention No. 131, Fifty Fourth Session (1970)

In its 54th session of ILO held on 3rd June, 1970 in Geneva, passed the Convention[90] concerning Minimum Wage Fixing, with special reference to developing countries on 22nd June, 1970. It was thought that the earlier conventions with regard to the Minimum Wages had played a valuable part in protecting disadvantaged groups of wage earners and that another Convention was needed to complement the earlier ones, which, while of general application, will pay special regard to the needs of developing countries.

2. *The Equal Remuneration Act, 1976*

In Part IV relating to the Directive Principles of State Policy Article 39 of the Constitution of India envisages that the State shall direct its policy, among other things, towards securing that there is equal pay for equal work for both men and women.[91] It is true that the doctrine of equal pay for equal work could not be accorded the status of fundamental right in our country. While our Constitution was being framed because of the work socio-economic position of our state, which was freed from the yoke of colonisation, only a few years back.

In 1951, ILO passed a convention called "Equal Remuneration Convention" (No. 100)[92], the full title of which is "Equal remuneration for men and women workers for work for equal value". With a view to honour the ILO convention and also to implement Article 39 of the Indian Constitution, the President of India promulgated an ordinance in September 1975 (International Women's Year) called "Equal Remuneration Ordinance". After receiving the consent of the Parliament it was turned into "Equal Remuneration Act of 1976".

Under the Act, the employer is obliged to pay equal remuneration to men and women workers for same work or work of a similar nature. By "same work or work of a similar nature" is meant work in respect of which the skill, effort, and responsibility required are the same, when performed under similar working conditions, by a man or a woman and the differences, if any, between the skill, effort and responsibility required of a man and those required of a woman are not of practical importance in relation to the terms and condition of employment.[93] The Act also prohibits the discrimination against women during and subsequent to the recruitment of women workers for the same work or work of a similar nature.

Adjudicating on the definition of same work or work of a similar nature, in the case of *Mackinnon Mackenzie and Co. Ltd* vs. *Audrey DCosta*[94], the Supreme Court, dealing with a case in which the lady stenographers were being paid less than their male counterparts, stated that while deciding whether the work is the same or broadly similar, "the Authority should take a broad view; ...in ascertaining whether any differences are of practical importance, the Authority should take an equally broad approach for the very concept of similar work implies differences in details, but these should not defeat a claim for equality on trivial grounds. It should look at the duties actually performed not those theoretically possible". Although labour legislations can be effective when implemented, a national framework for implementation of already existing rights is necessary since it is at the sites of implementation that practices of wage inequality and discrimination are practiced.

The Act imposes duty on employer to pay equal remuneration to men and women workers for same work or work of similar nature. It further provides that no employer shall, while making recruitment for the same work or work of similar nature, or on any condition of service subsequent to recruitment such as promotions, training or transfer, make any discrimination against women except where the employment of women in such work is prohibited or restricted by or under any law for the time being in force provided that the provisions of this section shall not affect any priority or reservation for Scheduled Castes or Scheduled Tribes, ex-servicemen, retrenched employees or any other class or category of persons in the matter of recruitment to the posts in an establishment or employment.[95]

The verdict of Hon'ble Supreme Court in *Randhir Singh* v. *Union of India*[96] is the most remarkable strength provider to the concept of equal pay for equal work whereby the Hon'ble Supreme Court relied upon the term 'socialist' used in the Preamble of the Constitution and held that even "if it does not mean each according to his need it must at least mean equal pay for equal work." In this context, Justice O. Chinappa Reddy held that the principle of equal pay for equal work was deducible from Article 14 and 16 of the Constitution of India, may be properly applied to the cases of unequal scale of pay based on classification, though those drawing a different scale of pay do identical work under the same employer. It was held by the Court that the principle of "Equal pay for equal work though not a fundamental right" is certainly a Constitutional goal and, therefore, of enforcement through constitutional remedies under Article 32 of the Constitution.[97]

The doctrine of equal pay for equal work is equally applicable to persons employed on a daily wage basis. They are also entitled to the same wages as other permanent employees in the department employed to do identical work.[98]

In *Air India* v. *Nargesh Meerza and Others*[99], the Central Government had made a declaration by virtue of a notification that the differences in the remuneration of air hostesses and flight stewards were not based on sex because Section 16[100] clearly authorizes restrictions regarding remuneration to be paid by the employer if a declaration under it is made by the appropriate government. An air hostess challenged the discriminatory employment conditions for air hostess and stewards along with other thing. The Supreme Court held that the benefit conferred under the Act is not absolute and unconditional. From a comparison of the mode of recruitment, the classification, promotional avenues and other matters, it is clear that air hostesses form an absolute separate category from the Assistant pursers in many respects such as different grades, different promotional avenues and different service conditions. No hostile discrimination is therefore, involved. Thus equal pay for equal work has been denied to the air hostess which resulted as tremendous setback to the working women.

In the case of *People's Union for Democratic Rights and Others* v. *Union of India*[101], it was alleged before the court that the workers engaged in construction work were being discriminated in matters of payment of wages on the basis of sex, which is violative of the provisions of the Equal Remuneration Act, 1976. It was contended in the writ petition that the women workers were getting paid only Rs. 7 per day whereas the fee fixed for the men was Rs. 9.25 (of which Re. 1 was being appropriated by the contractors which was also before adjudication by the Court) and that the balance amount was being appropriated by the *jamadars* and contractors. In this case, the Supreme Court held that the non-payment of equal wages was a violation of the Right to Equality under Article 14 of the Constitution of India and directed the Union of India and Delhi Administration to ensure that the provisions of the Equal Remuneration Act, 1976, were not violated.

In the case of *Rajendra Grover* v. *Air India Ltd. and Ors.*[102], adjudicated in the Delhi High Court, members of the male cabin crew moved the Court to challenge a directive issued by Air India Ltd. dated 27.12.2005 which allowed both male and female crew to perform the job of In-flight Supervisors. This effectively meant that male cabin crew could be expected to serve on a flight under the supervision of a woman In Flight Supervisor (IFS) which was challenged by the pre-1997 male cabin crew as unconstitutional. The Court held that there was nothing unreasonable about this directive and that 'in effect it removes the men-only tag on the function of the IFS' and found that it enabled the female cabin crew to break the 'glass ceiling'. The provisions of the Equal Remuneration Act (ERA) itself were not the subject of interpretation in this case, but the facts in the judgment reflect the level of discrimination between men and women even in terms of access to the same kinds of work. Fortunately, the Court was able to uphold the principles of non-discrimination in this judgment. Employers divide the kind of work done between men and women and technically evade the provisions of the Equal Remuneration Act, 1976.

The recommendations of ILO that equal remuneration must be made based on "work of equal value". must be incorporated into national laws. It is recommended that the Equal Remuneration Act, 1976, particularly Section 2(h), Section 4, and Section 5 are amended to include "work of equal value" in addition to or in lieu of the phrase "work of similar nature". Better implementation of the Act is also required to ensure that women workers in the unorganised sector get paid the same wages as the male workers for work of equal value.

In *Air India Cabin Crew Assn.* v. *Yeshaswince Merchant and others with Air India Officer Assn. and another* v. *Air India Ltd. and tagged cases*[103], where appeals were filed against the Division Bench Judgment of the Bombay High Court. In a batch of petitions filed by the respondents Air India Air Hostesses Association and its members, the High Court held that the age of retirement from flying duties of air hostesses at the age of 50 years with option to them to accept post for ground duties after 50 and up to the age of 58 years is discrimination against them based on sex which is violative of Articles 14, 15 and 16 of the Constitution of India as also Section 5 of Equal Remuneration Act, 1976 and contrary to the mandatory directions issued by the Central Government under Section 34 of the Air India Corporation Act, 1953.

Equal Pay: An International Perspective

Worldwide, women only make 77 cents for every dollar earned by men. As a result, there is a lifetime of income inequality between men and women and more women are retiring into poverty.[104] In 2006, women's average hourly pay (excluding overtime) was still 17.2 per cent less than that of men.[105] The right not to be discriminated against is a fundamental right which features in all the major human rights instrument. The vast majority of international instruments focus on pay inequality between men and women.[106]

There are two formulations in order to define workers' entitlement. One is 'equal pay for equal work'[107], and the other (which is more common) is 'equal pay for work of equal value'[108]. The former carries the risk that it might be given a narrow interpretation. 'Equal work' implies that the work done by the woman and the person with whom she seeks equality must be the same. The concept of 'work of equal value' is much more radical. On this approach, a woman might be able to claim equal pay with a man doing a different job, provided that their jobs are of equal value.[109]

United States of America: Equal Pay Act, 1963[110]

A landmark U.S. legislation mandating equal pay for equal work is a measure to end gender-based disparity. The National War Labour Board first advocated equal pay for equal work in 1942, and an equal pay Act was proposed in 1945. Eighteen years later, on June 10, 1963, President John F. Kennedy signed the Equal Pay Act into law. It was enacted as an amendment to the Fair Labour Standards Act of 1938, which regulates minimum wages, overtime, and child labour.[111] The prime provision forbids wage discrimination "between employees on the basis of sex" when employees perform "equal Work", on jobs in the same establishment requiring "equal skill, effort and responsibility, and which are performed under similar working conditions..."[112]

United Kingdom: Equal Pay Act, 1970

The Equal Pay Act, 1970 is an Act of the United Kingdom Parliament which prohibits any less favourable treatment between men and women in terms of pay and conditions of employment.[113] According to section 1(6)(a) of the Act, the Act applies to workers broadly defined, so it includes employees, workers and those self-employed people who undertake to perform work personally. The main mechanism for enforcing equal pay is individual litigation, though some claimants may be able to get help from the Equality and Human Rights Commission or from their trade union. To bring a claim under the Act, a woman must show that she is doing 'like work' or 'work of equal value' to that of a man 'in the same employment' her ('comparator').[114]

In *Leverton* v. *Clwyd*[115] it was held that the woman can only compare her treatment with that of a man at one of the employer's other establishments if 'common terms and conditions of employment' are observed at both.

III. Legislation Relating to Health and Welfare of Working Women

Chart given below shows Indian legislations providing for health and welfare benefits:

Sr. No.	*Act*	*About the Act*
1	The Factories Act, 1948	This Act provides for the regulation of the functioning of a factory and makes provisions for health, safety and welfare of the labour force employed in a factory. A factory has been defined by the Courts as any premises, including the precincts thereof, which carry on manufacturing processes. The Act applies only to those places where 10 or more workers are working with the aid of power or 20 or more workers are working without the aid of power.
2	The Plantation Labour Act, 1951	The Act provides for the regulation of condition of work of plantation workers and provide for their welfare. Though, in the first instance, it applies to tea, coffee, rubber, and cinnamon plantations, the State governments have been empowered to extend the provisions of this Act to other plantations with the approval of Central Government.
3	The Mines Act, 1952	The Act has been enacted to amend and consolidate the law relating to the regulation of labour and safety in mines. It seeks to regulate the working conditions in mines by providing for measures required to be taken for the safety and security of workers employed therein. The Act applies to all the mines defined under section 21(i).

(Contd.)

Sr. No.	Act	About the Act
4	The Beedi and Cigar Workers (Conditions of Employment) Act, 1966	This Act provides for the welfare and regulates conditions of work for workers engaged in Beedi and Cigar establishments and also applies to wage workers and home workers but not the self-employed workers/persons in private dwelling houses. The Act was enacted since employers were splitting their establishments into smaller units so that the provisions of the Factories Act, 1948, were not applicable to them.
5.	The Contract Labour (Regulation and Abolition) Act, 1970	The Contract Labour (Regulation and Abolition) Act, 1970, regulates the employment of contract labour and prohibits its use in certain circumstances. The primary object of the Act is to stop the exploitation of contract labourers carried out by contractors and establishments. It applies to all establishments and contractors who currently, or in the preceding year, employed 20 or more contract workers.
6.	Inter-State Migrant Workmen (Regulation of Employment and Condition of Service) Act, 1979	The Act was enacted in recognition of the exploitation of labourers by contractors who recruit labour for work outside the State by paying poor wages and engaging labour under extremely difficult work conditions. This Act is applicable to any establishment or contractors, which hires five or more inter-state migrant workers.
7.	Building and Other Construction Workers' (Regulation of Employment and Conditions of Service) Act 1996.	This is applicable to the establishments engaging ten or more building and other constructions workers. It seeks to regulate the employment and conditions of work for building and other construction workers and provides for their safety, health and other welfare measures. The establishments engaging less than ten workers are not covered under this Act.

Beneficial Provisions for Working Women provided under abovementioned legislations:

A. Crèches

The following has been extracted from a report of Committee for Legal Aid to Poor and Forum for Crèche and Childcare Service[116]: "The birth of a child brings overwhelming emotions, joy, and happiness in the minds of many, and the baby needs not only the love, care and attention of the family, but [of] the entire society.

The little, tender human beings are born to love all and to be loved by all. But what actually this vulnerable segment of our society receives is a matter of great irony....... We are a democracy. We have given unto ourselves a Constitution which defines and determines the manner of governance, keeping the concept of a welfare state at the forefront. Children between the age of 0 [and] 8... [who] come within the purview of child right[s] in early childhood, though [they] do not possess [the] voting right, are nevertheless citizens of our country for whom promises have been made in our Constitution.... Maternity and child-care support is seen as a major strategy to break the cycle of poverty. Day care and crèches have implication[s] for child survival and development, women's health, increased economic productivity and women's empowerment, school entry and retention, especially for the girl child, prevention of child labour, child prostitution and child abuse and, above all, an equitable development.... A holistic approach with a multi-pronged strategy is necessary that includes day-care services, food security, maternity entitlement, social security, education and adequate health-care systems."

A Crèche is a nursery.[117] It is a place where babies of working mothers are taken care of while the mothers are at work. From employers' point of view the provision of onsite crèche is beneficial as it reduces absenteeism of workers, reduces cost related to workplace injuries, greater daily output of women workers on the other hand from workers point of view, they appreciate relief from worrying about care and if not crèche, workers will look for other alternatives which may not be that convenient or affordable.[118]

Section 48 of the Factories Act, 1948 provides that in factory wherein more than 30 women workers are ordinarily employed there shall be provided and maintained a suitable room for use of children under the age of 6 years of such women. Such rooms shall provide adequate accommodation, and shall be adequately lighted and ventilated. Such rooms shall be maintained in a clean and sanitary condition and shall be under the charge of women trained in the care of children and infants.[119]

Here, it is also pertinent to mention International Labour, Organisation (ILO)'s, Welfare Facilities Recommendation which provides for special provisions for women for providing sitting arrangements to them while at work and for rest rooms to meet their needs.[120]

Night Work

The Working Time Regulations 1998[121] (WTR) provide that night time is ordinarily the period between 11 pm and 6 am. According to WTR regulation[122], a relevant agreement (that is, a collective agreement, a workforce agreement, or a written agreement between the worker and the employer) may specify different period as night time, provided that this period:[123]

a. Includes the hours between midnight and 5 am
b. Does not began earlier than 10 pm or end later than 7 am
c. Lasts for seven hours.

Various Indian legislations prohibit women from working at night.[124] While the Act[125] permits for State Governments to vary these limits by notification, it mandates that the notification cannot make a variation which allows a woman worker to work between 10 p.m and 5 a.m. This beneficial provision may also be criticised from the perspective that prohibiting women workers from working at night, based on sex is unreasonable and amounts to discrimination by the State since it take away the right of choice of a woman worker to work at night and legitimises the role of the State in enacting arbitrary laws which curtails the freedom of association and right to opportunity and employment of women at any time they choose. This prohibition has resulted in a decrease of the employment of women workers by employers because it means adding more people to the muster rolls as one entire shift of workers becomes unavailable for work. No prohibition through protective legislative can be made which denies women their right to equality of opportunity and treatment.

The Madras High Court in the case of *Vasantha R.* v. *Union of India*[126], struck down Section 66(1)(b) on the grounds that it was violative of Article 14, 15 and 16 of the Constitution of India. The petitioners were women workers who were working in the mill and some who were on the management of the various mills or factories filed petitions challenging the constitutionality and the batch of writ petitions was filed on the grounds that no discrimination should be practiced against women on account of their gender. The petitioner could not work in the third shift between 10 p.m. and 6 a.m. due to the statutory provisions banning night work of women. The Court held that, "potential employment cannot be denied on the sole ground of sex when no other factor arises" and struck down Section 66(1) (b). The Court laid out detailed guidelines in order to ensure the safety and welfare of women workers in the night shift.

The Union Government decided to amend section 66 (1) (b)[127] to provide for women working in late night shift.[128]

The position in international law, regarding the question of whether night work was detrimental to the health and welfare of women workers has changed over the decades. The ILO Conventions have shifted from the position of a blanket ban to a position which recognises that all work in night shifts need not be detrimental to the health of the woman.[129] The Protocol to Convention No. 89[130] stipulates that national laws or regulations may provide, in consultation with employers and workers' organisations, variations in the prescribed time limits and exemptions from the prohibition of the night work contained in Convention No. 89. Thereafter, the Night Work Convention, 1990 (No. 171) has also been adopted by the ILO on the premise that night work itself has effects which are detrimental to health, is generative of difficulties for the family and social life of the worker and provides for special compensation and regulations for men and women alike. It is necessary that Convention No. 171 is ratified by the Indian State and labour laws are harmonised to more egalitarian values.[131]

B. Separate Latrine and Urinal Facilities

Section 20 of the Mines Act, 1952 says that there shall be provided, separately for males and females in every mine a sufficient number of latrines and urinals of prescribed types so situated as to be convenient and accessible to persons employed in the mine at all times. It also provides that the latrines and urinals shall be properly lighted, ventilated and maintained in a clean and sanitary condition. It also empowers Central Government to specify the number of latrines and urinals to be provided in any mine, in proportion to the number of males and females and provide other matter relating to the sanitation. [132]

C. Prohibition of Work in Hazardous Occupation/Health and Safety Measures

Hazardous occupation or occupational hazard is a hazard experienced at the workplace. It can encompass many types of hazards including chemical hazard, biological (biohazard), psychosocial and physical hazard.[133]

In India, the Factories Act, 1948 prohibits employment of women in dangerous occupations. Section 22(2) of the Factories Act, 1948 provides that no woman shall be allowed to clean, lubricate or adjust any part of a prime mover or of any transmission machinery while the prime mover or transmission machinery is in motion, or to clean, lubricate or adjust any part of any machine if the cleaning, lubrication or adjustment thereof would expose the woman to risk of injury from any moving part either of that machine or of any adjacent machinery. Section 27 of the Factories Act, 1948 prohibits employment of women in any part of a factory for pressing cotton in which a cotton opener is at work.[134]

The ILO Constitution sets forth the principle that workers should be protected from sickness, disease and injury arising from their employment. Yet for millions of workers the reality is very different. An estimated 2.3 million people die every year from work-related accidents and diseases. More than 160 million people suffer from occupational and work-related diseases, and there are 313 million non-fatal accidents per year. The suffering caused by such accidents and illnesses to workers and their families is incalculable. In economic terms, the ILO has estimated that more than 4 per cent of the world's annual GDP is lost as a consequence of occupational accidents and diseases. Employers face costly early retirements, loss of skilled staff, absenteeism, and high insurance premiums due to work-related accidents and diseases. Yet many of these tragedies are preventable through the implementation of sound prevention, reporting and inspection practices. ILO standards on occupational safety and health provide essential tools for governments, employers, and workers to establish such practices and to provide for maximum safety at work.[135]

At international front ILO has adopted various general standards specifically dealing with occupational safety and health, as well as Codes of Practice. Nearly half of ILO instruments deal directly or indirectly with occupational safety and health issues.[136]

In the case of *Pearson* v. *Belgium Co. Ltd.*[137], the question was whether stationary parts of machine can be cleaned by a woman if the machine as a whole is in motion. It was held by the Court that if the machinery as a whole is not in motion even the stationary parts of the machine cannot be cleaned by a woman.

In *B.N. Gamadia* v. *Emperor*[138], it was held that both the legislature and judiciary have shown concern about the security of women workers and every precaution is being taken to protect them against the risk of employment.

D. Hours of Work

Working time has traditionally been regarded as a matter for collective bargaining or for managerial decision making. Nowadays, three important aspects of working time are regulated by legislation. First, the Working Time Regulation 1998 seek to regulate the working time of all the workers, by prescribing limits on the maximum number of hours that can be worked in the week and by requiring employers to give their workers daily and weekly rest breaks and annual holidays. Second, the law forbids discrimination against those who work part-time. Third, the law provides various kinds of leave to enable employees to combine work and family life: maternity leave, paternity leave and emergency leave.[139]

Legislations both at national and international positions have attempted to regulate the working hours of both men and women. Under the Factories Act, 1948, the daily hours of work of adult workers have been fixed at 9. Though the Act permits men under certain circumstances to work for more than 9 hours on any day, it does not permit women to work beyond this limit.[140]

Article 7 of ICESCR[141] says that, "The States Parties to the present Covenant recognise the right of everyone to the enjoyment of just and favourable conditions of work which ensure, in particular....(d) Rest, leisure and reasonable limitation of working hours and periodic holidays with pay, as well as remuneration for public holidays." Long working hours have been a concern of the ILO from its inception: the first convention to address working time is Convention 1 of 1919.[142] The basic ILO standards are that the working day should be limited to eight hours, the working week should be limited to forty-eight hours, and that there should be a continuous twenty-four hour rest period in every seven days. Once a worker has completed a year's continuous service, he or she should be entitled to three weeks' paid holiday.[143]

E. Legislations Relating to Social Security

According to Friedlander, social security is "a programme of protection provided by society against the contingencies of modern life—sickness, unemployment, old age, dependency, industrial accidents and invalidism against which an individual cannot be expected to protect himself and his family by his own ability and foresight."[144] The purpose of all social security legislations is three fold: Firstly, compensation—social security provides for income security and is based upon the idea during the spells of risks, the individual and his family should not be subjected to double calamity involving both destitution and loss of health; Secondly—restoration implying cure of the sick and lastly, prevention—social security is designed to avoid the loss of productive capacity due to sickness and to render the available resources which are used up by avoidable disease and idleness and thus increase the intellectual, material and moral well-being of community.

While Social Security is a programme that is vitally important to all Americans, it is especially important to the financial security of women. There are a number of reasons why this is so. First of all, women live longer than men. On average, women today who reach age 65 outlive men by two years. These additional years of longevity increase the risk that women may outlive their savings or that their pensions may lose their purchasing power.[145]

Despite the comprehensive increases that have occurred in women's participation in the labour force, and the economic benefits derived from that participation, women continue to have fewer assets and income in retirement, and depend more heavily than do men on Social Security as the primary source of their financial well-being in retirement. We owe it to our mothers, grandmothers and daughters to address this inequity and improve the Social Security programme for future generations.

Chart given below shows Indian legislations providing social security benefits:

Sr. No.	Act	About The Act
1	The Employees' State Insurance Act, 1948	The Act provides social security to Industrial workers in India. The Act extends to employees of factories, including government factories and seasonal factories. The Central or State Government is empowered to extend the provisions of this Act by notification to any establishment, which is industrial, agricultural, commercial or otherwise.
2	The Employees' Provident Funds and Miscellaneous Provisions Act, 1952	This Act provides the legal basis for three social security schemes, to act as safety net in cases of old age, disablement, widowhood or to provide for health or education related contingencies. These schemes are the Employee' Provident Fund Scheme, 1952; the Employees' Deposit Linked Insurance Scheme, 1976; and the Employees' Pension Scheme, 1995. The schemes require compulsory contributions from the employee and the employer, the rates of contributions being different for different industries.
3	The Payment of Gratuity Act, 1972	The Act envisages providing a retirement benefit to the workmen who have rendered long and unblemished service to the employer, and thus contributed to the prosperity to the employer.
4	The Workmen's Compensation Act, 1923	Originally enacted as the Workmen's Compensation Act in 1923, this legislation was renamed as the Employees Compensation Act in 2009. The Act establishes a statutory duty of the employer to pay monetary compensation to an employee, in case the latter acquires injury or contracts any illness, in course of his/her work. To be eligible for compensation, a person must be engaged in an employment listed in Schedule II of the Act, which has a range of occupations

Benefici al provision for working women provided under abovementioned legislations:

A. Sickness Benefit

According to the Employees State Insurance Act, 1948[146] sickness benefit[147] represents periodical payment made to an insured person (IP) for the period of certified sickness. This benefit is provided to an employee when he needs medical treatment and attendance is also given with wages on medical ground. Sickness benefit is roughly 50 per cent of average daily wages.

It is a qualifying type benefit and to become eligible to sickness benefit an IP should have paid contribution not less than 78 days during the corresponding contribution period. A newly entered person in insurable job has to wait till 9 months to become eligible for this benefit. Facility of this benefit is payable to 91 days in any two consecutive period. No benefit is admissible for the first two days of the spell of sickness which is called waiting period. This benefit is divided in two parts as follows:

(i) Extended Sickness Benefit

Insured persons suffering from long term ailment like T.B., mental diseases etc. and experiencing great hardships on expiry of 91 days, sickness benefit period can be converted in extended sickness benefit which is normally 25 per cent more than the sickness benefit rate. The ESIC has a common list of such diseases and it was last reviewed on 5 December, 1999 and came in effect from 1 January, 2000. Presently, this list includes 34 diseases in 11 groups.

(ii) Enhanced Sickness Benefit

This benefit is given to insured men and insured women for vasectomy and tubectomy. It is double the rate of sickness benefit i.e. about the full average daily wages. Duration of enhanced benefit is up to 7 days in the case of vasectomy and up to 14 days in tubectomy from the date of operation.

Any person in receipt of sickness benefit is required to remain in under medical care and treatment at dispensary/hospital or any other institution as recognised in the Act. Cash benefit is paid by local office either personally to an employee or is remitted by post.

Similarly, ILO Convention 130 concerning medical care and sickness benefit, 1969[148] provide under article 18 that each member shall secure to the persons protected, subject to prescribed conditions, the provision of sickness benefit in respect of the contingency referred to in sub-paragraph (b) of Article 7.[149]

B. Medical Benefit[150]

The ESI Act provides all kind of medical facilities and treatment to insured employee and his family during sickness, injury, accident and every kind of disease arising out of employment. The ESIC has now decided to modernise the ESI hospitals to provide better medical services to the beneficiaries.[151]

The medical benefit is divided into two categories as under:

(i) Full Medical Care

This benefit consists of hospitalisation facilities including specialist services, drugs, dressings and diets as required in-patient. All such kind of services is provided to workers and their family during ailment or illness.

(ii) Expended Medical Care

Expended medical care includes the facilities of consultation with the specialists and supply of special medicines and drugs as may be prescribed by the doctors during the out-patient care. Special laboratory tests and X-Ray services are also given.

C. Disablement Benefit

Disablement[152] benefit[153] is payable in the form of cash in installments, to an employee who is injured in the course of his employment and is, permanently or temporarily disabled, or contacts any occupational disease. Disablement is one of the very important provision which provides help to a workman at the time of disablement. Workers who work in dangerous working conditions sometimes, instead of having certain safety measures, met serious accidents and injuries which may result in loss of earning capacity of the concerned worker.

D. Dependent's Benefit

This benefit is provided to the dependents of such employee who get death after employment injury. The ESI Act divides dependents in two categories and in first category widow and children of the deceased employee is included whereas second category consists of parents, grandparents and others. Pension is given to the family members of expired employee. Widow receives this pension for whole life or until the second marriage however, minor children get it till the age of 18 years.[154]

Notes

1. Dr. Meenakshi Gupta, *Women Rights under Labour Laws,* Regal Publications, New Delhi, 2016, p. 37.
2. Ross Prizzia, "An International Perspective of Privatisation and Women Workers", *Journal of International Women's Studies,* November, 2005, p. 7.
3. Pragya Singh, *Women Education, Employment and Gender Discrimination,* Mohit Publications, New Delhi, 2010, pp. 3-4.
4. Centre for Social Research, *Analysis on Effectiveness of the Implementation of the Maternity Benefit Act, 1961",* National Commission for Women, Govt. of India, New Delhi (May 2014).
5. Nidhi Shukla, *Gender Justice and Domestic Violence,* Regal Publications, New Delhi, 2014, p. 3.
6. Meenakshi Poonia and Others, *Women and Human Rights in India,* Sonali Publications, New Delhi, 2011, p. 71.
7. Rashee Jain, *Text Book on Human Rights Law and Practice,* Universal Law Publications, New Delhi, 2016, p. 41.
8. Padmaja Mallavajjula, "Empowerment of women under socio-economic and political sphere in the light of Indian Constitution", *www.IndianJournals.com,* Accessed: January 3, 2018, 10:00am
9. The right not to be discriminated against features in almost every human right document. Article 7 of *UDHR* says that all are equal before the law and are entitled without any discrimination to equal protection of the law. All are entitled to equal protection against any discrimination in violation of this Declaration and against any incitement to such discrimination. Similar provision is made under article 26 of *the International Covenant on Civil and Political Rights, 1966 (ICCPR) and article 2(2) of International Covenant of Economic, Social and Cultural Rights, 1966 (ICESCR).*
10. Rashi, n. 7.
11. *Universal Declaration of Human Rights, 1948* set out principles that considers women as part of humanity and has granted them all rights as were granted to men. Similarly, *Convention on the Political Rights of Women, 1952,* obligates the State parties to ensure that women have right to vote in elections and to hold public office on equal

terms with men. Besides this, other United Nations effort include the *Convention on The Nationality of Married Women, 1957, Covenant on Consent to Marriage, Minimum Age for Marriage and Registration of Marriages, 1964, International Covenant on Civil and Political Rights, 1966 and international Covenant on Economic, Social and Cultural Rights, 1966, Declaration on the Protection of Women and Children in Emergency and Armed Conflict, 1974, Convention on Elimination of All Forms of Discrimination against Women, 1979, Declaration on the Elimination of Violence Against Women, 1993,* which aimed at removing gender disparity.

12. Mithilesh Kumar Sinha, "Women Empowerment: A New Roadmap Required", Bipin Kumar (ed.), *Globalisation and Women Empowerment: Multidimensional Approaches*, Deep & Deep Publications, New Delhi, 2009, pp. 105-106.
13. Nomination of Ruth Bader Ginsburg to be Associate Justice of the Supreme Court of the United States: Hearing before the S. Comm. on the Judiciary, 103d Cong. 206 (1993) (statement of Judge Ginsburg): Ayushi Singhal, "Analysing the Legal Viability of No Pregnancy Clauses in Film Contracts" *India Law Journal*, 2016, *http://www.indialawjournal.org/articles.php*, Accessed: April 1, 2018, 10:12am.
14. "Yashaswini Prasad, Standards for Women in Labour Law", *https://www.lawctopus.com/academike/standards-women-labour-law*. Accessed: March 14, 2018, 11:28 am.
15. *Maternity Protection Convention 2000 (No. 183)*, Convention concerning the revision of the *Maternity Protection Convention (Revised), 1952* (Entry into force: 07 Feb 2002), *http://www.ilo.org/dyn/normlex/en/f?p=NORMLEXPUB:12100:0::NO::P12100_ILO_CODE:C183*, Accessed: March 03, 2018, 01:04 pm.
16. Yashaswini Prasad, n. 11.
17. Raghavivishwanath, "Law and the Mother-Maternity Benefit Act", Lex Warrier, Vol. VI Issue IV, April 2015, *Lexwarrier.in*, Accessed: September 12, 2017, 02:45 pm.
18. Average daily wage means the average of women's wages payable to her for the days on which has worked during the period of three calendar months immediately preceding the date from which she absents herself on account of her maternity, the minimum rate of wage fixed under the *Minimum Wages Act, 1948* or one rupee a day whichever is higher.
19. According to section 46 (b) periodical payments to an insured woman in case of confinement or miscarriage or sickness arising out of pregnancy, confinement, premature birth of child or miscarriage, such woman being certified to be eligible for such payments by an authority specified in this behalf by the regulations (hereinafter referred to as maternity benefit) and section 50 provides that, "The

qualification of an insured woman to claim maternity benefit, the conditions subject to which such benefit may be given, the rates and period thereof shall be such as may be prescribed by the Central Government".

20. The coverage under *The ESI Act, 1948* is however at present restricted to factories and certain other specified categories of establishments located in specified areas. The Maternity Benefit Act therefore, applies to women employees employed in establishments which are not covered by ESI Act and also to women employees, employed in establishments covered by ESI Act, but who are out of its coverage because of the wage limit. Dr. Meenakshi Gupta, n. 6, p. 184.
21. *The Maternity Benefit Act, 1961* (Act 53 of 1961), The Ministry of Labour and Employment, Government of India *vide* Official Gazette notification dated 31 March 2017.
22. For the words "twelve weeks of which not more than six weeks", the words "twenty-six weeks of which are not more than eight weeks" shall be substituted. *The Maternity Benefit Amendment Act, 2017* (No. 6 of 2017).
23. In year 1952, the ILO Maternity Protection Convention (No. 103) prescribed at least 12 weeks of maternity leave. Since year 2000, the ILO, however, mandates the leave period to be 14 weeks (Convention No. 183). In addition, the accompanying Recommendation (No. 191) suggests that countries should try to increase the period of leave to 18 weeks. Although Convention No. 183 has only been ratified in 17 countries, 51 per cent of all countries in the world provide maternity leave for at least 14 weeks and 20 per cent provide it for at least 18 weeks. In fact, only 14 per cent of all countries provide less than 12 weeks of maternity leave.
24. "Child care leave" means the leave admissible to a female Government employee for a maximum period of two years (i.e. 730 days) during the entire service for taking care of her two eldest surviving children upto the age of 18 years only, provided under section 9 (3) of Haryana Civil Services (Leave) Rules, 2016. *http://www.finhry.gov.in/CSR2016/HCSLeaveEnglish.pdf: Accessed April 4,2018, 9:56 am.*
25. *The Maternity Benefit Amendment Act, 2017* (No. 6 of 2017).
26. Section 3 [b (a)], The Maternity Benefit Amendment Act, 2017, "Commissioning mother means a biological mother who uses her egg to create an embryo implanted in any other woman".
27. *K. Kalaiselvi v. Chennai Port Trust,* rep by the Chairman, 1, Rajaji Salai, Chennai.
28. The question of becoming parents through surrogacy came to be considered by the Supreme Court in a judgment in *Baby Manji Yamada v. Union of India* reported in (2008) 13 SCC 518.

29. AIR 1978 SC 12.
30. In its previous judgment in *Malayalam Plantations Ltd. v. Inspector of Plantations*, AIR 1975 Ker. 86, the court departed from this view and held that, maternity benefit was to be calculated with reference to the working days only, therefore in calculating the benefit the number of weeks for which a women worker is entitled to the benefit must be multiplied by six and not by seven.
31. The convention adopted by General Conference of the ILO says that: 1. While absent from work on maternity leave in accordance with the provisions of Article 3, the women shall be entitled to receive cash and medical benefits, 2. The rates of cash benefit shall be fixed by national laws or regulations so as to ensure benefit sufficient for the full and healthy maintenance of herself and her child in accordance with a suitable standard of living.
32. On this argument, court quoted 4 decisions in *A.M. Shaila and Anr. v. Chairman, Cochin Port Trust and Ors. On 1/7/1994 (1995 IILLJ 1193 Kerala 1)*. The difference of physical structure, the effect of long hours of work, and the natural function of motherhood place women in a separate class in the matter of employment *(Curt Muller v. The State of Oregon 208 US 412, 1908)*. The grouping of women as a separate class based on the conditions in which they may be required to work, is valid, *Jospeh Radice v. People of State of New York. (1923) 264 U.S. 292*. A law which seeks to protect women from moral and social hazards, by denying bartending license or denying employment at night does not offend equality and equal protection of law. *Valentine Goesaert v. Owen J Cleary (1948) 335. U.S. 464*. The well-being of women is object of public interest. A law meant to protect women "from the greed as well as passion of man" is not discriminatory. *(Curt Mullert v. The State of Oregon. 208 US 412, 1908)*.
33. *Municipal Corporation of Delhi v. Female Workers (Muster Roll)*, 2000 LLR 449.
34. Pragya Singh, n. 3.
35. *Brownmiller and Alexander, 1992.*
36. Janet Zollinger Giele and Leslie F. Stebbins, *Women and Equality in the Workplace*, ABC-CLIO, Inc. California, 2003, p. 66.
37. Over 50 countries have prohibited sexual harassment at work through national legislation or labour codes. India became one of these countries in 2013.
38. Pankaj Kumar and Sadhna Gupta (eds.), *Relocating Women's Equality*, Rawat Publications, New Delhi, 2015, p. 143.
39. M.D. Singh and Gurpreet Panny, "Sexual Victimisation of women in India", *India Socio-Legal Journal: An International Journal on Legal Philosophy*, Law and Society, Vol. XXX, No. 1 and 2, 2004.
40. "Lisette Alvarez (2011). "Justice for Jessica: A Human Rights Case Study on Media Influence, Rule of Law, and Civic Action in India".

Honours Theses, The Florida State University of College of Social Sciences", *https://fsu.digital.flvc.org/islandora/object/fsu:204451/datastream/PDF/view,* Accessed: March 22, 2018, 1:25 pm.

41. AIR 1996 SC 309 : 1996 Cri.LJ. 381.
42. *http://shodhganga.inflibnet.ac.in/bitstream/10603/63204/12/12_chapter%205.pdf,* Accessed: March 22, 2018, 2:27 pm.
43. AIR 1997 SC 3011.
44. Gibran Naushad and Susanah Naushad, "The Sexual Harassment of Women at Workplace: An Unmanned territory", *India Law Journal,* Vol. VIII Issue I, *http://www.indialawjournal.org/archives/volume8/issue-1/article9.html,* Accessed: September 15, 2017, 10:45 am.
45. AIR 1999 SC 625.
46. Article 1 of *CEDAW* provides, "For the purposes of the present Convention, the term "discrimination against women" shall mean any distinction, exclusion or restriction made on the basis of sex which has the effect or purpose of impairing or nullifying the recognition, enjoyment or exercise by women, irrespective of their marital status, on a basis of equality of men and women, of human rights and fundamental freedoms in the political, economic, social, cultural, civil or any other field".
47. Article 113 of *Beijing Declaration and Platform for Action, 1995* provides, The term "violence against women" means any act of gender-based violence that results in, or is likely to result in, physical, sexual or psychological harm or suffering to women, including threats of such acts, coercion or arbitrary deprivation of liberty, whether occurring in public or private life. Accordingly, violence against women encompasses but is not limited to the following:
    a. Physical, sexual and psychological violence occurring in the family, including battering, sexual abuse of female children in the household, dowry-related violence, marital rape, female genital mutilation and other traditional practices harmful to women, non-spousal violence and violence related to exploitation;
    b. Physical, sexual and psychological violence occurring within the general community, including rape, sexual abuse, sexual harassment and intimidation at work, in educational institutions and elsewhere, trafficking in women and forced prostitution;
    c. Physical, sexual and psychological violence perpetrated or condoned by the State, wherever it occurs.
48. AIR 2000 SC 988.
49. 2009 Lab IC (NOC) 693 (Bombay.)
50. "Judicial Response." *http://shodhganga.inflibnet.ac.in/bitstream/10603/12832/15/16_chapter%207.pdf,* Accessed: March 24, 2018, 1:50 pm.
51. Dr. Meenakshi Gupta, n. 6, p. 72.

52. The Bill introduced by the then Women and Child Development minister Krishna Tirath and approved by Union Cabinet in 2010.
53. Karan Guleria, "The Sexual Harassment of Women at Workplace (Prevention, Prohibition and Redressal, 2013", June 20, 2015, *http://www.legalservicesindia.com/article/article/sexual-harassment-of-women-at-workplace-prevention-prohibition-and-redressal-act-2013-1845-1.html,* Accessed: August 10, 2017, 1:30pm.
54. Writ Petition (Criminal) Nos. 173-177).
55. "National Crime Records Bureau (NCRB), Crime Clock 2002", *http://ncrb.nic.in/ciiprevious/data/cd-CII2002/cii-2002/crime%20clock.htm,* Accessed: July 12, 2017, 4:15 pm.
56. D.K. Srivastava and Minkang Gu, "Law and Policy issues on Sexual Harassment in China: Comparative Perspectives", *Or. Rev. Int,* 1 L. 46 n. 17, (2009).
57. "International Labour Organisation, When Working Becomes Hazardous, World of Work (1998)", *http://www.ilo.org/public/english/bureau/inf/magazine/26/violence.htm,* Accessed: September 14, 2017, 11:00 am.
58. "Julie Cogin & Alan Fish, "Sexual harassment—A touchy subject for nurses", *23 J, Health Org. & Management,* 2009, pp. 442-62.
59. "Equal Opportunities Commission, Work Review-Statistic", *http://www.eoc.org.hk/EOC/GraphicsFolder/ShowContent.aspx?ItemID=5157,* Accessed: September 05, 2017, 3:25 pm.
60. Jennifer Coburn, "Viewpoint: Sexual Harassment: Why is Society Shocked, National Org. Women", *http://www.now.org/nnt/01-97/shocked.html,* Accessed: July 12, 2017, 1:10 pm.
61. "SACHA Sexual Assault Centre, Statistics", *http://www.sacha.ca,* Accessed: September 15, 2017, 11: 55 am.
62. "Association of Women for Action and Research (AWARE), Survey Report 2007-08", *www.aware.org,* Accessed: April 20, 2017, 4:45 pm.
63. This movement was led by the United States. Title VII of the *United States Civil Rights Act, 1964* forbids sexual harassment (including same sex) in the field of employment.
64. *Sex Determination Act, 1984* (Act no. 4 of 1984).
65. Law No. 10.224.
66. The German regulation especially protects the employee against harassment and sexual harassment. Such categories are regarded as discriminatory categories in Germany. A specific form of harassment is sexual harassment, where the harassment takes place by unwanted conduct related to the sex of a person. This includes in particular unwanted sexual acts or requests to carry out sexual acts, physical contact of a sexual nature, comments of a sexual nature, as well as the unwanted showing or public exhibition of pornographic images. "Employment Law Overview, 2017, Germany, *http://*

knowledge.leglobal.org/wp-content/uploads/LEGlobal_Memo_Germany.pdf, Accessed: August 01, 2017, 2: 15 pm.

67. "A New Law on Sexual Harassment in France, Labour and Employment Client Service Group Bryan Cave, Paris September 24, 2012", *https://www.bryancave.com/images/content/1/8/v2/1837/ClientAlertHarc-lementENG.pdf,* Accessed: September 14, 2017, 1:45 pm.
68. The ILO adopted in 1928 Convention No.26 and Recommendation No.30 relating to wage fixing machinery in trades or parts of trades.
69. "Ms. A Srija, Implementation of the Minimum Wages Act, 1948—Case Study of India", *Global Journal of Human Social Science: F Political Science,* Vol. 4 issue 7, 2014, *http://niti.gov.in/writeraddata/files/.../Publication%20in%Global%20Journal.pdf, Accessed:* August 13, 2017, 9:15 am.
70. According to Article 39, "the State shall, in particular, direct its policy towards securing (a) that the citizen, men and women equally shall have the right to an adequate livelihood and (b) that there is equal pay for equal work for both men and women". Article 43 provides, "The state shall endeavour to secure, by suitable legislation or economic organisation or in any other way, to all workers, agricultural, industrial or otherwise, work, a living wage, conditions of work ensuring a decent standard of life, and full enjoyment of leisure and social and cultural opportunities in particular."
71. *The Minimum Wages Act* was enacted to fulfill the aspiration of the workers as contained in the resolution based on the *Geneva Convention* held in 1928, which reads: "If the labourers are to be secured the enjoyment of minimum wages and they are to be protected against exploitation by their employers, it is absolutely necessary that restraint should be imposed upon their freedom of contract and such restrictions cannot be in any sense be said to be unreasonable. On the other hand, the employers cannot be heard to complain if they are compelled to pay minimum wages to their labourers even though the labourers on account of their poverty and helplessness are willing to work on lesser wages", also see: Anirudh Shastree, "The Minimum Wages Act, 1948—An Evolutionary Panorama" *LSI* 2015, *http://www.legalservicesindia.com/article/article/evolution-of-minimum-wages-act-1948-1762-1.html,* Accessed: April 14, 2017, 2:30am.
72. Janet Zollinger, Gille and Leslie F, Stebbins, n. 36, p. 222.
73. *The Minimum Wages Act, 1948* (Act No. 11 of 1948).
74. (1992) I LLJ SC 340.
75. At the fifteenth session of the Indian Labour Conference held at New Delhi in July 1957, an important resolution was passed, which laid down that the minimum wage should be need-based and should ensure the minimum human needs of the industrial worker. Five

Norms were accepted as a guide for all wage-fixing authorities including Minimum Wage Committees, Wage Boards, Adjudicators, etc. "Report on the Working of the Minimum Wages Act—Labour Bureau", *labourbureau.nic.in/Mini%20Wages%202k5%20Intro.htm,* Accessed: April 14, 2018, 2:30 am.
76. *The Minimum Wages Act, 1948* (Act No. 11 of 1948).
77. *U. Uchinoyi* v. *State of Kerala,* 1961, I.L.L.J. 631.
78. *Ibid.*
79. There's an argument contrary to this decision according to which employers can argue that the responsibility for upholding workers right need not fall entirely on them. This approach is accepted by ILO, Article 3 of Convention 131 indicates that social security benefits are one of the factors to be taken into account when setting the wage level. Similarly, Article 23(3) of UDHR also makes it clear that the remuneration from employers can be supplemented, if necessary by other means of social protection.
80. Keeping in view the recommendation of NCRL and subsequent rise in price index, the NFLMW was fixed at Rs. 35/- per day in 1996. Quite recently the Ministry of Labour and Employment, Government of India, has increased the minimum wage from Rs. 160 fixed in 2015 to Rs. 176 w.e.f 1.06.2017.
81. *The Minimum Wages Act, 1948,* Ministry of Labour and Employment, Government of India.
82. Report, n. 75.
83. OECD promotes policies that will improve the economic and social well-being of people around the world. It is an international policy group that monitors and analyses 34 countries.
84. OECD, Directorate for Employment Labour and Social Welfare, 'Focus on Minimum Wages After the Crisis: Making them pay', May 2015.
85. "Libby Cane, The Minimum Wage around the World", May 6, 2015, 11:38 p.m.", *http://www.businessinsider.in/The-minimum-wage-around-the-world/articleshow/47181016.cms,* Accessed: September 04, 2017, 1:40 pm.
86. "Fair Labor Standards Act, 1938", *https://en.wikipedia.org/wiki,* Accessed: September 02, 2017, 10:00 pm.
87. A.C.L. Davies, *Perspectives on Labour Law,* Cambridge University Press, (2nd edition), U.K., 2009, p. 147.
88. *The National Minimum Wage Act, 1998.* Section 34.
89. Ministry of Labour and Employment, Labour Bureau. "Report on the working of The Minimum Wages Act, 1948 for the year 2008", Government of India.*http://labourbureau.nic.in/MW_Report_2008.pdf,* Accessed: September 10, 2017, 10:40 am.
90. *ILO's Minimum Wage Fixing Convention, 1970* (No. 131), the convention directs the State parties to establish a system of minimum

wages which covers all groups of wage earners, which shall have the force of law the failure to apply the same shall also attract penal or other sanctions. (Article 1 and 2), Accessed: March 31, 2018. 2:10 pm.

91. Janet Zollinger Giele and Leslie F. Stebbins, n. 36, p. 231.
92. ILO recommendations and conventions: Recommendation No. 90, also see: *Equal Remuneration, 1951, Discrimination (Employment and Occupation) Convention, 1958 (No. 111), Recommendation No. 111: Discrimination (Employment and Occupation), 1958, Convention No. 156: Workers with.Family Responsibilities, 1981.*
93. *The Equal Remuneration Act, 1976* (Act 25 of 1976), s. 2(8).
94. 1987 (2) SCC 469.
95. *The Equal Remuneration Act, 1976* (Act 25 of 1976 amended by Act 49 of 1987) Government of India, Ministry of Labour and Employment, s. 4 and 5.
96. AIR 1982 SC 879, also see: *D.S. Nakara v. Union of India*, AIR 1983 SC 130, *R. K. Ramachandaran Iyer v. Union of India*, AIR 1984 SC 541, *Delhi Veterinary Association v. Union of India*, AIR 1984 SC 1221, *Jeet Sigh v. MCD*, AIR 1987 SC 1781, *Bhagwan Das v. State of Haryana*, AIR 1988 SC 2014, *Delhi Municipal Karamchari Ekta Union (Regd.) v. State of Haryana, AIR* 1988 SC 1504, *State of U.P.* v. *J.P. Chaurasia*, AIR 1989 SC 19 at 26-27, *Mewa Ram v. All India Institute of Medical Sciences*, AIR 1989 SC 1256, *State of M.P. v. Pamod Bhartiya*, AIR 1993 SC 286, *S. Nagraj v. Stae of Karnatka* (1993) 4 SC 595 at 620, *Vijay Kumar v. State of Punjab*, AIR 1994 SC 265.
97. Dr. J.N. Pandey, *The Constitutional Law of India*, Central Law Agency, Allahabad, 2012, p. 413.
98. *Surinder Singh* v. *Engineer-in-chief*, C.P.W.D., AIR 1986 SC 534; *Dhirendra Chamoli* v. *State of U.P.*, (1986) 1 SCC 637; *Daily Rated Casual Labour* v. *Union of India*, (1988), AIR SCC 122.
99. AIR 1981 SC 1929.
100. According to Section 16 of the Equal Remuneration Act, 1976, where the appropriate government is, on a consideration of all the circumstances of the case, satisfied that the differences in regard to the remuneration, or a particular species of remuneration, of men and women workers in any establishment, or employment is based on a factor other than sex, it may, by notification, make a declaration to that effect, and any act of the employer attributable to such a difference shall not be deemed to be a contravention of any provisions of this Act.
101. AIR 1982 SC 1473.
102. *Rajendra Grover & Ors v. Air India Ltd* and Ors, 8th October 2007, Delhi High Court.
103. 2003 SCC (Land) 840.

104. *Equal Pay for Work of Equal Value, www.unwomen.org/en/news/in-focus/csw/equal-pay,* Accessed: September 13, 2017, 3:35 pm.
105. National Statistics, *Annual Survey of Hours and Earnings*. This figure is the internationally comparable mean. A.C.L. Davies, n. 87, pp. 22-27.
106. *ILO Convention 100 on Equal Remuneration 1951, Convention on Discrimination (Employment and Occupation) 1958,* Article 23(2) *of Universal Declaration of Human Rights, 1948* provides that, 'everyone, without any discrimination, has the right to equal pay for equal work', Article 26 of *International Convention on Civil and Political Rights, 1966, Article 2 of Convention of Elimination of All forms of Discrimination, 1979,* Article 5 of *International Convention on Elimination of all forms Racial Discrimination, 1969.*
107. The concept is similar to one embodied in Indian *Equal Remuneration Act, 1976* which provides that the deciding factor for the successful pursuit of a claim for equal wages under the Act is that the work being performed be either "same or similar nature". Nomita Aggarwal, *Women and Law in India,* New Century Publications, Delhi, 2002, p. 132.
108. Amendments to South African labour legislation namely, *The Employment Equity Amendment Act,* 47 of 2013 [EEA] and the *Employment Equity Regulations, 2014* [EER] came into effect on 01 August 2014. Regulation 4 of EER prescribes–"Meaning of work of equal value"-[Regulation 4]: "*4. Meaning of work of equal value*
    For the purpose of these Regulations, the work performed by an employee—
    (1) is the same as the work of another employee *of the same employer,* if their work is identical or interchangeable;
    (2) is substantially the same as the work of another employee employed by that employer, if the work performed by the employees is sufficiently similar that they can reasonably be considered to be performing the same job, even if their work is not identical or interchangeable;
    (3) Is of the same value as the work of another employee of the same employer in a different job, if their respective occupations are accorded the same value in accordance with regulations 5 to 7."
    http://www.labourguide.co.za/equal-pay-for-work-of-equal-value, Accessed: August 20, 2017, 3:09 pm.
109. A.C.L. Davies, n. 87, p. 146.
110. *The Equal Pay Act of 1963* (EPA) enacted by 88th United States Congress (Pub. L. No. 88-38) signed into law by President John. F. Kennedy on June 10, 1963
111. Seehttps://www.britannica.com/topic/Equal-Pay-Act, Accessed: 16-08-17, 1:09 pm.

112. U.S.C. 206(d)(1) (1970) provides: No employer having employees subject to any provisions of this section shall discriminate, within any establishment in which such employees are employed, between employees on the basis of sex by paying wages to employees in such establishment at a rate less than the rate at which he pays wages to employees of the opposite sex in such establishment for equal work on jobs the performance of which requires equal skill, effort, and responsibility, and which are performed under similar working conditions, except. where such payment is made pursuant to (i) a seniority system; (ii) a merit system; (iii) a system which measures earnings by quantity or quality of production; or (iv) a differential based on any other factor other than sex: Provided, that an employer who is paying a wage rate differential in violation of this sub-section shall not, in order to comply with the provisions of this sub-section, reduce the wage rate of any employee, *Albert H. Ross Frank* V. *McDermott Jr*, "The Equal Pay Act of 1963: A Decade of Enforcement" Vol. 16 issue 1, BCLR (1974), *http://lawdigitalcommons.bc.edu/cgi/viewcontent.cgi?article=1460&context=bclr,* Accessed: August 16, 2017, 5:05 pm.
113. The Act has now been mostly superseded by Part 5, chapter 3, of the Equality Act, 2010.
114. *Equal Pay Act, 1970*, S. 1(1) and (2).
115. CC [1989] AC 706; *British Coal v. Smith* [1996] 3 All ER 97.
116. Report of 'Committee for Legal Aid to Poor and Forum for Crèche and Childcare Service, New Delhi', which was published to influence public policy. The report was the outcome of a meeting held on 30 August 2004 as a collaborative effort of the Committee for Legal Aid to Poor (based in Cuttack, Orissa, India) and the Orissa regional chapter of the Forum for Crèche and Childcare Services. The committee is a pro-bono legal aid group established to protect and promote human rights and the rule of law. The forum is a network of non-government voluntary organisation committed to campaigning in India for the rights of survival, development and protection among poor and underprivileged 0-to-6-year-olds. The central office is in New Delhi.
117. This frequently mispronounced word is of French origin and should be pronounced as Krash, a, as, ale or day or kresh, e as in bed. Dr. Meenakshi Gupta, *Women Rights Under Labour Laws*, Regal Publications, New Delhi, 2016, p. 148.
118. ILO, workplace solution for children, Condition of work and employment programme, Geneva Switzerland.: *www.ilo.org/travail,* Accessed: August 17, 2017, 12:34pm.
119. Similar provision is provided under, Section 44 of the *Inter State Migrant Workmen (RECS) Act, 1979,* Section 12 of the Plantations Labour Act, 1951, Section 14 of the *Beedi and Cigar Workers (Conditions*

of Employment) Act, 1966, Section 35 of the *Building and other Constructions (Regulation of Employment and Conditions of Service) Act, 1996,* Section 58(d) of the *Mines Act, 1952.* See also: *The Working Women (Basic Facilities and Welfare) Bill, 2014,* Bill No. XL of 2014 still pending provide for the protection of women from discrimination, and for the basic facilities like crèche, recreational facilities, maternity benefits, hostel and transport facilities, etc. and for the welfare measures to be taken by the employers and the State for the women employees working in various sectors.

120. *ILO, Welfare Facilities Recommendation,* 1956 (No. 102).
121. *SI 1998 No. 1833.*
122. *WTR Regulation 2(*1).
123. Lucy McLynn, *Working Time and Holidays: A Practical Legal Guide,* Oxford University Press, New York, 2009, p. 147.
124. Section 66(1)(b) of the Factories Act, 1948 states that no woman shall be required or allowed to work in any factory except between the hours of 6 a.m. and 7 p.m. Section 25 of the *Beedi and Cigar Workers (Conditions of Employment) Act, 1966* stipulates that no woman shall be required or allowed to work in any industrial premise except between 6 a.m. and 7 p.m. Section 46(1)(b) of the Mines Act, 1952 prohibits employment of women in any mine above ground except between the hours of 6 a.m. and 7 p.m. Section 25 of the *Plantation Labour Act, 1951* says that except with the permission of State government no woman worker shall be employed in any plantation otherwise than between the hours of 6 a.m. and 7 p.m.
125. *The Factories Act, 1948.*
126. (2001) II LLJ 843 Mad, see also: *Triveni K.S. v. Union of India,* 2002 (5) ALT 223 (High Court of Andhra Pradesh).
127. This section was incorporated in the Act, after India's ratification of the *ILO Convention No. 89,* 1948.
128. *The Factories (Amendment) Bill, 2005* (Bill No. 104 of 2005), Ministry of Labour and Employment Government of India.
129. *ILO Night Work (Women) Convention,* 1919, No. 4; ILO Night *Work (Women) Convention* (Revised), 1934, No. 41; *Convention No. 89 Night Work* (Women) (Revised), 1948, *ILO Night Work of Women* (Agriculture) *Recommendation, 1921,* No. 13; *Recommendation No.* 178: *Night Work,* 1990.
130. *Protocol to the Night Work (Women) Convention* (Revised), 1948.
131. Anita Abraham, Devika Singh and Poulomi Pal, *Critical Assessment of Labour Laws Policies and Practices through Gender Lens,* National Resource Centre for Women, National Mission for Empowerment of Women, Ministry of Women and Child Development, Government of India, 2014.
132. Similar provision is provided in Rule 53 of the *Contract Labour (Regulation and Abolition) Act, 1970;* Section 19 of the Factories Act,

1948; Rule 42 of the *Inter State Migrant Workmen (RECS) Central Rules, 1980*; Section 9 of the *Plantations Labour Act, 1951;* Section 12 of the *Beedi and Cigar Workers (Condition of Employment) Act, 1966;* Section 33 of *Building and Construction Workers (Regulation of Employment and Condition of Service) Act, 1996.*

133. *https://en.wikipedia.org/wiki/Occupational_hazard,* Accessed: August 08, 2017, 4:00 pm.
134. Similar provision is provided in section 46(1) (b) of the *Mines Act, 1952* prohibits employment of women in any part of a mine which is below ground.
135. *http://www.ilo.org/global/standards/subjects-covered-by-international-labour-standards/occupational-safety-and-health/lang—en/index.htm,* Accessed: May 21, 2017, 10:20 am.
136. *ILO's Occupational safety and health convention, 1985* (No. 155); *Protocol of 2002 to Occupational safety and health convention, 1981; Occupational safety and health convention 1981* (No.164); *Occupational health services convention, 1985* (No. 161); *Occupational health services recommendation, 1985*(No. 171*); Protection of workers health recommendation, 1953* (No. 97); *Welfare facilities recommendation 1956* (No.102).
137. (1896) 1QB 244.
138. AIR 1926 Bombay. 57.
139. Janet Zollinger Giele and Leslie F. Stebbins n. 36, p. 97.
140. Section 54 and 66(1) (b) of the *Factories Act, 1948;* see also, section 30 and 31 of the *Mines Act, 1952;* section 19(2) and (3) of *the Plantation Labour Act, 1951;* section 28 of *Building and other Construction Workers' (Regulation of Employment and Conditions of Service)* Act, 1996: section 17 of the *Beedi and Cigar Workers (Condition of Employment) Act, 1966.*
141. *International Covenant on Economic Social and Cultural Rights, 1966.*
142. *ILO Convention 1 Hours of Work (Industry) 1919.* See also *Convention 30 on Hours and Work (Commerce and Offices) 1930, Convention 47 on Forty-Hour Week 1935, Convention 116 on Reduction of Hours of Work Recommendation 1962, Convention 14 on Weekly Rest (Industry) 1921, Convention 106 on Weekly Rest (Commerce and Offices) 1957. www.ilo.org,* Accessed: July 5, 2017, 12:25pm.
143. *ILO Convention 132 on Holidays with Pay* (Revised) 1970.
144. "Anukritibhatnagar and Deepikasehrawat, Social Security Legislation, April 1, 2010", *:https://www.slideshare.net/anukritibhat/social-security-legislation,* Accessed: September 21, 2017, 10:15 am.
145. "National Committee to Preserve Social Security & Medicare, Social Security and Women", Government Relations and Policy Department, March 2013.*http://www.eleanorshope.org/Portals/10/women-and-social-security.pdf,* Accessed: July 12, 2017, 3:01 pm.
146. This Act was passed on 19 April, 1948 and was inaugurated on February 24, 1952 in Kanpur and Delhi. This scheme improved the

defects of Workmen's Compensation Act, 1923. This Act was amended in 1951, 1966, 1975, 1984, and 2006 and recently in 2010. This Act is a major step in the direction of social insurance. It provides for the grant of cash benefits to the employees in the contingencies of sickness, employment injury and maternity. It also provides for medical benefit to the employees and their families.

147. *Employees' State Insurance Act, 1948* (Act No. 34 of 1948) Ministry of Labour and Employment, Government of India, section 49 provides that the qualification of a person to claim sickness benefit, the conditions subject to which such benefit may be given, the rates and period thereof shall be such as may be prescribed by the Central Government.
148. *ILO Convention 102 on Social Security (Minimum Standards), 1952.*
149. Article 7 The contingencies covered shall include—
    (a) need for medical care of a curative nature and, under prescribed conditions, need for medical care of a preventive nature;
    (b) Incapacity for work resulting from sickness and involving suspension of earnings, as defined by national legislation.
150. Article 8-17 of *ILO Convention 130 concerning medical care and sickness benefit, 1969* provide for medical care.
151. Section 56 read with Regulation 95-A of ESI Act, 1948 provides that if in respect of a person contribution ceases to be payable, he may be allowed medical benefit for such period and at such conditions as the regulations may specify.
152. *The Workmen Compensation Act,* 1923 defines disablement. The loss of earning capacity is called 'disablement'. Disablement can be classified as: (a) Total Disablement; and (b) Partial Disablement. It can further be distinguished into: (i) Permanent Disablement; (ii) Temporary Disablement. Section 2(g) partial disablement means where the disablement is of a temporary nature such disablement as reduces the earning capacity of a workman in any employment in which he was engaged at the time of the accident resulting in the disablement and where the disablement is of a permanent nature such disablement as reduces his earning capacity in every employment which he was capable of undertaking at that time: Provided that every injury specified in Part II of Schedule shall be deemed to result in permanent partial disablement; and section 2(l) total disablement means such disablement whether of a temporary or permanent nature as incapacitates a workman for all work which he was capable of performing at the time of the accident resulting in such disablement: Provided that permanent total disablement shall be deemed to result from every injury specified in Part I of Schedule I or from any combination of injuries specified in Part II thereof where the aggregate percentage of the loss of earning capacity as specified

in the said Part II against those injuries amount to one hundred per cent or more.

153. *The Employees' State Insurance Act, 1978,* Section 51 and 52A.

154. *Ibid.* Regulation 52A, also see: *ILO Convention 128 on Invalidity, Old Age and Survivors Benefit, 1967* among other things provide for survivors benefit.

Chapter 4

Working Women in India

A Present Scenario

The opening and the linking of the world-trade and market under the norms of liberalisation, privatisation and globalisation have not been only affecting different countries differently, but they are affecting different people and groups of the same country differently. The existing studies on gender and globalisation are exploring both the positive as well as the negative impact of globalisation on women across the globe. One view is that liberalisation, privatisation and globalisation will help women development as they will be provided with economic opportunities. The free flow of knowledge and information will open new horizons of knowledge and information to women, which were lacking earlier. The enhanced knowledge will help them to grow socially, economically as well as politically. They can share their work experience with the other women and the democratic and global governance will help to develop and implement the policies of women development more effectively than ever before was.

The other view is that the globalisation will increase the women exploitation as the privatisation and liberalisation are the sole guidelines of globalisation. The basis of both privatisation and liberalisation is making maximum profit by minimum investment. The employment opportunities which will be provided by development of industry and trade will be guided by the logic of maximisation of profit and minimisation of labour cost. The new opportunities and employment of women will be conditioned and will be provided only if the women offer themselves as cheap labour in comparison to male labour. The other observation is that the employments of women will double their burden as social conservatism and patriarchal division of labour will force the women living in developing societies to do the household chores along with their jobs.

The work participation and the economic rights of women are very complex issues and they are deeply embedded in the social fabrics of the society. Economic rights and economic status of women is somewhat related to the social status and social rights of women in a society. The economic rights of women include the right to employment, right to equal wages for equal work, maternity benefits and equal-share in the parental property as it is available to the male child of the family. Unfortunately, no standard definition of economic rights of women is available and the economic empowerment of women is always linked with the social and political issues. A number of national and international programmes link economic development of women with the alleviation of poverty, better health facilities, clean water, sanitation, education etc.

This chapter will focus on the impact of globalisation on the economic rights of women like the work participation or inclusion of women in the development process at national and international level. The rights of inheritance, marriage and property laws will also be analysed along with the latest developments for the development and empowerment of women at national and international level. For the purpose we will be analysing the policies and programmes of the Indian Government, which it enacted for the work participation and economic development of women in the pre- and post-globalisation era along with the international declarations and programmes for the work participation and for the rights of working of women.

Women represent half of the world's population and gender inequality exists in every nation on the planet earth. Women play a very strategic role in the development of society in particular and development of economy in general. Women is the leading planner of the family, the first trainers and the supplier of labour and play a focal role in the development of different sectors like agriculture, industry, service, etc. and she also contributes to the creation of an enlightened society. Women contribute directly or indirectly to economic development of the family and the nation. Though nature has given the genetic power of reproduction especially to women, the socio-economic status of women is very poor and the ill-effects of poverty are more on women than on men. Burden of work is increasing with the development of human civilisation, the dual burden of rearing the children along with household task has increased with the dawn of modernisation and industrialisation and as she came out to work as paid worker.

The work participation and economic empowerment of women can help to solve a majority of social and political problems which women are facing due to the lack of economic independence. Poverty and the social coercion are creating a lot of hurdles in the work participation and economic empowerment of women; they are forced to sell their labour at a lower price than men. The poverty alleviation, education and skill training are considered as the major instruments for the economic empowerment of women. Empowering women and removal of poverty are considered as the two sides of the same coin. If a woman is educated and empowered; her potential can be utilised for the economic development of the family as well as for the nation. Mahatma Gandhi said, "You educate a man and you educate an individual. You educate a woman and you educate an entire family."[1]

The promises and the efforts of the global governance are aimed at improving the condition of women across the globe. The emerging trends are linking women rights with human rights and claims for equal and universal rights of women across the globe. It is held that "Irrespective of their caste, colour, creed, language, social and political status as well as nationality, women shall be considered as one group and all the human rights shall also be provided to them as they are provided to men. The post-cold war efforts of the United Nations and the democratisation of most of the world have led to the development and empowerment of women across the globe. The emphasis of the national and international governance is on the deepening of democracy and expansion of human rights to every deprived strata of the society.

The old concept of the national government and political control of the nation is now being transformed with the new concept of human governance, which aims at the inclusion of the deprived sections of the nation in the socio-economic and political mainstream of the nations and extending of the human rights to every citizen. It was in 1975 when General Assembly of UN passed a resolution (resolution 3010) which state that year of 1975 should be International Women's Year. In December 1975, the UN General

Assembly passed a further resolution (resolution 31/136) that 1976-1985 should be the "Decade of Women", the first world conference on women was held in Mexico City in 1975. It resulted in the Declaration of Mexico on the Equality of Women and Their Contribution to Development and Peace.[2]

A unique mechanism for the development and empowerment of women at the international level came into existence at the very foundation of UNO and Division for the Advancement of Women (DAW) was established in 1946. The Commission on the Status of Women (CSW) was established under the auspices of United Nations Economic and Social Council (ECOSOC) in 1946. CSW is dedicated exclusively to gender equality and the advancement of the status of women. It is the principal global policy-making body, meeting annually to evaluate progress on gender equality, identify challenges, set standards and formulates concrete policies to promote gender equality and the advancement of women worldwide. CSW prepare reports and makes recommendations and presents the same before the ECOSOC.[3]

Convention on the Elimination of All Forms of Discrimination Against Women (1979), International Research and Training Institute for the Advancement of Women (INSTRAW) (1976), Office of the Special Adviser on Gender Issues and Advancement of Women (OSAGI) 1997, United Nations Development Fund for Women (UNIFEM) established in 1976 are worth mention to the credit of the United Nations.[4]

The First World Conference on Women was held in 1975 at Mexico and the progress of this single conference was so impressing that within five years the Second World Conference on Women was held in 1980 at Copenhagen. The efforts and commitment of CSW was furthered by Third World Conference on Women in 1985 at Nairobi and finally Fourth World Conference on Women at Beijing in 1995. The Beijing Conference proved to be a landmark event that set the pace for women empowerment. The Beijing Platform for Action was pegged on the pillars of human rights and gender equality. The principle of gender equality has been accepted by most of the democratic countries, including India.[5] It was recognised by the national governments at the Twenty-third Special Session of General Assembly entitled "Women 2000: Gender, Equality, Development and Peace for Twenty First Century": these goals and commitments determined in the Platform for Action have not been fully implemented. All the national governments have agreed upon for further actions and initiatives at local, national, regional and international levels.

The claims, efforts and commitments of the national governments come under a cloud when one analysis the objectives of the capitalised and privatised global economy. A drastic change in the global economy has been observed and the national states are forced to adopt the *New Economic Policy* and the *Structural Adjustment Programmes*, under which the states are advised to cut the fiscal-budgets and welfare measures since 1990s.[6]

The old concept of the welfare state is withering away and the maximisation of profit and development have come to the forefront, the labour welfare and other social issues have been pushed to a back seat. The labour laws have been modified and amended to facilitate the global capital and investment in the nations and the labour welfare and security have been decreased by the states under the labour laws reform policies.[7]

The deepening of democracy and the inclusion of the weaker sections into the mainstream has been facing a serious challenge as the political democracy and political equality has become meaningless in the unequal economic world. The challenges of the global competitive market and the social conservatism are creating hurdles in the economic development of women.[8]

Global Investment and Special Economic Zones

The use of the capital intensive techniques and acquiring of the big chunk of the agriculture and forest land under the policy of Special Economic Zones (SEZ) and Export Processing Zones (EPZ) in the developing nations has resulted in further marginalisation of tribal, rural and indigenous people along with unskilled labour from the market. The marginalisation of the unskilled and indigenous labour from land definitely has an impact on the women's lives.

Women's unpaid work has increased because of privatisation of economy and withering away of the welfare policies by the state in the developing countries. The private contractors and owners of the private firms don't follow the labour laws and thus workers are forced to work for longer hours and under inhuman conditions. It is necessary to mention that the absolute majority of the workers who work in the unorganised sector are constituted by women. The hire and fire policy which has been adopted by industry in the liberalised and privatised economies has also forced the labour to dance to the tunes of the management as the unemployment level in the developing countries is very high as compared to the developed countries.[9]

Women dominate the workforce in EPZs in most developing countries. For instance, in Philippines the share of women workers in total EPZs workforce was 74 per cent in 1980. It remained the same even in 1994. In Korea, it was 70 per cent in 1990. It declined to 60 per cent in 1993. In Dominican Republic, it was 60 per cent in 1995. In Bangladesh and Sri Lanka, it was above 70 per cent. Some scholars argue that the high proportion of female employment implies that the creation of SEZs does not reduce the local unemployment rate. This is because prior to being employed in the SEZs majority of them were not part of labour force.[10]

Studies have shown that increased employment opportunities have empowered women and have made them more independent and improved their relative status and bargaining power within their household. Madani in Dominican Republic found that SEZ wages were the main source of income for 38 per cent of women working in these zones and that almost half of them were single, divorced or widows.[11] According to Dunn many of the women workers were bread winners for their household as well. ILO in 1998 reported that in Guatemala 45 per cent and in Honduras 22 per cent of women reported that they were the only bread winners of their family. It has been established in literature that the economic participation of women their presence in the workforce in quantitative terms is important not only for lowering the disproportionate levels of poverty among women but also for raising household income and encouraging economic development in countries as a whole.[12]

The vast majority of workers in SEZ firms are young women aged 16–25 years. It is found that women are paid less than men for similar jobs[13] and are subjected to sexual harassment and violence. Further, there is evidence that the type of employment generated in SEZ firms is generally poor. Female employment is concentrated in low paying and low productive jobs. As the nature of employment in SEZs involves higher technology inputs, women are thrown out of employment. It has been observed that the proportion of women in SEZs has declined with the passage of time in many countries.[14] As wages rise, more men are attracted to SEZ employment and as production requirements increase (such as supervisors or skilled workers), demand for male workers increases.

Thus, SEZs are a mechanism of exploitation of women and not of their empowerment, though country-specific experiences may vary. ILO in 1998 concludes that SEZs do play an important role in employment generation in developing countries but employment generation by itself does not ensure human development and poverty alleviation. Thus, the crucial question is whether employment in EPZs results in higher wages, better working conditions and higher standard of living. The general perception is that minimum wages paid in the zones are lower than those paid outside the zones. This is because labour laws are not extended to the zone firms and where these laws are applicable, they are not enforced strictly.

The Special Economic Zones Policy was announced in April 2000 with the objective of making the Special Economic Zones an engine for economic growth, supported by quality infrastructure and an attractive fiscal package both at the Central and State level with a single window clearance. A Special Economic Zones Act was passed in the year 2005. As a result of this Act and rules coming into force, it was envisaged that the SEZs would attract a large flow of foreign and domestic investment in infrastructure and production capacity leading to generation of additional economic activity and creation of employment opportunities.

The Act was rapidly passed through the Indian Parliament with a very brief discussion on 10th May, 2005. Though the law was passed with ease and with very little discussion, a good deal of adverse reaction has visited the SEZ endeavour later particularly when once the process of land acquisition to set up the zones was initiated. There were many protests against SEZs by both affected parties and civil society. However, the SEZ could not become popular in India and they are just limited to some pockets of Gujarat, Maharastra, and Gurgaon etc.[15]

The fact of the marginalisation of women labour in the capitalised world market was recognised by the Fourth World Conference on Women, held in Beijing in 1995 and 5 Strategic objectives were adopted to improve the economic condition of women. These objectives are aimed to:

- Promote women's economic rights and independence, including access to employment, appropriate working conditions and control over economic resources.
- Facilitate women's equal access to resources, employment, markets and trade.
- Provide business services, training and access to markets, information and technology, particularly to low-income women.
- Strengthen women's economic capacity and commercial networks.
- Eliminate occupational segregation and all forms of employment discrimination.[16]

The Beijing Platform for Action asserted women's rights as human rights and committed to specific actions to ensure respect for those rights. The UN Division for Women in its review of the Fourth World Conference observed: "The fundamental transformation that took place in Beijing was the recognition of the need to shift the focus from women to the concept of gender, recognising that the entire structure of society, and all relations between men and women within it, had to be re-evaluated. Only by such a fundamental restructuring of society and its institutions could help women to take their rightful place as equal partners with men in all aspects of life."[17]

To empower women economically certain special provisions are made in CEADAW to address the problems of working women: The right to work is claimed as an inalienable right of all human beings, the right to the same employment opportunities including the application of the same criteria for selection in matters of employment, the right to free choice of profession and employment, the right to promotion, job security and all benefits and conditions of service and the right to receive vocational training and retraining, including apprenticeships, advanced vocational training and recurrent training, the right in equal remuneration including benefits and to equal treatment in respect of work of equal value; as well as quality of treatment in the evaluation of the quality of work, the right to social security particularly in cases of retirement unemployment, sickness invalidity and old age and other incapacity to work as well as the right to paid leave, the right to protection of health and to satisfy in working conditions, including the safeguarding of the function of reproduction etc.[18]

Five years after the Mexico Conference, the Second World Conference on Women was held in Copenhagen in 1980. The resulting Programme of Action called for stronger national measures to ensure women's ownership and control of property as well as improvements in women's rights with respect to inheritance, child custody and loss of nationality.[19] In 1985, the Third World Conference on Women was held in Nairobi and the main objective of this conference was to review and appraise the achievements of the United Nations Decade for Women: Equality, Development and Peace. This conference was convened at the time when the movement for gender equality had finally gained the global recognition, and 15,000 representatives of non-governmental organisations (NGOs) participated in a parallel NGO Forum.[20] This event is also described as "the birth of global feminism". Realising that the goals of the Mexico City Conference had not been adequately met, the 157 participating governments adopted the Nairobi Forward-looking Strategies up to the Year 2000.[21] An early result of the Nairobi Conference was the transformation of the Voluntary Fund for the UN Decade for Women into the UN Development Fund for Women (UNIFEM).[22]

In the lead-up to the Millennium Development Goals (MDGs) Summit in September 2010, the Secretary-General launched a global effort convening 40 key leaders to define a collective strategy for accelerating progress on women's and children's health. In the aftermath of the Millennium Declaration of the September 2000 Summit, gender issues were integrated in many of the subsequent Millennium Development Goals (MDGs) and explicitly the Goal No. 3 was devoted to promote gender equality and women empowerment.

The new tools, techniques and innovations adopted by both national and international agencies for the development and empowerment of women. International institutions like World Bank and International Monetary Fund along with other agencies of UNO have been working with a rigous for the development and empowerment of women at the global level. The concept of gender mainstreaming[23], gender budgeting[24] and gender audit has become the focus of development grants in these days.

The Global Efforts and the Real Position of Women

The UN efforts and the promises of democratic and good governance of the globalised world are creditable. However, the agenda and policies for the women development and empowerment, which are on the agenda of every democratic country especially after the 1990s has, come under question from every corner of society. The discriminated and exploited women can be seen all-over the world. There is no end to women's suffering and their tales are endless. The global efforts for the development and empowerment of women are too far behind their expected goals.

Women constitute almost 50 per cent of the world's population but the developing countries like India have shown disproportionate sex ratio whereby female's population has been comparatively lower than males.[25] As far as their social status is concerned, they are not treated as equal to men and are discriminated at all places. In the Western societies women have got equal rights and status with men in all walks of life. But gender disabilities and discriminations exist in India even today. The paradoxical situation is prevailing to such an extent that a woman is sometimes considered as a goddess and at other times merely as a slave.

Women comprise an average of 43 per cent of the agricultural labour force in developing countries, varying considerably across regions from 20 per cent or less in Latin America to 50 per cent or more in parts of Asia and Africa.[26] Despite the regional and sub-regional variation, women make an essential contribution to agriculture across the developing world. Women farmers control less land than do men, and also have limited access to inputs, seeds, credits, and extension services. Less than 20 per cent of landholders are women.[27] Gender differences in access to land and credit affect the relative ability of female and male farmers and entrepreneurs to invest, operate and benefit from new economic opportunities.[28]

Women are responsible for household and food preparation in 85-90 per cent of cases as per the record of surveys of World Health Organisation conducted in a wide range of countries.[29]

Women and children bear the main negative impacts of fuel, water collection and transport, with women in many developing countries spending from 1 to 4 hours a day collecting biomass for fuel.[30] A study of time and water scarcity in 25 sub-Saharan African countries estimated that women spend at least 16 million hours a day collecting drinking water; men spend 6 million hours; and children 4 million hours.[31]

Women continue to participate in labour markets on an unequal basis with men. In 2013, the male population ratio stood at 72.2 per cent, while the ratio for females was 47.1 per cent.[32] Globally, women are paid less than men. Women in most countries earn, on average, only 60 to 75 per cent of men's wages.[33] Contributing factors include the fact that women are more likely to be wage workers and unpaid family workers; that women are more likely to engage in low-productive activities and to work in the informal sector, with less mobility to the formal sector than men[34]; the view of women as economic dependents; and the likelihood that women are in unorganised sectors or not represented in the unions.[35]

Women bear disproportionate responsibility for unpaid care work. Women devote 1 to 3 hours more a day to housework than men; 2 to 10 times the amount of time a day to care (for children, elderly, and the sick), and 1 to 4 hours less a day to market activities.[36] In the European Union for example, 25 per cent of women report care of other family members and personal responsibilities as the reason for not being in the labour force, versus only three per cent of men.[37] This directly and negatively impact women's participation in the labour force. Women are more likely than men to work in informal employment. In South Asia, over 80 per cent of women in non-agricultural jobs are in informal employment, in sub-Saharan Africa, 74 per cent, and in Latin America and the Caribbean, 54 per cent. In rural areas, many women derive their livelihoods from small-scale farming, almost always informal and often unpaid. More women than men work in vulnerable, low-paid, or undervalued jobs.[38] As of 2013, 49.1 per cent of the world's working women were in vulnerable employment, often unprotected by labour legislation, compared to 46.9 per cent of men. Women were far more likely than men to be in vulnerable employment in East Asia (50.3% versus 42.3%), South-East Asia and the Pacific (63.1% versus 56%), South Asia

(80.9% versus 74.4%), North Africa 54.7%, the Middle East (33.2% versus 23.7%) and Sub-Saharan Africa (nearly 85.5% versus 70.5%).[39]

Gender differences in laws affect both developing and developed economies, and women in all regions. Almost 90 per cent of 143 economies studied by World Bank show at least one legal difference restricting women's economic opportunities.[40] Of those, 79 economies have laws that restrict the types of jobs that women can do[41] and husbands can object to their wives working and prevent them from accepting jobs in 15 economies.[42]

Despite the hard facts presented on women's conditions in the liberalised, privatised and global world, the economic position of women has improved relatively; however, liberlisation and privatisation have marginalised women from the mainstream labour market due to the lack of skill and education backwardness. Simultaneously, educated and urbanite women are taking the full advantage of job opportunities, which are provided by the investors and companies.

Globalisation and Economic Empowerment of Women in India

India is increasingly portrayed as a highly globalised nation and a poster state of globalisation.[43] The extensive economic and trade reforms were carried out by the Indian Government in 1990s with the objective of reducing controls and easing policies to achieve greater integration with the world economy and to stimulate economic growth. The process of integrating and opening of the Indian economy for global investment and global market is often referred to as liberalising, privatising and globalising Indian economy. It is to note that under the norms of liberalisation, privatisation and globalisation, the Indian Government was forced to modify its earlier model of mixed-economy and to encourage the privatisation of economy under the New Economic Policy (NEP) and Structural Adjustment Programme (SAP).

The integration of Indian economy with the global economy has not only impacted the old model of economic development and the structure of the Indian economy, but it also has larger social implications for the Indian society. The impact of liberalistion, privatisation and globalisation may in case of the different social groups looking up to their position in the old state sponsored and mixed-economy model of the Indian State. It will be perceived in the different ways not only by the rich and the poor but also by other social groups like: women, disabled, children, *dalits*, tribals rural and urban groups etc.

In recent years, globalisation and its implications for gender have been much discussed and commented upon in academic circles around the world and the fact of the marginalisation of women in the economic sphere has been recognised by various studies at International conferences.[44] The fact of marginalisation of women has been also recognised by the General Secretary of U.N. In his concluding remarks on International Women Day 2015 he said that "Today we join the people of the world in celebration of the progress made for women rights, women's empowerment and gender equality. Research scholars also acknowledge that progress has been slow and uneven and in some cases women and girls face new and more complex challenges."[45] Expressing the urgency and necessity of the women's development UN General Secretary urged that "To be truly transformative, the post-2015 development agenda must prioritize gender equality and women's empowerment. The world will never realise 100 per cent of its goals if 50 per cent of its people cannot realize their full potential."[46]

In the Indian context many comprehensive studies have been conducted by the governmental and non-governmental organisations to examine the economic impact of globalisation on women. These studies have noted an increase in gender inequality since the economic reforms were initiated under the NEP and SAP.[47] But these studies lack the comprehensive analysis of economic development on women at the national level and were limited to the analysis of a district, a state and a particular policy of the states and Central Government in a limited area or a region. Some studies have explored the impact of economic development in the context of globalisation, but only in a localised context and their geographical scope does not extend to all the states of India.

The researchers' attempt is to examine the gender inequality and economic development particularly after the globalisation. This chapter will examine gender inequality, work participation of women and globalisation in India in a holistic method. A special emphasis will be given to examine the inclusion and exclusion of gender in the development discourse and process of development in the globalised India.

The Government of India has ratified various international conventions and human rights instruments committed to secure equal rights to women. These are CEDAW (1979), the Mexico Plan of Action (1975), the Nairobi Forward Looking Strategies (1985), the Beijing Declaration as well as the Platform for Action (1995) and other such instruments. The year 2001 was observed as the year of women's empowerment in India. During the year, landmark documents 'the National Policy for the Empowerment of Women' and many other programmes and schemes for the development and empowerment of women like National Credit Fund for Women, Food and Nutrition Board (FNB), Information and Mass Education (IME) etc. were adopted by the Indian Government in this year.

The Constitution of India aimed at creating a society in which the development of all sections of society on the equal basis could become possible. Equal citizenship along with equal, legal and political rights and state welfare measures can reduce economic inequality. [48] Planned development was considered to be the most efficient way for solving the problems of poverty, illiteracy and social conservatism, which had caused various imbalances and discriminations among vast numbers of people. The attempts were aimed at the inclusion of the weaker section of society and empowering them through the state sponsored welfare economy.[49]

The Planning Commission in its landmark document entitled "Plans and Prospects for Social Welfare in India, initially has spelled out social welfare services as intending to cater to the special needs of persons and groups who by the reason of some handicap social, economic, physical or mental are unable to avail or are traditionally denied the amenities and services provided to the other members of the community."[50] *The committee on Status of Women,* in its report "towards equality", has recommended that "women are considered to be handicapped by social customs and social values, therefore, social welfare services have specially endeavoured to rehabilitate them.[51]

The First Five Year Plan defined three major areas in which it had paid special attention to women's development namely Education, Social welfare and Health under the welfare model of the state. To implement welfare measures for the benefit of the poor women, the Central Social Welfare Board (CSWB) was established. The CSWB recognised and realised the need for organising women into Mahila Mandals or women's clubs as an approach to community development.[52] Although the Second Five Year Plan concentrated on the overall agricultural development, it was also determined to recognise women's labour rights. It provided protection against the injuries at work, maternity benefits and crèches for their children. It advocated the immediate implementation of equal pay for equal work and provision for training to enable women to compete for higher jobs. The Third and Fourth Five Year Plans concentrated on women's education as education was considered the key to the socio-economic and political development of women.[53]

The Fifth Five Year Plan was implemented during the International Decade for Women's and the submission of the Report of the Committee on the Status of Women in India (CSWI) "Towards Equality". The CSWI had comprehensively examined the rights and status of women in the context of changing social and economic conditions and the problems related to the advancement of women. The CSWI reported that the dynamics of social change and development had adversely affected a large section of women and created new imbalances and disparities.[54]

Need for training women in respect of income generating activities and their protection was stressed in the Fifth Five Year Plan. Further it recommended a strategic programme of functional literacy to equip women with skills and knowledge to perform their functions as good housewives. Under the health programmes, the primary objective was to provide minimum public health facilities integrated with family planning and nutrition for vulnerable groups, children, pregnant and lactating mothers.[55]

It was realised in the 1970s that constitutional guarantees of equality would be meaningless and unrealistic unless women's right to economic independence is acknowledged and their training in skills as contributors to the family and the national economy did not improved. Consequently, National Plan of Action (1976) provided the guidelines based on 'United Nations' World Plan of Action for Women' came into force. The National Plan of Action identified areas of health, family planning, nutrition, education, employment, legislation and social welfare for formulating and implementing of action programmes for women and called for planned interventions to improve the conditions of women in India. Women's Welfare and Development Bureau was established in 1976 to act as a nodal point within the Government of India to co-ordinate policies and programmes and initiate some other measures for women's development.

The Sixth Five Year Plan stressed the need for economic independence, educational advancement and access to health care and family planning as essential for women development.[56] The impact of women movements and the global feminism which emerged in the'1970s have also showed their presence in India in the eighties.[57] It was first ever in the history of women's movements in India that women groups made an effort to integrate women in the economy and their pressure on the government for the inclusion of women into India's economy had become considerable.[58] But efforts of women groups could not achieve the desired goals as the means of production; exchange and distribution were controlled by men, which allowed women very limited space to evolve a Development Alternative with Women (DAWN).[59] Then efforts of the highly educated and politically connected women were aimed to save women from further marginalisation and to pressurise the government for the inclusion of women in the national development.

The period of 1980s is very crucial for the political governance and economic survival of the country. On the one hand, communalism, terrorism and violation of the human rights by the state forces dominated the political governance and the issues of *Mandal, Mandir* and *Masjid* forced a severe crises of governance[60] and on the other, the mounting burden of debt leading to a balance of payment crisis forced the government to discontinue with the social responsibility towards the mass of poor women in the rural, tribal and urban areas.[61]

This decade witnessed the strengthening of women movement and the mass mobilisations of women on a wide range of issues like water, drought, riots, communal tensions, police brutality against forest people, agricultural labourers, industrial workers, white-collar women employees; problems about promotions and transfers, sexual harassment at workplace, harassment for dowry and bride price, witch hunting, widow burning, sexual violence against women, coercion in family, fetuses, female infanticide child care facilities etc.[62] It was during the eighties that a gender analysis of the development schemes supported by the states and Central Government as well as by the international aid agencies and the voluntary organisations was started by the women academicians and women organisations in India.[63]

The Seventh Five Year Plan sought to generate awareness among women about their rights and privileges. The long term objectives of developmental programmes in the Seventh Plan were to raise economic and social status of women in order to bring them into the mainstream of national development and to recognise the importance of women in contributing to the various socio-economic, political and cultural activities. The Seventh Plan emphasised the need to open new avenues of work for women and perceived them as crucial resource for the development of the country. Another salient and crucial recognition was the need for organisation of women workers and uniting of women for their rights.[64]

The decade of nineties is marked by an approach of gender and development (GAD). Here the focus was on the power relations determined as a result of interplay of complex class, caste, ethnicity, religion, races and gender. It was the emergence of the era of partnership with a clear cut understanding that women constitute half of the world's workforce and get only 1/10th of the world's income and own only 1/100th of the world's wealth.[65]

The strategy in the Eighth Plan was to ensure that the benefits of development from different sectors did not bypass the women and special programmes were implemented to complement them. The main objective of Eighth Plan was to extend the reach of services to women both qualitatively and quantitatively. Panchayati Raj Institutions were involved in the designing and implementation of women's programmes. The Ninth Five Year Plan was an attempt to bring the women's issues within the policy-making spheres and it came into effect from April 1, 1997. The problems like feminisation of poverty, inadequate investment in social sectors, increasing violence against women and stereotyped portrayal of women in private and state sponsored media especially television were focused upon. The necessity for information and training opportunities, reservations and social services etc., and people's involvement were considered necessary for the success of any programme and were also desired to be solved by the state and civil society initiatives.[66]

Tenth Five Year Plan aimed at empowering women through translating the recently adopted National Policy for Empowerment of Women (2001) into action and ensuring survival protection and development of children through rights based approach.[67]

Eleventh Five Year Plan focused on women and work and the attempts were made to enhance women education and skills through public-private partnership in general and technical education. Special allocation of funds and new schemes were made to save the girl child and to raise the sex ratio for the age group 0–6 to 935 by 2011–12 and to 950 by 2016–17. Further, this plan intended to ensure that 33 per cent of the direct and indirect beneficiaries of all government schemes are women and girl children. It also proposed to ensure that all children enjoy a safe childhood, without any compulsion to work.[68]

Gender Budgeting and National Perspective Plan for Women 1988–2000

Twenty first century started with the new promises of good governance and inclusive growth in India. The government took two major steps to increase the accountability of public sector towards women through the gender budgeting in 2001. Gender budgeting in India takes two forms: the Gender Budget Statement (also known as Statement 20) and Gender Budgeting Cells located in government ministries and departments. The Gender Budget Statement was institutionalised in India in the 2005-2006 financial year. 3 key actors in the formulation of the Gender Budget Statement are the Ministry of Finance, the Ministry of Women and Child Development, the Planning Department at the national level and the Planning Commissions at the state level. The Gender Budget Statement is a component of the annual "Union Budget of India", being India's national budget, which is issued by the Ministry of Finance. There are two parts to the Gender Budget Statement. Part A lists "schemes" for which the beneficiaries are solely women and girls, while Part B lists the schemes for which at least 30 per cent of the expenditure flows to women and girls. Thus, the Gender Budget Statement indicates the quantity of public financial resources for which women and girls are the sole and partial beneficiaries. In this respect, India's Gender Budget Statement is a quantitative form of gender budgeting. To support ministries and departments in undertaking gender budgeting, in 2007, the Ministry of Women and Child Development issued a handbook explaining gender budgeting and providing guidance on the practical steps to be followed. The handbook is an example of the capacity building efforts designed to promote meaningful gender budgeting in India. While initially a national initiative, gender budgeting is being promulgated at the state level. In February 2013, the Ministry of Women and Child Development issued an advisory letter to the Chief Secretaries of the State Governments, in which the State Governments were advised to (a) formally adopt gender budgeting in all departments, municipal bodies and zila panchayats (district councils), (b) establish a "High Powered Committee/Task Force on Gender Budgeting", and (c) address gender issues in the Planning Department's "annual plan development circular". The progressive institutionalisation of gender budgeting is also evident in budget speeches and circulars.[69]

The second major step is the National Policy for the Empowerment of Women, 2001 views empowerment as an enabling process that must lead to their economic as well as social transformation. Government has sought to operationalise this approach through legislative and programmatic interventions as well as by mainstreaming gender into the development planning process. Numerous such initiatives were taken during the Eleventh Plan period. These initiatives need to be consolidated and built on during the Twelfth Five Year Plan to enable women to challenge and change the contexts in which they live. Focused efforts through development programmes, both multi-sectoral as well as targeted, along with governance reforms would be a prerequisite. Women, especially the vulnerable and marginalised, would need to be provided a level playing field to access social, economic and legal entitlements as a right.[70]

Twelfth Five Year Plan has been entitled as Faster, Sustainable and More Inclusive growth. It has addressed the shortcomings of the Eleventh Five Year Plan including the decline in women employment. Recognising that economic independence is the key to improving the position of women within the family and in society, the Plan would need to focus on enhancing women's access to control over resources. Amongst others, this would entail not only increasing their presence in the workforce but, more importantly, improving the quality of women's work and ensuring their upward mobility on the economic ladder.

The theory of patriarchy puts the question of women empowerment in a proper perspective.[71] The Planning Commission is pushing for special dispensation for single women, particularly those who are single by choice, under various government schemes in the 12th Plan. In addition to reserving a certain percentage of jobs for single women under centrally sponsored schemes, the plan has proposed promoting and strengthening federations of single women at the block and district level.[72]

It is observed in the Census of 2011 that 833 million people continue to live in rural India. A very large proportion of them are either wholly or significantly dependent on their livelihood on farm activity be it crop agriculture, horticulture, animal husbandry or fisheries. Women participation in favour related work, both in agriculture and in animal husbandry in framing policies/schemes for the 12th Five Year Plan, the special needs of women are taken care of. The Mahila Kisan Sashaktikaran Pariyojana (MKSP) which is a sub-component of NRHM (National Rural Health Mission) has been recently launched to meet the specific needs and to give leverage to the enormous potential of empowering rural women in the farm sector, and also in the rural sector and also in the rural non-farmer sector.[73]

Policies and Programmes for Development and Empowerment of Women

The schemes of the Ministry like Vocational Programme for Empowerment of Women and Swawlamban enable economic empowerment. Working Women Hostels and Creches provide support services. The Ministry also supports autonomous bodies like National Commission for Women, Central Social Welfare Board, Rashtriya Mahila Kosh and Indira Awas Yojana which work for the welfare and development of women. These schemes were started under the Tenth Plan and were continued in the Eleventh Plan.

The following are the details pertaining to the above schemes intended for the development and empowerment of women:

Vocational Programme for Empowerment of Women

This programme has been launched with ILO assistance just to provide equitable opportunities for women's employment in the industry, service sectors and also in self-employment. In this programme, diverse types of training like secretarial practice, electronics, hair and skin care, dress making instrument mechanic, data programming, computer software, architecture basic skills, embroidery business advanced skills and instructional skills etc.

Support to Training and Employment (STEP)

The Vocational programmes seek to provide skills and new knowledge to poor and assetless women in the traditional sectors. Under this project, women beneficiaries are organised into viable and cohesive groups or cooperatives. A comprehensive package of services such as health care, elementary education, crèche facility, market linkages, etc. is provided besides access to credit. Skill development is provided in ten traditional skills amongst women. This is a Central Scheme launched in 1987. The Ministry is at present getting the programme evaluated. Based on the results of the evaluation, the scheme is proposed to be revamped. Further, the possibilities of providing training and skills to women both in traditional and non-traditional sectors and integrating with Rashtriya Mahila Kosh for credit linkages are being considered. A sum of Rs. 240 crore was proposed for the scheme in the XIth Plan.

Rashtriya Mahila Kosh (RMK)

The RMK was set up in 1993 as a national instrument for extending credit to poor and needy women in the informal, unorganised sector and had sanction worth Rs. 1113.50 crore (Upto October 31, 2002.) More than 4.28 crore women have benefited through 1046 NGOs. The objective of RMK is to create an environment for increase in the outlay of RMK's funds to the needy women through the intervention of women self-help groups (SHGs). The SHGs promote saving, build up a thrift fund and create leaders who manage the activity. Handling money is considered as a process of empowerment of women. It leads to a greater empowerment, whey they learn to apply the funds for income generation and for improvement of their economic status.[74]

Swa-Shakti

The project jointly founded by IFAD, World Bank and the Government of India was launched in October, 1999 and culminated on 30th June, 2005. The objective of the programme was to bring out socio-economic development and empowerment of women through promotion of women SHGs, micro credit and income generating activities. The project was conceived as a Pilot Project implemented in 335 blocks of 57 districts in 9 states. The project established 17,647 SHGs covering about 2,44,000 women. This was a Centrally Sponsored Project.

Swayamsiddha

This was an integrated scheme for women empowerment through formation of Self Help Groups (SHGs) launched in February, 2001. The long term objective of the programme was holistic empowerment of women through a sustained process of mobilisation and convergence of all the ongoing sectoral programmes by improving access of women to micro-credit, economic resources, etc. This is a Centrally Sponsored Scheme. The Scheme was able to provide a forum for women empowerment, collective reflection and united action. The scheme was culminated in March, 2007. The programme was implemented in 650 blocks of the country and 67,971 women SHGs have been formed assisting 9,89,485 beneficiaries. The scheme came to an end in March 2007.

It is proposed to take up *Swayamsiddha* with a wider scope during the XIth Plan. It is also proposed to implement a woman's empowerment and livelihood project in four districts of Uttar Pradesh and two districts of Bihar with assistance from IFAD. The schemes of *Swayamsiddha* and *Swashakti* would be merged and implemented as *Swayamsiddha,* Phase-II in the XI Plan. The Mid-Term Appraisal Report of the Tenth Plan has also recommended merger of these two schemes as these have similar objectives. The next phase would be a country wide programme with larger coverage in states lagging behind on women development indices. Convergence is the basic concept in *Swayamsiddha*. The lessons learnt in *Swayamsiddha* and *Swashakti* would be incorporated in the universalised *Swayamsiddha* giving an integrated set of training inputs relating to social and economic empowerment, including skill development and training in traditional and non-traditional sectors. The estimated requirement during the XIth Plan period for both phase II of *Swayamsiddha* as well as the IFAD Project is Rs. 3000 crore.

National Rural Employment Guarantee Scheme (NREGS)

NREGS is a demand driven programme. However, it has been provided in the National Rural Employment Guarantee Scheme that while providing employment, priority shall be given to women in such a way that at least 1/3rd of the beneficiaries are women who have been registered and requested for work under the scheme.

Swarnajayanthi Gram Swarozgar Yojana (SGSY)

The Swarnajayanti Gram Swarozgar Yojana (SGSY) was launched in April 1999 after restructuring the Integrated Rural Development Programme (IRDP) and allied programmes. It is the only Self Employment Programme currently being implemented for the rural poor. The objective of the SGSY is to bring the assisted *swarozgaris* above the poverty line by providing them income generating assets through bank credit and government subsidy. The scheme is being implemented on cost sharing basis of 75:25 between the centre and states. Up to December 2007, 27.37 lakh self-help groups (SHGs) have been formed and 93.21 lakh *swarozgaris* have been assisted with a total outlay of Rs. 19,340.32 crore.[75]

It is envisaged in the guidelines that 50 per cent of the groups formed in each block should be exclusively for women who will account for at least 40 per cent of the total *Swarazgaris*. Under the scheme, women are encouraged in the practice of thrift and credit which enables them to become self-reliant.

Through assistance in the form of resolving fund, bank credit and subsidy, the programme seeks to integrate women in the economy by providing increased opportunities of self-employment, thereby empowering them economically and socially.

Women Employment and Empowerment in India: An Analysis

Although women development was a matter of serious concern for the policy-makers in India from the dawn of Independence, the women employment and work participation could only become a matter of concern for the policy-makers and women studies in 1970s. The inception of women studies in India in 1970s questioned the state sponsored welfare measures of the state of women development and urged the authorities concerned to evolve new alternatives for women development in India.

It is to be noted that in 1960s and specially before the advent of specialised women's studies decline in female work participation had been noticed, but it was generally thought to be transitory phenomena as the economy moved from subsistence agriculture and household industry to modern Industry.[76] It was also assumed that the decline would be automatically corrected by a "countervailing force", identified with the increase in income.[77] Analysis of historical trends in developed countries, particularly in Europe, had given rise to the development of the view which held that income increase initially aggravated the downward trend in female work participation; further gains in income reversed the decline.[78] Such assumptions and perspectives were, of course, proven to be erroneous in case of India on several counts.

It was after the Report of the Committee on the Status of Women in India (CSWI) in 1974 that the decline in the women work participation was thought to be the problem of developmental process in India. The long term overall decline, both in percentage of workers to total female population and in their percentage to the total labour force, began to be viewed as evidence that women's economic participation had been adversely affected by the nature of the development process in India.

The CSWI postulated that ruination of domestic industry from the colonial period onwards (with relatively greater ruin in the female labour intensive sectors) had eroded the non-agricultural occupations of women, while externally the process of limited modernisation had excluded them from the limited opportunities in the modern sector. The result was a permanent shift of women to the periphery of the economy.[79]

From the latter half of the 1970s and throughout the 1990s studies on the Women Work Participation Rate (WWPR) attempted to further explain the processes of underpinning the decline in female employment in India while simultaneously focusing on the question of actual underenumeration or undercounting of women's work in national data sets. There were sufficient and observable evidences to show that the vast majority of women were not idle but were actively contributing to their household economy. The question, therefore, arose as to why and how their work was not being counted. Considerable attention was paid to problems in measurement of the extent of decline in the Female Work Participation Rate (FWPR), especially in the context of changes in the definition of workers across censuses and the ensuing problems of comparability.[80]

At the conceptual level, the need to evolve alternative methods of capturing women's work and the inadequacy of the existing modes of data collection on women's work were linked to the invisibility of a large part of women's productive labour and its contribution to family subsistence labour in both the monetised and non-monetised segments of the economy.[81] The two sectors where such invisibility prevailed to a great extent were agriculture and household industry. The two decades of discussion and debates contributed to generating a greater awareness of the need to make women's work more visible in the macro data, particularly in agriculture.[82]

The census as the primary source of historical trends was the data based at the heart of these initial discussions and it is only from the 1990s onwards that the quinquennial National Sample Survey Office (NSSO) became more central. In the 1990s, there was an understandable eagerness to assess the impact of the structural shift in the policy framework towards liberalisation, without having to wait for the 2001 census report. Given publication delays and the limitations of the published economic data of the 2001 census, the National Sample Survey (NSS), which is thought to be more amenable to capturing women's economic activities, has continued to be the principle data source for most of the studies and analyses of women's work and employment trends even after 2001.

A continue debate on the invisibility of women's work, including issues of definitional limitations in data sources, was in a sense circumscribed during the 1990s by a wave of discussions on the informal sector that came into its own in the 1980s. Arguably, it could be said that the new preoccupation with the informal sector shifted the focus from the classical developmental dualistic approach comprising agriculture (as the backward subsistence sector) and industry (as the modern sector) to a more diffused set of occupations and employments that could always be catalogued and categorised within the dualistic framework. While there were clear failings in the formulaic assumptions of traditional developmental approaches, which were brought out by empirical evidence on informal and unorganised sector employment, the discussions on the informal sector contributed little to the great question of agrarian social relations. In relation to women, home-based work became a primary point of discussion that united the earlier discourses on the invisibility of women's work and the later preoccupation with the informal sector.[83]

Further evidence of the uncounted labour of women in economic activities came from the 1998 'time use survey' conducted by the Central Statistics Office (CSO) in some states, which showed that the Women Participation Rate Survey (WPRS) for women as per the time use data was 58.2 per cent and 30 per cent for rural and urban areas respectively against 25.3 per cent and 12.8 per cent according to current weekly status in the closest NSSO employment survey.

The time use survey was used to press a case for computing a value to women's unpaid labour on the grounds of giving it visibility in official statistics and providing a base for unpaid workers to claim their due share from the state exchequer to improve their conditions. Implicit to the valuation argument was a critique of the gross domestic product (GDP) in its present form as "a limited variable to project the status of well-being in an economy."[84]

National Sample Survey Office's report, "Key Indicator of Employment and Unemployment in India, 2009-10" shows that the distributing trend of a steep fall in the Female Work Participation Rate (FWPR) that began in 2007-08 has continued. With an increase of 22.3 million in the male workforce between 2004-05 and 2009-10 being virtually cancelled out by a fall of more than 21 million in the female workforce, of employment trend in India acquired a new urgency.

This chapter will examine some of the explicit as well as non-explicit trends in women's employment from 1993-1994 to 2009-

10 and will argue that they indicate a continuing crisis in this domain under liberalisation led growth. Trends in the distribution of male and female workers in terms of employment status and broad industrial categories for the same period are also outlined.

Decline of Female Work Participation Rate

Before making an analysis on women empowerment through the employment and unemployment situations during various survey rounds by the Government of India, it is pertinent to mention that after 68th round (2011-12) employment and unemployment survey of **NSSO** by (Ministry of Statistics and Programme Implementation) has not published the survey reports. So, after 2011-12 we have collected data from **Labour Bureau** survey reports on employment-unemployment by (Ministry of Labour and Employment). The number highlighted as bold in this chapter show the declining rate of work participation of women.

Labour Force indicates the supply of labour in the country. As per the definition by Labour Bureau, Labour Force Participation Rate shows the proportion of a country's working-age population that engages actively in the labour market either **'working'** (employed) or **'seeking or available for work'** (unemployed) or both during a major part of the reference period. [(*see* Table-B(1) and Figs. 4.1 & 4.2].

In Table B(1), the LFPR based on the different approaches, as estimated from various NSS Employment and Unemployment Survey rounds (Ministry of Statistics and Programme Implementation) and Labour Bureau Employment and Unemployment survey reports (Ministry of Labour and Employment). The corresponding rates are obtained from 38th (1983), 43rd (1987-88), 50th (1993-94), 55th (1999-00), 62nd (2005-06), 64th (2007-08), 66th (2009-10), 68th (2011-12) survey rounds of NSSO and 4th (2013-14), 5th (2015-16) Annual Employment-Unemployment survey rounds of Labour Bureau.

Between 38th (1983) and 43rd (1987-88) rounds of NSSO, the percentage share of rural female Labour Force Participation Rate has increased by 0.2 per cent and urban female LFPR remained at the same level according to the principal status while rural and urban male LFPR has declined by 0.8 per cent and 0.3 per cent respectively according to the (ps). Labour force of rural female

Table-B (1): Labour Force Participation Rates (in%)

Year	*Rural Male*		*Rural Female*		*Urban Male*		*Urban Female*	
	ps	psss	ps	psss	ps	psss	ps	psss
1983	54.0	55.5	25.2	34.2	53.1	54.0	12.9	15.9
1987-1988	53.2	54.9	25.4	33.1	52.8	53.4	12.9	16.2
Growth Rate								
1983 to 1987-88	**-0.8**	**-0.6**	0.2	**-1.1**	**-0.3**	**-0.6**	00	0.3
1993-1994	54.9	56.1	23.7	33.0	53.8	54.3	13.2	16.5
1999-2000	53.3	54.0	23.5	30.2	53.9	54.2	12.6	14.7
Growth Rate								
1993-94 to 1999-2000	**-1.6**	**-2.1**	**-0.2**	**-2.8**	0.1	**-0.1**	**-0.6**	**-1.8**
2005-2006	55.1	56.1	22.9	31.4	56.1	56.6	13.1	15.2
2007-2008	55.1	55.9	22.0	29.2	57.3	57.6	12.6	14.6
Growth Rate								
2005-06 to 2007-08	00	**-0.2**	**-0.9**	**-2.2**	1.2	1.0	**-0.5**	**-0.6**
2009-2010	54.8	55.6	20.8	26.5	55.6	55.9	12.8	14.6
2011-2012	54.7	55.3	18.1	25.3	56.0	56.3	13.4	15.5
Growth Rate								
2009-10 to 2011-12	**-0.1**	**-0.3**	**-2.7**	**-1.2**	0.4	0.4	0.6	0.9
2013-2014	74.2	76.4	29.1	36.4	73.8	74.0	18.5	19.7
2015-2016	77.3	78.0	26.7	31.7	69.1	69.1	16.2	16.6
Growth Rate								
2013-14 to 2015-16	3.1	1.6	**-2.4**	**-4.7**	**-4.7**	**-4.9**	**-2.3**	**-3.1**

Source: Government of India, Estimated LFPR reported in various NSS reports on employment and unemployment 38th, 43rd, 50th, 55th, 62nd, 64th, 66th and 68th rounds NSSO, Central Statistical Organisation, and 4th and 5th Annual Employment-Unemployment survey rounds of Labour Bureau by Ministry of Labour and Employment, Government of India.

decreased by 1.1 per cent, urban female labour force increased by 0.3 per cent and rural male labour force decreased by 0.8 per cent, urban male labour force decreased by 0.6 per cent according to principal status and subsidiary status taken together (psss).

Between 50th (1993-94) and 55th (1999-2000) rounds of NSSO, labour force of rural female decreased by 2.8 per cent, urban female labour force decreased by 1.8 per cent and rural male labour force decreased by 1.6 per cent and urban male labour force decreased by 0.1 per cent according to principal status and subsidiary status taken together (psss).

Between 62nd (2005-06) and 64th (2007-08) rounds of NSSO, labour force of rural female decreased by 2.2 per cent, labour force of urban female 0.6 per cent and labour force of rural male

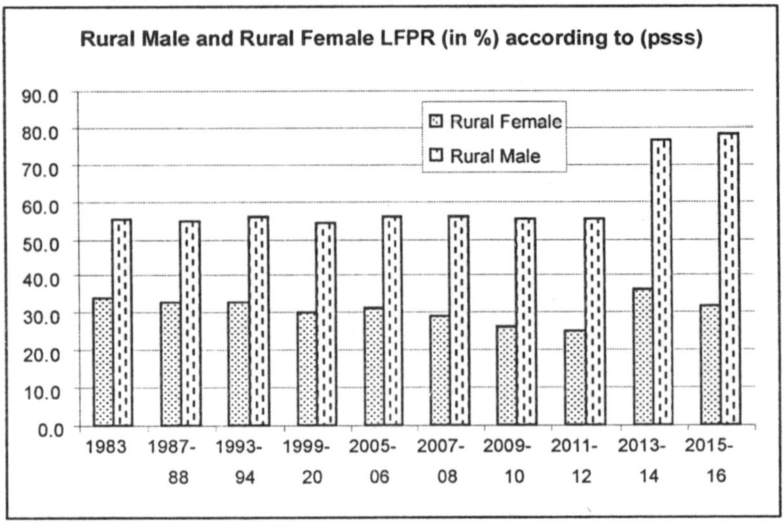

Fig. 4.1: Labour Force Participation Rate.

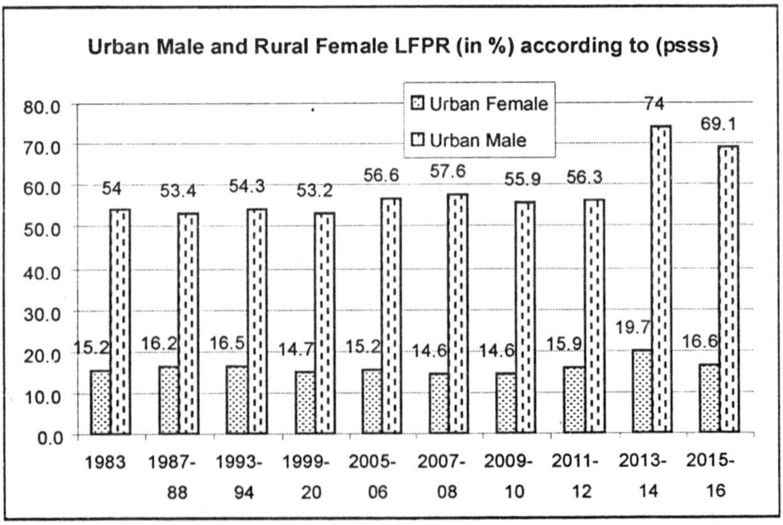

Fig. 4.2: Labour Force Participation Rate.

decreased by 0.2 per cent while urban male labour force increased by 1.0 per cent according to principal status and subsidiary status taken together (psss).

Between 66th (2009-10) and 68th (2011-12) rounds of NSSO, rural female labour force decreased by 1.2 per cent, urban female labour force increased by 0.9 per cent and rural male labour force decreased by 0.3 per cent, urban male labour force increased by 0.4 per cent according to principal status and subsidiary status taken together (psss).

Between 4th (2013-14) and 5th (2015-16) survey rounds of Labour Bureau, LFPR has increased by 3.1 per cent for males and decreased by 2.4 per cent for females in the rural areas according to principal status. In the urban areas LFPR has decreased by 4.7 per cent for males and 2.3 per cent for females according to (ps). LFPR of Rural female declined from 36.4 per cent to 31.7 per cent and urban female labour force declined from 19.7 per cent to 16.6 per cent. While rural male labour force increased by 1.6 per cent and urban male labour force declined from 74.0 per cent to 69.1 per cent according to (psss) during the same period.

Worker Population Ratio (WPR)

The second important parameter of the labour force is the Worker Population Ratio (WPR). Worker Population Ratio shows the proportion of workers/employed persons in the total population for the specific age group as per the definition of Labour Bureau. [see Table-B(2) and Fig. 4.3]

In the Table-B(2), Between 38th (1983) and 43rd (1987-88) rounds of NSSO, Female Worker Population Ratio has decreased by 0.1 per cent and Male WPR decreased by 0.9 per cent. During the same period, Rural Female WPR decreased less than Male WPR i.e. 0.3 per cent and 1.1 per cent respectively. Urban Female WPR decreased by 0.2 per cent and urban male WPR decreased by 0.4 per cent.

Between 50th (1993-94) and 55th (1999-2000) rounds of NSSO, Rural Female WPR decreased less than Rural Male i.e. 0.3 per cent and 1.6 per cent respectively. Urban Female WPR decreased by 0.4 per cent and Urban Male WPR remained at the same level.

Between 62nd (2005-06) and 64th (2007-08) rounds of NSSO, Female WPR decreased by 0.9 per cent however, Male WPR increased by 0.5 per cent. Rural Female WPR decreased by 0.8 per cent and Rural Male WPR increased by 0.1 per cent. Urban Female WPR decreased by 0.3 per cent While Urban Male WPR increased by 1.6 per cent.

Table-B (2): Worker Population Ratio (in%) According to (ps)

Year	*Rural*			*Urban*			*Rural + Urban*		
	Male	*Female*	*Person*	*Male*	*Female*	*Person*	*Male*	*Female*	*Person*
1983	52.8	24.8	39.1	50.0	12.0	32	52.1	21.8	37.4
1987-1988	51.7	24.5	38.5	49.6	11.8	31.5	51.2	21.7	36.9
Growth Rate 1983 to 1987-88	**-1.1**	**-0.3**	**-0.6**	**-0.4**	**-0.2**	**-0.5**	**-0.9**	**-0.1**	**-0.5**
1993-1994	53.8	23.4	39.0	51.3	12.1	32.7	53.2	20.6	37.5
1999-2000	52.2	23.1	38.0	51.3	11.7	32.4	52.0	20.3	36.5
Growth Rate 1993-94 to 1999-2000	**-1.6**	**-0.3**	**-1.0**	**00**	**-0.4**	**-0.3**	**-0.2**	**-0.3**	**-1.0**
2005-2006	53.7	22.4	38.4	53.4	12.1	33.6	53.6	19.9	37.3
2007-2008	53.8	21.6	38.1	55	11.8	34.2	54.1	19.0	37.1
Growth Rate 2005-06 to 2007-08	0.1	**-0.8**	**-0.3**	1.6	**-0.3**	0.6	0.5	**-0.9**	**-0.2**
2009-2010	53.7	20.2	37.4	53.9	11.9	33.9	53.8	18.0	36.5
2011-2012	53.5	17.6	35.9	54.2	12.5	34.2	53.7	16.1	35.4
Growth Rate 2009-10 to 2011-12	0.2	**-2.6**	**-1.5**	0.3	0.6	0.3	0.1	**-1.9**	**-1.1**
2013-2014	71.6	27.2	52.1	70.9	16.2	44.6	71.4	23.8	49.9
2015-2016	74.1	24.6	50.4	66.8	14.3	41.4	72.1	21.7	47.8
Growth Rate 2013-14 to 2015-16	2.5	**-2.6**	**-1.7**	**-4.1**	**-1.9**	**-3.2**	0.7	**-2.1**	**-2.1**

Source: Government of India, Estimated LFPR reported in various NSS reports on employment and unemployment 38th, 43rd, 50th, 55th, 62nd, 64th, 66th and 68th rounds NSSO, Central Statistical Organisation, 4th and 5th Annual Employment-Unemployment survey rounds of Labour Bureau by Ministry of Labour and Employment, Government of India.

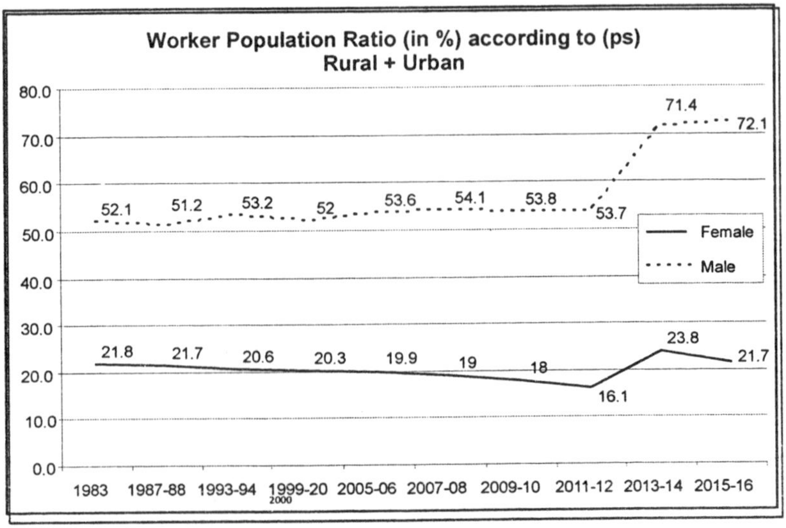

Fig. 4.3: WPR (ps).

Between 66th (2009-10) and 68th (2011-12) survey rounds of NSSO, Female WPR decreased by 1.9 per cent however Male WPR remained at the same level. Rural Female WPR decreased by 2.6 per cent and Rural Male WPR increased by 0.2 per cent. Urban Female and Male WPR increased by 0.6 per cent and 0.3 per cent respectively.

Between 4th (2013-14) and 5th (2015-16) annual survey rounds of Labour Bureau, Female WPR declined from 23.8 per cent to 21.7 per cent and Male WPR increased by 0.7 per cent. During the same period, Rural Female WPR decreased by 2.6 per cent and Rural Male WPR increased by 2.5 per cent. Urban Female WPR decreased by 1.9 per cent and Urban Male WPR decreased by 4.1 per cent.

Table-B (3): Worker Population Ratio (in %) According to (psss)

Year	*Rural*			*Urban*			*Rural + Urban*		
	Male	*Female*	*Person*	*Male*	*Female*	*Person*	*Male*	*Female*	*Person*
1983	54.7	34.0	44.5	51.2	15.1	34.0	53.8	29.6	42.0
1987-1988	53.9	32.3	43.4	50.6	15.2	33.7	53.1	28.5	41.2
Growth Rate 1983 to 1987-88	**-0.8**	**-1.7**	**-1.1**	**-0.6**	0.1	**-0.3**	**-0.7**	**-1.1**	**-0.8**
1993-1994	55.3	32.8	44.4	52.1	15.5	34.7	54.5	28.6	42.0
1999-2000	53.1	29.9	41.7	51.8	13.9	33.7	52.7	25.9	39.7
Growth Rate 1993-94 to 1999-2000	**-0.2**	**-2.9**	**-2.7**	**-0.3**	**-1.6**	**-1.0**	**-1.8**	**-2.7**	**-2.3**
2005-2006	54.9	31.0	43.3	54.0	14.3	35.0	54.7	27.0	41.3
2007-2008	54.8	28.9	42.2	55.4	13.8	35.4	55.0	25.0	40.4
Growth Rate 2005-06 to 2007-08	**-0.1**	**-2.1**	**-1.1**	1.4	**-0.5**	0.4	0.3	**-2.0**	**-0.9**
2009-2010	54.7	26.1	40.8	54.3	13.8	35.0	54.6	22.8	39.2
2011-2012	54.3	24.8	39.9	54.6	14.7	35.5	54.4	21.9	38.6
Growth Rate 2009-10 to 2011-12	**-0.4**	**-1.3**	**-0.9**	0.3	0.9	0.5	**-0.2**	**-0.9**	**-0.6**
2013-2014	74.3	35.1	57.1	71.4	17.5	45.5	73.5	29.6	53.7
2015-2016	75.7	30.2	53.9	67.1	14.8	41.8	73.3	25.8	50.5
Growth Rate 2013-14 to 2015-16	1.4	**-4.9**	**-3.2**	**-4.3**	**-2.7**	**-3.7**	**-0.2**	**-3.8**	**-3.2**

Source: Government of India, Estimated LFPR reported in various NSS reports on employment and unemployment 38th, 43rd, 50th, 55th, 62nd, 64th, 66th and 68th rounds NSSO, Central Statistical Organisation, 4th and 5th Annual Employment-Unemployment survey rounds of Labour Bureau by Ministry of Labour and Employment, Government of India.

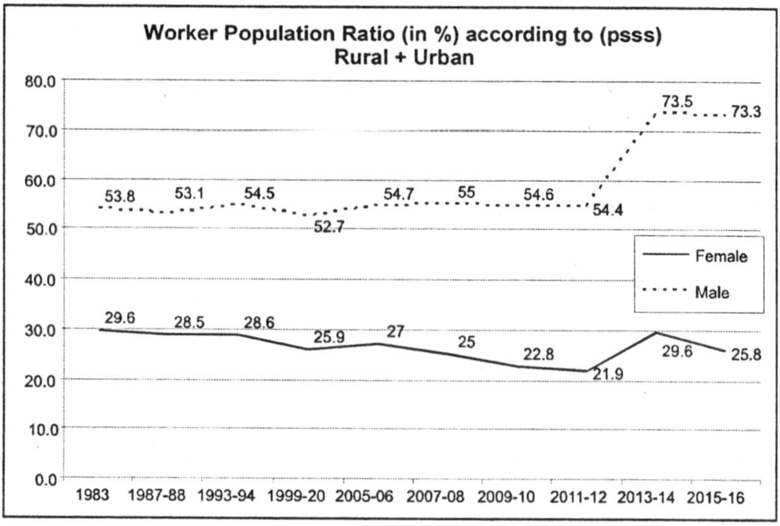

Fig. 4.4: WPR (psss).

In the Table-B(2), between 38th (1983) and 43rd (1987-88) rounds of NSSO, Female WPR decreased by 1.1 per cent and Male WPR decreased by 0.7 per cent. During the same period, Rural Female WPR decreased more than Male WPR i.e. 1.7 per cent and 0.8 per cent respectively. Urban Female WPR decreased by 0.1 per cent and urban male WPR decreased by 0.6 per cent.

Between 50th (1993-94) and 55th (1999-2000) rounds of NSSO, Female and Male WPR decreased by 2.7 per cent and 1.8 per cent respectively. Rural Female WPR decreased more than Rural Male WPR i.e. 2.9 per cent and 0.2 per cent respectively. Urban Female WPR decreased by 1.6 per cent and Urban Male WPR decreased by 0.3 per cent.

Between 62nd (2005-06) and 64th (2007-08) rounds of NSSO, Female WPR decreased by 2.0 per cent and Male WPR increased by 0.3 per cent. Rural Female WPR decreased by 2.1 per cent and Rural Male WPR decreased by 0.1 per cent. Urban Female WPR decreased by 0.5 per cent however, Urban Male WPR increased by 1.4 per cent.

Between 66th (2009-10) and 68th (2011-12) survey rounds of NSSO, Female WPR decreased by 0.9 per cent and Male WPR decreased by 0.2 per cent. Rural Female WPR decreased by 1.3 per cent and Rural Male WPR decreased by 0.4 per cent. Urban Female and Male WPR increased by less corresponding rates i.e. 0.3 per cent and 0.9 per cent.

Between 4th (2013-14) and 5th (2015-16) annual survey rounds of Labour Bureau, Female WPR decreased by 3.8 per cent and Male WPR decreased by 0.2 per cent. During the same period, Rural Female WPR decreased by 4.9 per cent and Rural Male WPR decreased by 1.4 per cent. Urban Female WPR decreased less than Urban Male WPR in the corresponding rates i.e. 2.7 per cent and 4.3 per cent.

Gender Differentials by Category of Employment

To analyse the women empowerment through the work participation in the economy, it is very important to see the nature of work through different category of employment. Women are engaged less in regular/wage salaried employment than men, while in casual labour women's participation is high than men in India [see Table-B(4) and Figs. 4.5 and 4.6].

It may be observed from the Table B (4) that between 38th (1983) and 43rd (1987-88) rounds of NSSO, self-employed male has decreased by 0.6 per cent and self-employed female has increased by 1.4 per cent while Regular/wage salaried male has increased by 0.15 per cent and female increased by 1.8 per cent according to principal status. The percentage share of male casual labour has increased by 0.75 per cent while female casual has declined by 0.15 per cent according to (ps). Self-employed male has increased by 0.55 per cent, female has increased by 0.1 per cent and regular/wage salaried male workers has decreased by 0.15 per cent, female workers has increased by 1.3 per cent and casual male labour has increased by 0.7 per cent but female workers has decreased by 1.6 per cent according to the principal status and subsidiary status taken together during the same period.

Between 66th (2009-10) and 68th (2011-12) survey rounds of NSSO, the number of self-employed female workers has increased by 3.1 per cent and male workers increased by 0.8 per cent. Regular/wage salaried female employees increased more than male workers in the corresponding rates i.e. 2.35 per cent and 1.5 per cent. While female casual labour decreased by 5.05 per cent and male casual labour decreased by 2.3 per cent according to principal status and subsidiary status taken together (psss).

Table-B (4): Distribution of Usually Employed Persons by Category of Employment (in %)

Rural+Urban

Year	Category of Employment											
	Usual status (ps)						*Usual status (psss)*					
	Self-employed		*Regular/wage salaried employees*		*Casual labour*		*Self-employed*		*Regular/wage salaried employees*		*Casual labour*	
	Male	*Female*	*Male*	*Female*	*Male*	*Female*	*Male*	*Female*	*Male*	*Female*	*Male*	*Female*
1983	49.85	45.7	27.55	17.75	22.6	36.55	50.7	53.85	27.0	14.3	22.3	31.85
1987-88	49.25	47.1	27.4	19.55	23.35	33.35	50.15	53.95	26.85	15.6	23.0	30.25
Growth Rate 1983 to 1987-88	**-0.6**	1.4	0.15	1.8	0.75	**-0.15**	0.55	0.1	**-0.15**	1.3	0.7	**-1.6**
1993-94	48.9	44.25	25.7	19.45	25.4	36.3	49.7	52.2	22.25	15.55	25.5	32.25
1999-2000	47.8	44.2	25.45	21.2	26.75	34.6	48.25	51.3	25.25	18.2	26.5	30.5
Growth Rate 1993-94 to 1999-2000	**-1.1**	**-0.05**	**-0.25**	1.75	1.35	**-1.7**	**-1.45**	**-0.9**	3.0	2.65	1.0	**-1.75**
2005-06	49.1	49.2	28.8	17.3	23.4	33.5	48.2	53.8	28.5	14.85	23.3	31.35
2007-08	48.7	43.3	25.7	24.25	25.65	32.45	49.05	50.3	25.55	21.0	25.45	28.75
Growth Rate 2005-06 to 2007-08	**-0.4**	**-5.9**	**-3.1**	6.95	2.25	**-1.05**	0.85	**-3.5**	**-2.95**	6.15	2.15	-2.5
2009-10	46.95	42.85	25.35	24.95	27.7	32.2	47.3	48.4	25.2	21.85	27.5	29.75
2011-12	47.85	45.15	26.9	28.15	25.3	26.75	48.1	51.5	26.7	24.2	25.2	24.7
Growth Rate 2009-08 to 2011-12	0.9	2.3	1.55	3.2	**-2.4**	**-5.45**	0.8	3.1	1.5	2.35	**-2.3**	**-5.05**
2013-14	50.5	45.7	16.9	15.0	29.2	37.2	51.0	49.1	16.5	12.1	29.3	36.8
2015-16	48.4	39.9	17.6	14.8	30.2	42.1	48.6	42.9	17.4	12.5	30.2	41.9
Growth Rate 2013-14 to 2015-16	**-2.1**	**-5.8**	0.7	**-0.2**	1.0	4.9	**-2.4**	**-6.2**	0.9	0.4	0.9	5.1

Source: Government of India, Estimated LFPR reported in various NSS reports on employment and unemployment 38th, 43rd, 50th, 55th, 62nd, 64th, 66th and 68th rounds NSSO, Central Statistical Organisation, 4th and 5th Annual Employment-Unemployment survey rounds of Labour Bureau by Ministry of Labour and Employment, Government of India.

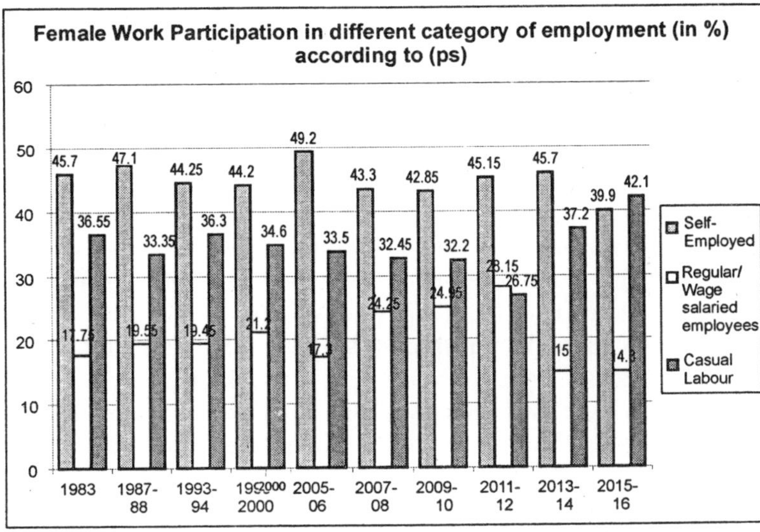

Fig. 4.5: Category of Employment (ps).

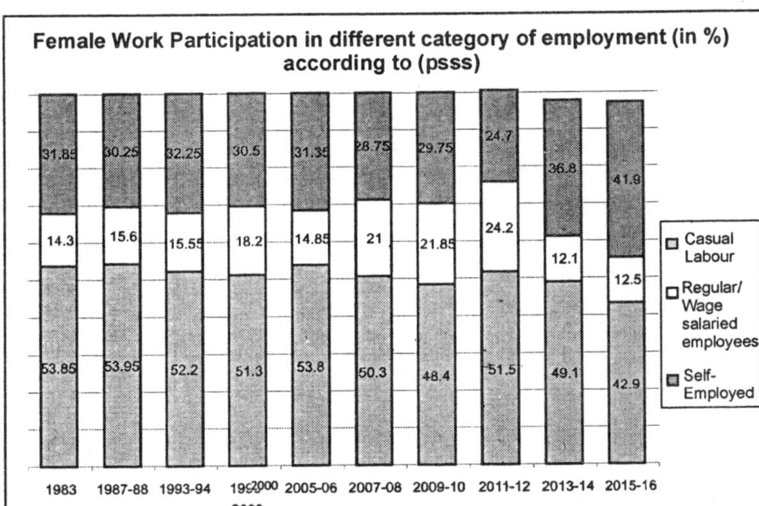

Fig. 4.6: Category of Employment (psss).

Between 4th (2013-14) and 5th (2015-16) rounds of Labour Bureau, according to principal status self-employed women workers has decreased by 5.8 per cent and male self-employees has decreased by about 2 per cent. Regular/wage salaried female employees has decreased by 0.2 per cent and male workers decreased by 0.7 per cent while casual labour percentage share for both male and female has increased as the corresponding rates i.e. 1.0 per cent and 4.9 per cent according to (ps). Female self-employed workers declined from 49.1 per cent in 2013-14 to 42.9 per cent in 2015-16 while regular/wage salaried female employees increased by 0.4 per cent and male employees increased by 0.9 per cent. Female casual labour increased more than male casual labour in the corresponding rates i.e. 5.1 per cent and 0.9 per cent during the same period according to principal status and subsidiary status taken together (psss).

Between 38th (1983) round of NSSO and 5th (2015-16) round of Labour Bureau, Female self-employed workers have decreased by 10.95 per cent and male workers have decreased by 2.1 per cent. Female regular/wage salaried employees have decreased by 1.8 per cent and male employees decreased by 9.6 per cent while female casual labour has increased by 10.05 per cent and male casual labour has increased by 7.9 per cent during the same period according to principal status and subsidiary status taken together (psss).

Women's Participation in Unpaid Domestic Activities

It became necessary to mention here that due to the discontinuation of NSSO survey rounds of employment and unemployment situations in India since 2011-12, we are forced to shift to the Labour Bureau's Annual Reports on Employment-Unemployment survey from 2012-2013. It is pertinent to mention that the variables determined by the NSSO and Labour Bureau are differ on the gender issue or women work participation as the male and female work participation is not classified differently in some variables. It is due to the missing of some variables like Female Activity Status Distribution, Level of Education Attainment and LFPR of Women Excluding those Undergoing Education, Distribution of the usually employed persons by level of general education, Industrial Classification of Women Workers, WRPS in Organised Sector, Employment of Women Workers in Public and Private Sector, Women Employment in Different Branches of Public Sector and in the Larger and Smaller Establishments in Private Sector that we are not able to give data and information on the work participation of women in above variables after 2011-12.

With the decline in the labour force participation a commensurate rise is in their participation is noted in the education and unpaid domestic activities by women. But the prominent activity that the largest share of women is seen to engage in domestic activities including allied activities. Moreover, its prominence is rising at a very fast pace throughout the period.

Table-B (5): Total Female Activity Status Distribution (UPS)

Activity Status	*Rural*						
	1983	1987-1988	1993-1994	1999-2000	2004-2005	2009-2010	2011-2012
Self-Employed unpaid family work	21	22	**18.5**	**11.4**	13.6	**10.2**	**9.4**
Regular Wage work	1.6	2.1	**1.3**	**0.9**	1.2	**1.1**	1.3
Casual Wage work	18	**17**	17	**11**	**9**	9	**6.8**
Unemployed	0.6	1.4	**0.5**	0	0.8	**0.5**	0.5
Education	7.6	**7.2**	11.7	18.4	21.3	23.8	25.1
All Domestic (a+b)	29.8	**27.3**	34.4	36.3	**35.5**	39.9	42.2
(a) Domestic Activities only	15.9	**15.1**	15.7	20.3	**17.5**	22	**18.5**
(b) Domestic+allied work	13.9	**12.2**	18.7	**16**	18	**17.9**	23.7
Others	21.4	23.1	**16.2**	22.4	**18.4**	**15.6**	**14.7**
Total	100	100	100	100	100	100	100
	Urban						
Self-Employed/Unpaid Family Work	8.3	8.5	**7.9**	**4.5**	5.4	**4.2**	4.6
Regular Wage work	8.4	9	**7.8**	**4.6**	5.7	**5.3**	6.1
Casual Wage work	7	**6**	6	**3**	**2**	2.4	**1.8**
Unemployed	1.5	1.9	**1.8**	**0.9**	1.4	**0.9**	0.9
Education	18.2	18.4	21.8	25.1	25.1	25.6	26
All Domestic (a+b)	38.5	**38.1**	40.2	45.4	45.7	48.2	48
(a) Domestic Activities only	30.8	**29.5**	30.5	38.4	**35**	39.9	**36.4**
(b) Domestic and allied work	7.7	8.6	9.7	**7**	10.7	**8.3**	11.6
Others	18.1	**17.9**	**14.1**	16.9	**14.5**	**13.4**	**12.6**
Total	100	100	100	100	100	100	100

Source: Government of India, NSS reports on Employment and Unemployment in India, 38th, 43rd, 50th, 61st, 66th and 68th rounds, NSSO, Central Statistical Organisation.

The unpaid domestic activities accounted for 30 per cent of the women in 1983 but by 2011-2012 their number increased to 42 per cent among the rural women and for urban women, from 38.5 per cent to 48 per cent. The share of females attending educational institutions increased from 7.6 per cent in 1983 to 25 per cent in 2011-12 for the rural areas and for urban areas it increased from 18.2 per cent to 26 per cent during the same period [Table-B (5)].

Level of Income and Domestication of Women

The relation between household income level and women's participation in domestic activity seems to be more robust. There is a positive relation between level of income and participation in domestic activities. A large number of women seem to enter domestic participation related with income levels visible in all years, both for urban and rural areas. Though in the initial years there was tendency of decline in domestic work participation of urban women in the high income groups, this trend has been reversed in the recent years.

According to the life cycle hypothesis, gender relations may throw more light on the understanding the declining labour participation and increasing unpaid domestic activity among women. The declining labour participation across all adult age-groups, with rising income levels may be a strategy to reduce the "double burden" of paid and unpaid work among women. In the historical process patriarchal societies have encouraged gender specific roles wherein most unpaid domestic activities are assigned to women. A typical patriarchal set up of the society approves such roles through the social mechanism of valorising domestic activities and stigmatising paid work among women so that social mobility is linked to the gender roles played out. Rising income levels apparently provides women an option between paid and unpaid work. Yet, even after considering the opportunity costs of wages and probability of finding a job, the household decision may be for women to withdraw from the labour force responding to the incentive of improving social status. Women thus engaged in status production for the household more intensely by withdrawing from paid labour and expand more on domestic activities which encourage status oriented roles such as child care, healthcare, religious activities etc. This enhances the status for the household and in turn ensures economic security for women.

Disaggregation of the domestic activities provides with further evidence that could probably link the rise in domestic activities among females with double burden and social stigma. Within the domestic activities an important feature is that over the period

1983 to 2009-10 there has been a tendency for urban female activity to get concentrated in pure domestic activities, instead of domestic and allied activities. As per NSS definition, domestic activities consists of "Engaging in the free collection of goods (vegetables, firewood, cattle feed, etc.), sewing, tailoring, weaving, etc., for household use". These allied activities add a third dimension to the burden of women's work. In the urban areas, the share of women with domestic and allied (D & A) activities had remained between 7 per cent and 11 per cent throughout the period 1983 to 2009-10, while pure domestic activities increased from 31 per cent to 40 per cent. The relatively low level of participation in Domestic and Allied activities among urban women may be due to the expanding service delivery and amenities such as cooking gas, tap water, etc. thus providing them some relief from the double burden. However, the relief from the drudgery of domestic and allied activities in urban areas does not encourage women to redirect their time to the labour market. Rather their participation is focused on pure domestic activities, which is shown in the rising participation rate in the category throughout the period.

For the rural areas, the domestic and allied activities have been higher than urban areas fluctuating in the range of 12 per cent to 19 per cent, while pure domestic activities remained between 15 per cent and 22 per cent. Though women are withdrawing from work in rural areas too, they do not seem to withdraw from domestic and allied activities but get involved in pure domestic activity and domestic and allied activities in equal share. The low level of monetisation of economic transaction and the need for high levels of social transactions for subsistence may require rural women to engage with the world outside the domestic activities frequently. The richest segment of the population, both in the rural and urban areas entering only pure domestic activities and not the labour market, which probably points towards stigma associated with paid work. With the rise in income levels, the stigma imposed by the society seems to be more stringently followed.

The receding preference for domestic and allied activities, apart from reduction of double burden and stigma, may also be indicative of another gender norm, i.e., relative invisibility in public places. Unlike pure domestic activities, other activities such as domestic and allied activities, unpaid family labour and paid labour require greater interaction with the local world outside the household. It is this type of an engagement with the outside their place of residence that is losing preference among urban women and rural women in the higher income groups.[85]

Participation in Education and Level of Income

It is pertinent to mention that in general, as expected the low income groups have lower participation while higher income groups have higher participation in education. Moreover, both in the rural areas and urban areas the participation in education has risen considerably during the last 30 years. However, while participation in education seems to increase with income levels during 1983, the income-based differences are being phased out gradually. By 2009-10, the gap between the lowest income group and highest income group in all age group of rural and urban areas has declined and has become more or less uniform. This implies that women's education is becoming universal in nature, and independent of their income levels. The young girls are attending schools across all section of Indian society and the participation of the girl child in education is encouraged through the state-driven *Sarva Shiksha Abhiyan* and the other programmes of universal child education. The other determinant of the economic upliftment of women is related to education and employment. Table-B(6) explains the impact of education on the LFPR.

Education is widely regarded as one of the key tools of empowerment of women that enhances their autonomy. The change in preference among the female children and young adult females towards education should essentially prepare females for entry into the labour market equipped with more years of education and skills than in case of their counterparts in preceding generations.

Now, to get a clearer picture of the role of education on enhancement of women's activity status if looked at the labour participation patterns at different levels of educational attainment [Table B-(6)]. A new dimension to calculate the LFPR is added here to exclude those who are undergoing education as they are potential entrants to the current labour market though they may enter it in future. From Table-B(6), it can be inferred that the incentive for the educated women to join the labour force had been declining throughout the period given in Table-B(6). During the

Table-B (6): Level of Education Attainment and LFPR of Women Excluding those Undergoing Education

	1983	*1987-1988*	*1993-1994*	*1999-2000*	*2004-2005*	*2009-2010*
Rural						
Not Literate	44.8	46.5	**43.1**	**28.7**	30.8	**25.8**
Literate but less than primary	44.7	**35.6**	44.0	**28.6**	33.2	**30.0**
Primary	43.0	45.3	**41.9**	**30.8**	33.2	**30.6**
Middle	37.5	41.8	**36.2**	**25.5**	32.2	**28.7**
Secondary	50.2	53.8	**40.3**	**26.2**	32.0	**24.9**
Graduate and above	56.7	63.0	**61.2**	**46.2**	**41.9**	**32.4**
Total	44.6	45.7	**42.8**	**28.6**	31.7	**27.2**
Urban						
Not Literate	29.3	**28.7**	**28.1**	**15.6**	17.4	**13.8**
Literate But less than primary	29.3	**27.4**	28.5	**15.0**	19.2	**16.6**
Primary	26.0	26.9	27.1	**14.4**	19.6	**17.6**
Middle	22.4	25.1	**23.8**	**13.5**	15.3	16.0
Secondary	42.8	**40.6**	**34.6**	**16.8**	**15.1**	**12.5**
Graduate and above	61.1	61.6	**57.2**	**33.7**	**32.3**	**26.0**
Total	30.9	31.4	**30.6**	**16.8**	19.8	**17.3**

Source: Government of India, estimated from NSS unit Level data, 38th, 43rd, 50th, 55th, 61st and 66th, NSSO, Central Statistical Organisation.

period 1987 to 2009-10, the LFPR for the highest educated, graduates and above, declined from 63 per cent to 32.4 per cent in the rural areas while it declined from 61.6 per cent to a mere 26 per cent in the urban areas. The decline in the LFPR of educated women has been such that currently there is hardly any difference between the less educated and more educated in their LFPR. The only consistent pattern is that across all levels of education, even among the non-literate, women are withdrawing from the labour market.

The above analysis throws up an apparently paradoxical situation. On the one hand, female education up to school level seems to be valued as expressed though high participation rate in school education, while on the other, the LFPR trends suggest that higher education seems as an incentive to women for withdrawing from the labour market, which can be observed from the above Table also. As it become evident from the table, the female educational attainment and participation in domestic activities move in the same direction. Whatever the level of education, the share of women engaged in domestic activities seems, by and large, to have increased throughout the period 1983 to 2009-10. This probably points out that education, which is arguably a liberating process, makes the income level of women engaged in education increase. The second important factor for the improvement of female education is the state driven agenda of universal education with special focus on the girl child.

Three lines of argument support this trend. First, studies do point out that education among women does not necessarily increase their "autonomy" in substantive internalisation of patriarchal norms.[86] Secondly, the withdrawal of women from the labour market across all levels of education, especially the most conspicuous withdrawal of women with educational attainment of graduation and above, probably points out towards discouraging worker effect owing to various forms of discriminations within the labour market including occupational segregation, wage discrimination and social stigma towards women's work. Third, it may also be due to the gender-based patterns of parental investment in education. Women are encouraged to enter arts and science education, which have much lower labour demand compared to technical and professional education. But technical and professional education also incurs substantial costs compared to arts and science education and therefore may be preferentially allocated to male children in the society.[87] Moreover, education for women in patriarchal societies may be aimed at enhancing the women's status in relation to their reproduction capacity and hence may not require technical and professional education [see Table-B(7) and Fig. 4.7].

In the Table–B (7) Gender differentials are presented of usually employed persons at different levels of educational attainment during various survey rounds of NSSO. During the period 1993-94 to 2011-12, the percentage share of graduate and above level of females has increased by 6.6 per cent while the percentage share of male for the same has increased by 5.15 per cent.

During the same period, secondary level of education of usually employed women has increased by 2.5 per cent and for male, it has increased by 3.35 per cent only. In the year 1993, 64.1 per cent usually employed women were not literate and 31.45 per cent was for the male during the same period. In 2011-12, illiteracy rate of usually employed has decreased by about 22 per cent for females and 11.75 per cent for males. Middle educational

Table-B (7): Distribution of the Usually Employed Persons by Level of General Education According to Usual Principal Status (ps)

Level of general education	*1993-94*		*1999-2000*		*2004-05*		*2009-10*		*2011-12*		*1993-94/ 2011-12*	
	Male	*Female*	*Male*	*Female*	*Male*	*Female*	*Male*	*Female*	*Male*	*Female*	*Male*	*Female*
Not Literate	31.45	64.1	28.05	59.5	23.7	52.7	19.9	43.7	19.7	42.05	**-11.75**	**-22.05**
Literate and up to primary	27.7	16.15	24.7	16.1	26.25	18.95	23.3	20.75	23.35	20.4	**-4.35**	4.25
Middle	15.35	5.55	17.45	9.3	18.7	9.3	18.85	11.55	18.25	10.8	2.9	5.25
Secondary	11.25	4.7	13.05	5.1	11.95	5.1	15.05	6.45	14.6	7.2	3.35	2.5
Higher Secondary	5.85	2.9	6.7	3.15	6.75	3.15	8.4	3.9	8.55	4.85	2.7	1.95
Diploma/certificate	_	_	_	2.05	2.3	2.05	1.8	1.7	2.0	1.55	2.0	1.55
Graduate and above	8.4	6.55	10.0	8.7	10.4	8.7	12.7	12.05	13.55	13.15	5.15	**-18.15**

Source: Government of India, Estimated LFPR reported in various NSS reports on employment and unemployment 50th, 55th, 61st, 66th and 68th rounds NSSO, Central Statistical Organisation.

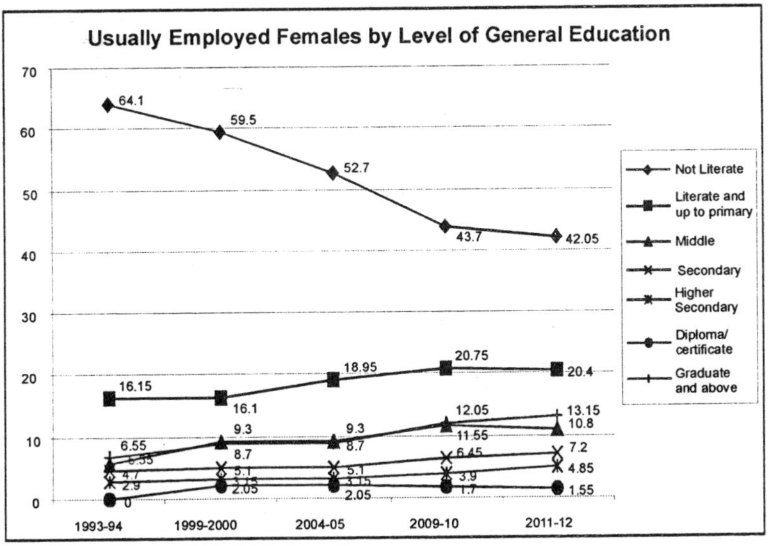

Fig. 4.7: Usually Employed by Level of Education.

attainment level of usually employed females has increased by 5.25 per cent and for males it has increased by only 2.9 per cent during the same period.

Industrial Distribution of Workforce

Three lines of argument support this trend. First, studies do point out that education among women does not necessarily increase their "autonomy" in substantive internalisation of patriarchal norms.[88] Secondly, the withdrawal of women from the labour market across all levels of education, especially the most conspicuous withdrawal of women with educational attainment of graduation and above, probably points out towards discouraging worker effect owing to various forms of discriminations within the labour market including occupational segregation, wage discrimination and social stigma towards women's work. Third, it may also be due to the gender-based patterns of parental investment in education. Women are encouraged to enter arts and science education, which have much lower labour demand compared to technical and professional education. But technical and professional education also incurs substantial costs compared to arts and science education and therefore may be preferentially allocated to male children in the society.[89] Moreover, education for women in patriarchal societies may be aimed at enhancing the women's status in relation to their reproduction capacity and hence may not require technical and professional education [see Table-B(8) and Figs. 4.8 & 4.9].

Table-B (10) presents the Industrial classification of women workers in rural and urban areas in the 7 survey rounds of NSSO. In between 38th (1983) and 68th (2011-12) rounds, women workers has declined by 11.7 per cent in the agriculture sector in rural areas. Women workers in mining and quarrying was 0.4 per cent in 1983 and 0.3 per cent in 2011-12 while women work participation in manufacturing has increased by 3 per cent and in electricity, gas and water increased by 1 per cent only in the rural areas.

In 1983, 0.9 per cent women were engaged in construction work. In 2011-12, it has increased by only 4.2 per cent in rural areas. Women work participation in Trade and Hotel and Restaurant has increased by 1.4 per cent from 1983 to 2011-12 while work participation in Transport Storage and Communication remained at the same level and in other services women work participation has increased by 2.8 per cent in the rural areas.

In urban areas, women workers percentage share in agriculture sector, declined from 25.5 per cent in 1983 to 8.7 per cent in 2011-

Table-B (8): Industrial Classification of Women Workers (UPS) as Percentage Share

Industry	*1983*	*1987-88*	*1993-94*	*1999-2000*	*2004-05*	*2009-10*	*2011-12*	*Growth Rate 1983 to 2011-12*
				Rural				
Agriculture	86.2	82.5	84.7	84.1	81.4	78.9	74.5	**-11.7**
Mining & Quarrying	0.4	0.5	0.5	0.4	0.4	0.3	0.3	**-0.1**
Manufacturing	6.5	7.5	7.5	7.7	8.7	7.6	9.5	8.0
Electricity, Gas & Water	-	-	-	-	0	0	1.0	1.0
Construction	0.9	3.2	1.1	1.2	1.7	4.2	5.1	4.2
Trade & hotel & Restaurant	2.2	2.4	2.2	2.3	2.8	3.1	3.6	1.4
Transport storage & communication	0.1	0.1	0.1	0.1	0.2	0.3	0.1	00
Other services	3.1	3.7	4.3	4.3	4.6	5.7	5.9	2.8
Industry				*Urban*				
Agriculture	25.5	21.8	19.3	14.6	14.7	11.8	8.7	**-16.8**
Mining & Quarrying	0.8	0.9	0.7	0.4	0.2	0.3	0.3	**-0.5**
Manufacturing	26.0	26.9	23.6	23.2	25.4	25.8	26.6	0.6
Electricity, Gas & Water	0.2	0.3	0.3	0.2	0.2	0.4	1.1	0.9
Construction	3.7	4.3	4.9	5.5	4.5	5.1	4.6	0.9
Trade & hotel & Restaurant	9.9	10.9	10.7	16.4	13.1	12.4	13.0	3.1
Transport storage & communication	1.7	1.2	1.5	2.0	1.6	1.5	2.7	1.0
Other services	31.4	33.6	38.8	37.8	40.2	42.7	43.3	11.9

Source: Government of India Estimated from NSS unit Level data, 38th, 43rd, 50th, 55th, 61st and 66th, 68th survey rounds, Central Statistical Organisation.

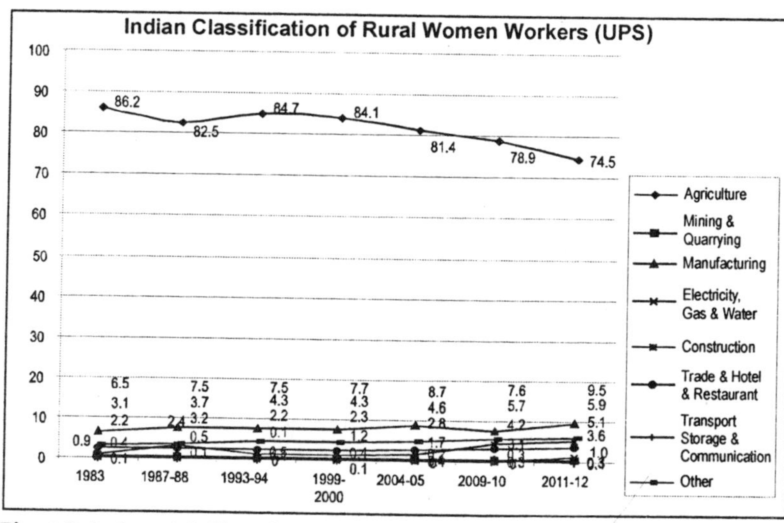

Fig. 4.8: Industrial Classification of Rural Women Workers.

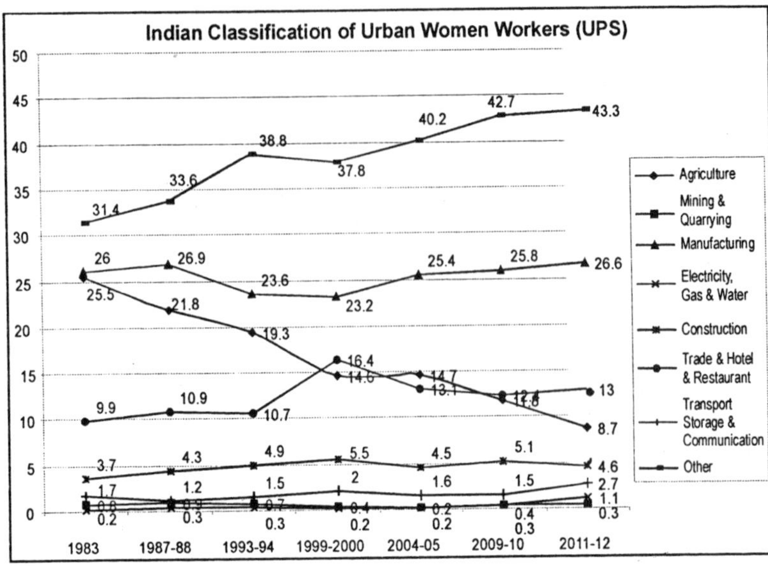

Fig. 4.9: Industrial Classification of Urban Women Workers.

12. In mining and quarrying work participation has decreased by 0.5 per cent and in the Manufacturing it has increased by 0.6 per cent only. In Electricity, Gas and Water and construction it has increased by only 0.9 per cent between 1983 to 2011-12 in the urban areas. During the same period the proportion of women workers in Trade and Hotel and Restaurant has increased by 3.1 per cent, in Transport storage and Communication increased by about 1 per cent only and in the other services increased by 11.9 per cent in the urban areas.

It is probably the case that women from households who suffer from multiple and overlapping modes of marginalisation through caste, class, physical disabilities and other forms of exclusion enter the workforce in non-traditional sector and occupations as low-paid vulnerable workers in sectors such as "Construction" and "Other services". However, their share of employment has been rising in the manufacturing sector during the recent period.

The process of entry of this vulnerable segment of women into the labour market is by and large, through the transition from feudal agrarian economy to the capitalised agricultural projects. The share of households with no land for cultivation or marginal landholders had been increasing since 1982-83 from 51 per cent to

66.5 per cent in 2008-09 while the share of all larger classes had been declining (GoI: 2011). Along with the rise in the number of the landless and of marginalised landholders there had been a widening of inequality in rural landholdings.[90] With consolidation of landholding by the capitalist farmers on the one hand, land alienation and land fragmentation on the other, peasants and households enter into monetised labour relations.

Women in Organised and Unorganised Sector: An Analysis

Workers in organised sector are distinguished by regular salaried jobs with well-defined terms and conditions of employment, clear-cut rights and obligations and a comprehensive social security. The unorganised sector on the other hand has no such clear-cut employer-employee relationship and lacks social protection. Having no fixed employer, these workers are casual, contractual, migrant, name-based, own-account workers who attempt to earn a living from whatever meager assets and skills they possess.

National Commission on labour has defined unorganised labour as those who have not been able to organise themselves in pursuit of common objectives on account of constraints like casual nature of employment, ignorance and illiteracy, small and scattered size of establishments and position of power enjoyed by employers because of the nature of industry. According to National Sample Survey Organisation (2010), of the total number of women workers in India around 96 per cent are in the unorganised sector, whereas merely 8 per cent are in the organised sector.

Women in Organised Sector

Women's share in organised sector has shown an increasing trend [Table-B (12)] from 2.8 Million (12.2%) in 1981 to 4.8 Million (17.2%) in 1999. Between 1991 and 1999, rise in the percentage points of women was 3.1; in contrast the share of men has been declining. However, women's participation in the organised sector is still very low, as compared to men [see Table-B(9) and Fig. 4.10].

It may be observed from the Table-B(9) that women's employment in the organised sector has risen up from 2.8 million in 1981 to 4.8 million in 2001 and it has increased by 4.8 million in 2001 to 5.85 million 2010. [see Table-B(10) and Fig. 4.11]

Table-B (9): WPRS in Organised Sector (Millions)

Year	*Women*	*Men*	*Total*
1981	2.8	20.1	22.9
1991	3.8	23.0	26.7
2001	4.8	23.3	28.1
2002	4.93	**22.8**	**27.7**
2003	4.96	**22.2**	**27.1**
2004	**4.93**	**22.1**	**27.0**
2005	5.01	**21.4**	**26.4**
2006	5.12	**21.3**	**26.4**
2007	5.31	21.6	26.9
2008	5.51	21.7	27.2
2009	5.58	22.5	28.0
2010	5.85	22.9	28.7

Source: Government of India, Ministry of Labour, New Delhi

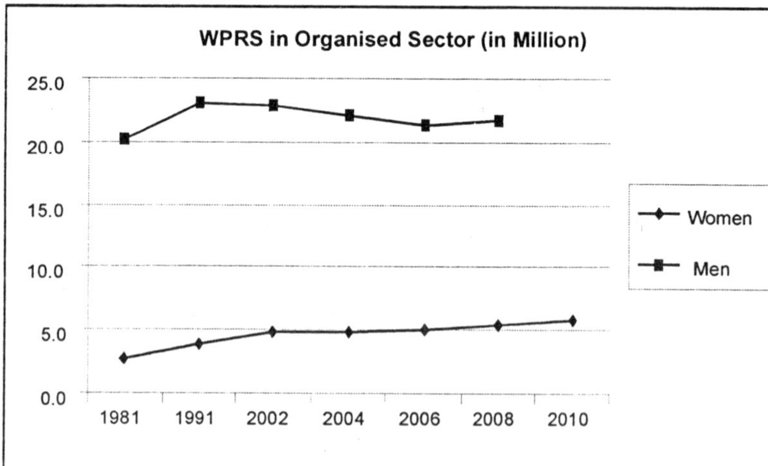

Fig. 4.10: WPRS in Organised Sector.

The number of women employed in the public and private sector has increased to 49.34 lac in 2004 from 47.74 lac in 1998, while the number of men employed has fallen to 215.09 lac from 233.92 lac during the same period. As provided in the Table 4.11, the private sector has been hiring women much more aggressively than the public sector. The number of men employed in the public sector has risen to 4.6 and 28.9 lac in 2004 from 27.63 lac in 1998 while women staff in the private sector has grown from 1.64 per cent to 20.44 lac.

Table-B (10): Employment of Women Workers in Public and Private Sector in India (in Lac)

Year	*Public Sector*	*Private Sector*	*Total*
1990	22.50	13.93	36.43
1994	25.64	15.89	41.53
2001	28.10	20.18	48.29
2004	29.90	20.44	49.34
2008	30.40	24.72	55.12
2009	30.91	24.89	55.80
2010	31.96	26.63	58.59

Source: Government of India, Ministry of Labour, New Delhi.

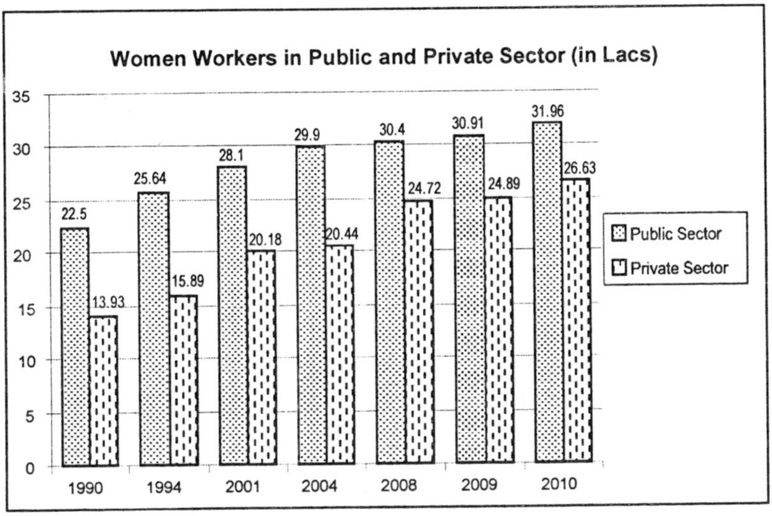

Fig. 4.11: Women Workers in Public and Private Sector.

There were 30.40 lac in the public sector and the remaining 24.72 lac in the private sector in 2008. Women's employment in public sector and private sector registered an increase of 1.56 per cent and 1.91 per cent respectively during the period 2008-2010.

Branch-wise and Size-wise Composition of Women Employment

The distribution of women's employment by different branches of public sector and by size of establishments in the private sector is presented in Table-B(11).

Table-B (11): Women Employment in Different Branches of Public Sector and in the Larger and Smaller Establishments in Private Sector (in lac)

Sr. No.	Sector	2008	2009	2010	2009/2008	2010/2009
1.	Public Sector	30.40	30.41	31.38	0.04	3.20
	Central Govt.	2.38	2.34	2.30	**-1.80**	**-1.64**
	State Govt.	15.88	15.71	16.09	**-1.07**	2.38
	Central Govt. (Quasi)	3.84	3.86	4.08	0.35	5.76
	State Govt. (Quasi)	2.56	2.58	2.78	0.72	7.60
	Local Bodies	5.71	5.90	6.12	3.35	3.68
2.	Private Sector	24.72	24.85	27.01	0.52	8.68
	Larger Estt.	22.29	22.43	23.57	0.60	5.11
	Smaller Estt.	2.43	2.42	3.43	0.21	41.69
	Grand Total	55.12	55.27	58.40	0.27	5.66

Sources: Government of India, Ministry of Labour, New Delhi Due to non-availability of data as per NIC-1998 information in respect of J & K Manipur and Mizoram, Daman & Diu and Pondicherry not included in Total in 2010.

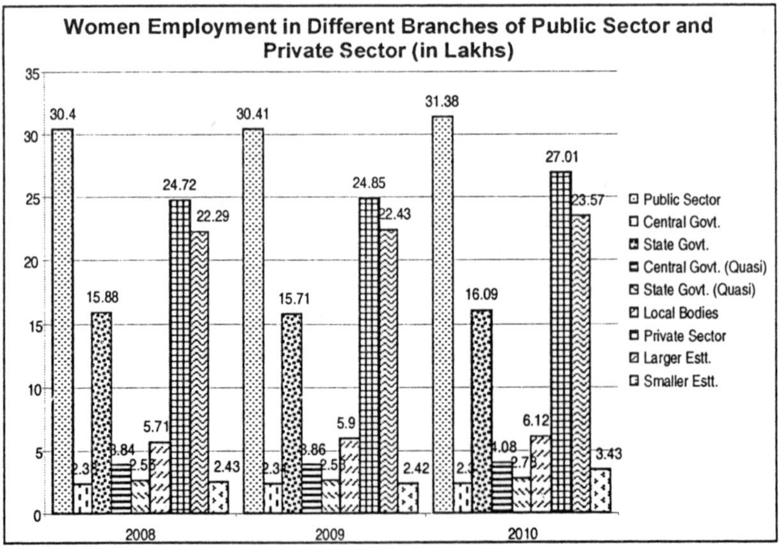

Fig. 4.12: Women Employment in Different Branches.

The branch-wise distribution of women's employment shows an overall increase in employment of women in public sector (3.20%) in all constituents of public sectors except Central Government and state government which recorded negative growth of women employment. The highest increase was recorded in state Government Quasi (7.60%) followed by Central Government Quasi (5.76%) local bodies (3.68%) and state government (2.38) whereas Central Government recorded a negative growth of (1.64%) in women's employment. There was an overall increase of 8.68 per cent in women's employment in the private sector. The women employment recorded a growth of 5.11 per cent in larger establishment and 41.69 per cent in smaller establishments during the period under review.

Women in Unorganised Sector

Unorganised sector of economy is considered as the most vulnerable as no social security is provided in this sector. Unfortunately in India, the absolute majority of women labour, which is about 94 per cent at present, is engaged in the unorganised sector of Indian economy. There is no clear law on the hire and fire policy of labour in the unorganised sector. Looking into the vulnerability of women working in the unorganised sector, the Government of India has formulated some Acts and programmes for women workers in the unorganised sector.

Domestic Workers and Social Security Act, 2010: Women and child are more vulnerable to exploitation, so the government has formulated this Act for providing them better working conditions including registration

Mahatma Gandhi National Rural Employment Guarantee Act (MGNREGA): MGNREGA has played a remarkable role in employment of women workers in the unorganised sector. It has created better working conditions and ensured equal wages to men and women.

Unorganised Sector Worker's Act 2008: The workers' felicitation centre (WFC) is responsible for implementing the Act. Under this Act, following schemes have been launched Janani Suraksha SXW Yojna, National Family Benefit Scheme, Rashtriya Swasthya Bima Yojana, etc.

Cooperative intervention: Cooperatives provide employment opportunities to women workers for earning income. Cooperatives try to strike a balance between individual need and community need by empowering women. The employment in the organised sector requires minimum qualification and most of these educated women workers are drawn from middle class and richer section of society, very few women from lower classes would get a chance to secure jobs in the organised sector. The national commission on labour enlists some characteristics and constrains of the unorganised sector, namely; casual nature of employment, ignorance and illiteracy and superior strength of the employers operating in single and in groups.

Almost 400 million people (more than 85% of the working population in India) work in unorganised sector and of these about 120 million are women. According to an estimate, by the National Commission on Self-employed Women (1988), of the total number of women workers in India, about 94 per cent are in the informal or unorganised sector whereas just 6 per cent are in the organised or in the formal sector. Thus, there is no exaggeration in saying that the unorganised sector in India is the women's sector.[91] The proportion of employment in the organised sector for males was 10.43 per cent in 1971, and has declined to 8.29 per cent in 2001; with regard to females, the proportion of employment in the organised sector has declined from 6 per cent to 4 per cent in 1971 to 2001.[92]

On an average, unorganised sector workers earn one fourth the wage of organised sector workers, often doing similar jobs. It is estimated that 118 million workers or 96 per cent of the female work force are involved in agriculture sector. Still agriculture is the main employer of women as informal workers, 75 per cent the total female work force and 85 per cent of rural women are employed in agriculture as wage workers or workers on own/ contracted household farms. As men migrate to non-farm jobs, there has been an increasing feminisation of agriculture. But ever as the face of the farmer became increasing female; few women have direct access to agricultural land affecting their ability to optimise agricultural productivity.

The non-agricultural segment of the informal sector engages 27 million workers or 23 per cent of the female work force. It is estimated that more than half the 31 million construction workers in India (90% of them informal) are women. The seasonality of work and the lack of alternate avenues lead to their exploitation and ensure that these women remain the poorest and most vulnerable.

In the organised sector employment of women has increased nearly four times between 1971 and 2001, registering a total increase in female employment from 31.3 million to 127 million. Even more significant is the fact that the rapid increase in female employment has taken place during 1981-91. The trend remained the same for the period 1991-2001 in terms of increase in female employment. The fact of the male dominance in the labour force in the organised sector has remained true that men share 82.2 per cent of the employment against women during this period has been more in the unorganised sector than in the organised sector.

The most important feature of women labour in India is that they are employed in the unorganised sector as contract labourers. Studies conducted in several parts of the country indicate the awful conditions of the women workers in this sector. They continue to face discrimination and ignorance and traditional attitudes, illiteracy, lack of skills, seasonal nature of employment, heavy physical work of different types, lack of job security, lack of a comprehensive legislation to cover these workers in the unorganised sector and their salaries are arbitrarily fixed, without regard to the minimum wages legislations, which adversely affect the income of the wage workers in general, and women workers in particular. In the unorganised sector wage workers constituted 36 per cent and the remaining 64 per cent were self-employed.[93]

The higher level of unemployment and underemployment among women has lead the researcher to conclude that their proportion below the poverty line is likely to be higher than that of men. Women who are drawn from rural areas are unskilled labourers. The life of the unorganised sector workers is very tough and they are exploited in many ways. The exploitation is not only done on the class lines but also on the lines of male domination over females. Sexual harassment is common but unreported due to fear of loss of employment. Despite the advances women have made in many societies, women's concerns are still given second priority almost everywhere. Their contribution is not given due credit. Women workers in the unorganised sector lag behind the males in terms of level and quality of their employment. There are still cases where women workers are deprived of the benefits and amenities like equal remuneration vis-à-vis their male counterparts, maternity benefits, proper child care services and indifferent attitude of the employers towards women workers.[94]

After analysing the government policies, programmes and legislation on the economic development and empowerment of women and their actual participation in the world of work and economy, some of the basic problems for economic backwardness of women from independence to the globalised India can be identified.

It can be said that the vicious circle of poverty is continuing in India and the women face the worst of poverty, they lack access to the resources, education as well as access to the mainstream labour market. Unfortunately, the women labour-force is still working under the social conservatism and their economic contribution to the family income is still considered as secondary. The immediate increase of women work participation after the globalisation has decreased within the small span of a decade. The government attempt to improve the women's skill through education has also met with its worst as the women work participation showed the decreasing trends with the rise of female education in India.

The indicators like workforce participation rate shift in the pattern of employment in different sectors, employment status, unemployment rates and increased numbers of women in the unorganised sector point towards the marginalisation of women labour in India. The condition and position of women work participation in the unorganised sector of the Indian economy also shows the reverse. The government efforts and claims to improve the work participation are proving contradictory. The defeminisation of the labour market and the use of the capital intensive techniques have forced the unskilled women labour to leave their traditional work to join the domestic and allied domestic work.

No doubt there are laws to protect women and prevent exploitation of women in the inside and outside the home, but these laws are not strictly implemented. The very vastness of the country, the scattered nature of women workers, the lack of education and legal literacy and the indifferent attitude of the government, bureaucracy and the general status of women in society cause vulnerability to women.

The need of the hour reveals that only unanimous efforts and co-ordination of the both, the governmental and non-governmental organisations should be started at the social, economic and political levels to improve the economic condition of women in India.

The trade unions and voluntary organsations can play a vital role in making them conscious of health and education and above all their right to be provided through education and training. Therefore, a credible employment strategy needs to focus on enhancing educational level of the workers, social status of workers including women, specific industries that can absorb a higher proportion of women labour and create quality jobs.

So there has been a rise in the work participation rate among women, or in other words, that the number of women as workers has been recorded as being more in recent years. However, in reality the employment opportunities for women continue to be unsatisfactory. Due to structural reforms, women are working under hazardous conditions with a lot of insecurity and low wages.

Notes

1. R.S. Bawa and Manjit Singh, "Globalisation, Development and India", Ranjit Singh Ghuman, *et al.*, (eds.), *Globalisation and Change*, Rawat Publication, New Delhi, 2010, p. 105.
2. Madhudan Pandit, *Human Rights and Social Justice*, Swastika Publications, Delhi, 2011, pp. 91-93.
3. Asha Kapur Mehta, "Globalisation and Women", Raj Mohini (ed.), *Globalisation, Culture and Women's Development*, Rawat Publications, Jaipur, 1999, pp. 54-61.
4. D. Padmavthi, "Empowerment of Women Through Micro Finance", Rameswari Pandya (ed.), *Women Welfare and Empowerment in India*, New Century Publications, New Delhi, 2008, pp. 331-333.
5. Deepak Nayyar, "Toward Global Governance", Deepak Nayyar (ed.), *Governing Globalisation: Issues and Institutions*, Oxford University Press, New Delhi, 2006, pp. 13-18.
6. Vibhuti Patel, *Women's Challenges of the New Millennium*, Gyan Publishing House, New Delhi, 2002, pp. 21-25.
7. Kaushik Basu, "India and the Global Economy: Role of Culture, Norms and Beliefs", *Economic and Political Weekly*, vol. XXXVI, no. 40, October, 2001, pp. 187-189.
8. "Globalisation and the welfare state — Global Economic.", www.global-economic-symposium.org/.../globalisation...welfare-state/., Accessed: 14-12-2017, 10:50 am.
9. Jane Harrigan and Paul Mosley, "Evaluating the Impact of World Bank Structural Adjustment Leading: 1980-87", *The Journal of Development Studies*, vol. II, no. 3, April, 1991, pp. 63-94.
10. T. Kusago and Z. Tzannatos, "Export Processing Zones: A Review in Need of Update", World Bank Discussion Paper No. 9802, World Bank, Washington, DC, January 1998, pp. 633-722.

11. D. Madani, *A Review of the Role and Impact of Export Processing Zones*, World Bank Policy Research Paper no. 2238, World Bank, Washington DC, 1999, pp. 542-592. also see: N. Heyzer, *Dughters in Industry: Work, Skills and Consciousness of Women Workers in Asia,* Asian and Pacific Development Centre, Kuala Lumpur, 1988, pp. 97-102.
12. WEF, "Women's Employment: Measuring the Global Gender Gap, World Economic Forum", http://www.weforum.org/pdf/Global_Competitiveness_Report/*Report/gender_gap.pdf,* Accessed:18-6-2015, 10:15 am.
13. Hooshang Amirahmadi and Wu Weiping, "Export Processing Zones in Asia", *Asian Survey,* Vol. XXXV, No. 9, 1995, pp. 828-49, also see: P. Lang and S. Young "Foreign Direct Investment and Technology Transfer: A Case Study of Foreign Direct Investment in North East China", *Transnational Corporations,* vol. V, no.1, 1996, pp. 57–83.
14. Kusago and T. zannatos, n. 10, pp. 65-69.
15. *Ibid.*
16. V.S. Ganesamurthy, "Women in India: A Situational Report", V.S. Ganesamurthy (ed.), *Women in Indian Economy,* New Century Publications, New Delhi, 2008, pp. 35-36.
17. Pandit, n. 2, p. 92.
18. Ganeshamurthy, n. 16, pp. 34-35.
19. *Ibid.*, p. 39.
20. Rajeshwar Prasad, "Globalisation, Culture and Women's Development", Raj Mohini Sethi (ed.), *Globalisation, Culture and Women's Development,* Rawat Publications, Jaipur, 1999, pp. 50-52.
21. Ganeshamurthy, n. 16, p. 35.
22. Tajpreet Kaur Kang, "Globalisation and Employment Status of Women in India", Rameswari Pandya (ed.), *Women Welfare and Employment in India,* New Century Publications, New Delhi, 2008, pp. 255-256.
23. Parveen Devgan, "Welfare Development and Empowerment of Women: The Indian Experience", Rameshwari Pandya, *Women Welfare and Employment in India,* New Century Publications, New Delhi, 2008, pp. 255-256.
24. Bhumika Jhamb, *et al.*, "The Paradox of Gender Responsive Budgeting", *Economic and Political Weekly,* vol. XLVIII, no. 20, May, 2013, pp. 36-38, also see: Yamini Mishra and Navanita Sinha, "Gender Responsive Budgeting in India", *Economic and Political Weekly,* vol. XLVII, no. 17, April, 2012, pp. 50-56.
25. M. Rajeshwari Shettar, "A Study on Issues and Challenges of Women Empowerment in India", *IOSR Journal of Business and Management* (IOSR-JBM), vol. XVII, no. 4, April. 2015, pp. 13-19.
26. G.K., Chadha, "World Agriculture Under Strain: Are Developing Countries Heading Towards Technological Orphanage?", Ranjit

Singh Ghuman, *et al.* (eds.), *Globalisation and Change*, Rawat Publications, New Delhi, 2010, pp. 31-35.
27. *Ibid.*, pp. 35-37.
28. World Bank, "Gender Equality and Development", *World Development Report, 2014*, Washington, DC., USA, 2015, p. 3.
29. Anupam Hazra, *India's Social Sector and Millennium Development Goals*, Rawat Publications, New Delhi, 2013, pp. 207-208.
30. World Bank, n. 29, p. 50.
31. World Health Organisation, *Progress on Drinking Water and Sanitation: 2012 Update*, United Nations Children's Fund, Geneva, 2012, pp. 206-210.
32. Hazra, n. 29, pp. 138-140.
33. World Bank, n. 28, pp. 46-50.
34. *Ibid.*, p. 239.
35. Tinku Paul, "Rural Women Work Force", Rameshwari Pandya, *Women Welfare and Empowerment in India*, New Century Publications, New Delhi, 2008, p. 416.
36. World Bank, n. 28, p. 216.
37. R.S. Bawa and Manjit Singh, "Globalisation, Development and India: Issues and Politics", Ranjit Singh Guhman, *et al.* (ed.), *Globalisation and Change*, Rawat Publications, New Delhi, 2010, p. 108.
38. Chadha, n. 26, p. 40.
39. "ILO, Global Employment Trends, 2014", *http://www.ilo.org/wcmsp5/groups/public/—dgreports/—dcomm/—publ/documents/publication/wcms_233953.pdf*, Accessed: 3-1-2015: 10:00 am.
40. World Bank, "Women, Business and Law 2014: Removing Restrictions to Enhance Gender Equality" *World Development Report 2014*, Washington DC, USA, p. 238.
41. *Ibid.*
42. World Bank, n. 28, p. 259.
43. M. Ahluwalia, *State Level Performance under Economic Reforms in India*, Centre for Research on Economic Development and Policy Reform, Stanford University, Stanford, 2001, pp. 117-127.
44. Bade Onimoda, "Adjustment Policies: Policy Options Before the Developing Nations", Pam Rajput & Hem Lata Swarup, *Women and Globalisation*, Asish Publishing House, New Delhi, 2002, pp. 2-3.
45. "Secretary-General's Message for 2015", *www.onwomen.org/en.*, Accessed: 3-3-2017: 10:00 am.
46. *Ibid.*
47. Rashmi Umesh Arora, "Bank Credit and Development: A Study of Uttar Pradesh", *The Journal of Developing Areas*, vol. VI, no. I, 2012, pp. 124-142.
48. T.N., Kitchlu, "Women Rights, Legislative Measures" *Yojana*, vol. XXXV, no. 20, 15 Nov., 1991, New Delhi, p. 16.

49. Neera Desai and Amit Kumar Gupta, *Women and Society in India*, Ajanta Publications, Delhi, 1987, p. 44.
50. *Ibid.*, p. 1.
51. Government of India, "Towards Equality", *Report of the Committee on the Status of Women in India*, Ministry of Human Resources and Development, New Delhi, 1975, p. 356.
52. *Ibid.*
53. *Ibid.*
54. *Ibid.*, p. 308.
55. M.K. Widge, "Gender Issue in Development", *Yojana*, vol. XXXVII, no. 10, 15 June, 1992, p. 12.
56. Kalbagh Chetana, "A Better Deal for Women by 2000 AD", Kalbagh Chetana (ed.), *Social and Economic Dimensions of Women's Development*, Discovery Publishing House, New Delhi, 1992, p. 124.
57. Barbare Epstein, "What Happened to the Women's Movement", *Monthly Review*, vol. XXXXXIII, no.1, 2001, pp. 1-13.
58. Patel, n. 6, pp. 47-48.
59. Geeta Sen and Carer Grown, Development *Alternative with women: DAWN Network*, Monthly Review Press, Delhi, 1987, p. 87.
60. *Ibid.*,
61. Shirin Kudchetkar and Sabiha Al-Issa, *Women against Violence, Violence against Women*, Pencraft International Press, New Delhi, 1998, p. 68.
62. Arvind Gupta, *Social Movements in India*, Patriot Publishers, New Delhi, 2013, pp. 73-75.
63. Patel, n. 6, p. 49.
64. Government of India, "National Perspective Plan for Women 1988–2000 AD", *Report of the Core Groups*, Department of Women and Child Development, Ministry of Human Resource Development, New Delhi, 1986, p. 14.
65. Kanakalatha Mukund, *Women Welfare Programmes in A.P.*, 1990, Centre of Economic and Social Studies, Hyderabad, 1990, p. 204.
66. Government of India, *Eighth Five Year Plan (1992–97)*, Planning Commission, New Delhi, 1992, pp. 291–292.
67. Government of India, *Tenth Five Year Plan (2002-2007)*, Planning Commission, New Delhi, 2002, pp. 202-209.
68. Government of India, *Twelfth Five Year Plan* (2012-2017), Planning Commission, New Delhi, 2012, pp. 192-197.
69. Jhamb, n. 24, pp. 37-38.
70. Chetana, n. 56, p. 127.
71. Editorial, "Good News for Single Women in 12th Plan", *The Hindu*, 14 May, 2013.
72. *Ibid.*
73. *Ibid.*, pp. 124-125.
74. Ravi Parkash Yadav, *et al.*, "Empowerment of Women in India", Rameshwari Pandya (ed.), *Women Welfare and Empowerment in India*,

New Century Publication, New Delhi, 2008, p. 254.
75. Government of India (2008), *Economic Survey: 2007-08*, Ministry of Finance, New Delhi, p. 246.
76. *Ibid.*
77. Kamalanath Naryana, "Women in Working Force in India", *Economic and Political Weekly*, vol. III, no. 2, 1968, p. 927.
78. J.N. Sinha, "How to Use 1961 Census Working Force Data: A Comment", *Economic and Political Weekly*, vol. II, no. 15, April, 1967, p. 89.
79. Nirmala Benerjee, "Whatever Happened to the Dreams of Modernity, The Nehruvian Era and Women's Position", *Economic and Political Weekly*, vol. XXXIII, no. 17, April, 1998, pp. 2203-05.
80. Devaki Jain, "Domestic Work: Its Implication for Enumeration on Women's Work and Employment", K. Saradamoni (ed.), *Women, Work and Society*, Indian Statistical Institute, Calcutta, 1995, pp. 79-82.
81. *Ibid.*, p. 81.
82. *Ibid.*
83. Government of India, *Report on the Conditions of Work and Promotion of Livelihood in the Unorganised Sector*, National Commission for Enterprises in the Unorganised Sector, New Delhi, 2007, pp. 132-136.
84. *Ibid.*
85. Vinod Abraham, "Missing Labour or Consistent Defeminisation", *Economic & Political Weekly*, vol. XVIII, no. 31, August, 2013, pp. 103-104.
86. A.M. Basu, "Why Does Education Lead to Lower Fertility? A Critical Review of Some of the Possibilites", *World Development*, vol. XXX, no.10, 2002, pp. 1780-89.
87. *Ibid.*
88. A.M. Basu, "Why Does Education Lead to Lower Fertility? A Critical Review of Some of the Possibilities", *World Development*, vol. XXX, no. 10, 2002, pp. 1780-89.
89. *Ibid.*
90. Vikas Rawal, "Ownership Holdings of Land in Rural India: Putting the Record Straight", *Economic and Political Weekly*, vol. XXXXIII, no. 10, March, 2008, p. 87
91. Neha Mittal, "Women Workers in Unorganised Sector: Socio-Economic Perspective", *Asian Journal of Multidimensional Research*, vol. 1, no. 3, August, 2012, p. 184.
92. Government of India, *Census, 1971,1981,1991 and 2001*, Office of the Registrar General & Census Commissioner, Ministry of Home Affairs, New Delhi.
93. Mittal, n. 91, pp. 184.
94. *Ibid.*

Chapter 5

Conclusion

Women in the workforce earning wages or salary are part of a modern phenomenon, one that developed at the same time as the growth of paid employment for men, but women have been challenged by inequality in the workforce. Until modern times, legal and cultural practices, combined with the inertia of longstanding religious and educational conventions, restricted women's entry and participation in the workforce. Economic dependency upon men and consequently the poor socio-economic and political status of women have had the same impact, particularly as occupations have become professionalised over the 19th and 20th centuries.

Women constitute almost 50 per cent of the world population and yet represent a staggering 70 per cent of the world's poor.[1] They are also considered as a group that is weak due to their marginalisation of the socio-economic and political set-up of the world. Women's lack of access to higher education had effectively excluded them from the practice of well-paid and high status occupations. Entry of women into the higher professions like, law and medicine was delayed in most countries due to women being denied entry to universities and qualification for degrees; for example, Cambridge University only fully validated degrees for women late in 1947, and even then only after much opposition and acrimonious debate.[2]

Women continue to participate in labour markets on an unequal basis with men. Globally, women are paid less than men. Women in most countries earn on average only 60 to 75 per cent of men's wages.[3] Contributing factors include the fact that women are more likely to be wage workers and unpaid family workers; that women are more likely to engage in low-productivity activities and to work in the informal sector, with less mobility to the formal sector than men[4]; the view of women as economic dependents; and the likelihood that women are in unorganised sectors or not represented in unions.[5] Women perform 66 per cent of the world's work, produce 50 per cent of the food, but earn 10 per cent of the income and own 1 per cent of the property.[6]

The new concept for favourable discrimination to increase the work participation of women and provide them some special protections and facilities to women on gender lines are linked with the industrialisation, modernisation and democratisation. The establishment of ILO and UNO at the International level can be seen as the positive development for the development of democracy, liberty, equality, justice, global, peace from above which is to be supported by the movements from the below.

The demand of positive discrimination and special laws for the protection of the rights of women in general and working women in particular is linked with the principles of liberty, equality, justice and democracy in the connotations of political theory nowadays. The advent of globalisation has been predicted as a new era for the socio-economic and political development of the world in general and the developing economies in particular. The experts argue that the linking of world economy and opening of world-trade through the liberalisation and privatisation of the economies will not only affect different countries differently, but its impact will be different on different people and groups in the same countries.

The widespread use of information technology, media, free-flow of knowledge and the easy interaction among people of different countries and regions has been viewed as a positive development for the socio-political development of the developing societies. The global connectivity of women movements and the rise of global feminism have proved crucial for the work participation and empowerment of women.

In the historical context the work participation of women and the development of labour laws and policy initiatives in India are linked with the Nehruvain era of state sponsored mix economy and the constitutional provisions for the women. Women response to the economic opportunities, social exposure and the global demand for the political empowerment of women are also linked to the socio-economic and political set-up of Indian society. The studies on work participation, development and empowerment of women in India revolve around the social and political responses of the Indian society to the new socio-economic and political developments and their influence on the status and rights of women.

Women movements in India have been linked to the Western education and an organised campaign for the socio-economic and political rights of women in India. Although the social awareness against the evil practices like *sati*, child marriage, *devdasis* etc., were initiated by the Indian intelligentsia and social reformists but reformists could bring reforms only with the support of colonial bureaucracy. However, the political and economic issues like work participation, political participation and right to property were only raised by the Indian women who got education in the West during the freedom struggle.

The issue of socio-economic and political rights of women was raised by the various women organisations during the freedom struggle; however, the colonial judiciary didn't adopt a secular approach while deciding the issue of the property rights of women and referred it to religious texts and other old customs which undermined the rights of women. As a free nation India started its journey with great promises of socio-economic and political justice to the weaker and backward classes of India under the state sponsored mixed-economy and social sector. The constitutional initiatives for social democracy and the socio-economic and political justice were furthered by the constitutional amendments and legal and policy initiatives taken by the Indian Government from time to time.

The provisions for the upliftment and development of women have always remained a serious issue for the policy frame-work and legal initiatives of the Indian state along with other weaker and backward sections of the Indian society. The Constitution of India guarantees right to equality to women in every sphere of life: right to equality before the law (Article 14), no discrimination by the State [Article 15(1)], equality of opportunity (Article 16), and equal pay for equal work [Article 39(d)]. In addition, it allows special provisions to be made by the State in favour of women and children [Article 15(3)], renounces practices derogatory to the dignity of women [Article 51(A) (e)], and also allows for provisions to be made by the State for securing just and human conditions of work and for maternity relief for women (Article 42). To ensure the protection and promotion of women, Indian Parliament has enacted special laws along with the constitutional provisions. The Minimum Wages Act, 1950, The Mines Act, 1952, The Immoral Traffic (Prevention) Act, 1956, Dowry Prohibition Act, 1961, Child Marriage Restrain Act, 1961, The Beedi and Cigar Workers (Conditions of Employment) Act, 1966, The Indecent Representation of Women (Prohibition) Act, 1986, National Commission for Women Act, 1990, Protection of Women from Domestic Violence Act, 2005, The Sexual Harassment of Women at Workplace (Prevention, Prohibition and Redressal) Act, 2013,

The Government of India has ratified various international conventions and human rights instruments committed to secure equal rights to women. These are CEDAW (1979), the Mexico Plan of Action (1975), the Nairobi Forward Looking Strategies (1985), the Beijing Declaration as well as the Platform for Action (1995) and other such instruments. The year 2001 was observed as the year of women's empowerment in India. During the year, landmark documents 'the National Policy for the Empowerment of Women' and many other programmes and schemes for the development and empowerment of women like National Credit Fund for Women, Food and Nutrition Board (FNB), Information and Mass Education (IMF) etc. were adopted by the Indian Government in this year.

The policy initiatives to improve the women condition have been initiated with the very dawn of state sponsored development under the mix-economy model. The First Five Year Plan defined three major areas in which it had paid special attention to women's development namely Education, Social welfare and Health under the welfare model of the state. To implement welfare measures for the benefit of the poor women, the Central Social Welfare Board (CSWB) was established. The CSWB recognised and realised the need for organising women into Mahila Mandals or women's clubs as an approach to community development.[7] Although the second five year plan concentrated on the overall agricultural development, it was also determined to recognise women's labour rights. It provided protection against the injuries at work, maternity benefits and crèches for their children. It advocated the immediate implementation of equal pay for equal work and provision for training to enable women to compete for higher jobs. The Third and Fourth Five Year Plans concentrated on women's education as education was considered the key to the socio-economic and political development of women.[8]

The Fifth Five Year Plan emphasised the need for the training of women in respect of income generating activities, it recommended a strategic programme of functional literacy to equip women with skills and knowledge to perform their functions as good housewives. Under the health programmes, the primary objective was to provide minimum public health facilities integrated with family planning and nutrition for vulnerable groups, children, pregnant and lactating mothers.[9]

The Sixth Five Year Plan stressed the need for economic independence, educational advancement and access to health care and family planning as essential for women development.[10] The impact of women movements and the global feminism which emerged in the 1970s have also showed their presence in India in the eighties.[11] It was first ever in the history of women's movements in India that women groups made an effort to integrate women in the economy and their pressure on the government for the inclusion of women into India's economy had become considerable.[12] But efforts of women groups could not achieve the desired goals as the means of production; exchange and distribution were controlled by men, which allowed women very limited space to evolve a Development Alternative with Women (DAWN).[13] Then efforts of the highly educated and politically connected women were aimed to save women from further marginalisation and to pressurise the government for the inclusion of women in the national development.

The period of 1980s is very crucial for the political governance and economic survival of the country. On the one hand, communalism, terrorism and violation of the human rights by the state forces dominated the political governance and the issues of *Mandal, Mandir* and *Masjid* forced a severe crises of governance[14] and on the other, the mounting burden of debt leading to a balance of payment crisis forced the government to discontinue with the social responsibility towards the mass of poor women in the rural, tribal and urban areas.[15]

This decade witnessed the strengthening of women movement and the mass mobilisations of women on a wide range of issues like water, drought, riots, communal tensions, police brutality against forest people, agricultural labourers, industrial workers, white-collar women employees; problems about promotions and transfers, sexual harassment at workplace, harassment for dowry and bride price, witch hunting, widow burning, sexual violence against women, coercion in family planning, fetuses, female infanticide and child care facilities etc.[16] It was during the eighties that a gender analysis of the development schemes supported by the states and Central Governments as well as by the international aid agencies and the voluntary organisations was started by the women academicians and women organisations in India.[17]

The Seventh Five Year Plan sought to generate awareness among women about their rights and privileges. The long term objectives of developmental programmes in the Seventh Plan were to raise economic and social status of women in order to bring them into the mainstream of national development and to recognise the importance of women in contributing to the various socio-economic, political and cultural activities.

The Seventh Plan emphasised the need to open new avenues of work for women and perceived them as crucial resource for the development of the country. Another salient and crucial recognition was the need for organisation of women workers and uniting of women for their rights.[18]

The decade of nineties is marked by an approach of gender and development (GAD). Here the focus was on the power relations determined as a result of interplay of complex class, caste, ethnicity, religion, races and gender. It was the emergence of the era of partnership with a clear cut understanding that women constitute half of the world's workforce and get only 1/10th of the world's income and own only 1/100th of the world's wealth.[19]

The main objective of Eighth Plan was to extend the reach of services to women both qualitatively and quantitatively. Panchayati Raj Institutions were involved in the designing and implementation of women's programmes. The Ninth Five Year Plan was an attempt to bring the women's issues within the policy-making spheres and it came into effect from April 1, 1997. The problems like feminisation of poverty, inadequate investment in social sectors, increasing violence against women and stereotyped portrayal of women in private and state sponsored media especially television were focused upon. The necessity for information and training opportunities, reservations and social services etc., and people's involvement were considered necessary for the success of any programme and were also desired to be solved by the state and civil society initiatives.[20] Tenth Five Year Plan aimed at empowering women through translating the recently adopted National Policy for Empowerment of Women (2001) into action and ensuring survival protection and development of children through rights based approach.[21] Eleventh Five Year Plan focused on women and work and the attempts were made to enhance women education and skills through public-private partnership in general and technical education. Special allocation of funds under new schemes was made to save the girl child and to raise the sex ratio for the age group 0–6 to 935 by 2011–12 and to 950 by 2016-17. Further, this plan intended to ensure that 33 per cent of the direct and indirect beneficiaries of all government schemes are women and girl children. It also proposed to ensure that all children enjoyed a safe childhood, without any compulsion to work.[22]

Gender Budgeting and National Perspective Plan for Women 1988–2000

Gender budgeting in India takes two forms: the Gender Budget Statement (also known as Statement 20) and Gender Budgeting Cells located in government ministries and departments. The Gender Budget Statement was institutionalised in India in the 2005-2006 financial year. 3 Key actors in the formulation of the Gender Budget Statement are the Ministry of Finance, the Ministry of Women and Child Development, the Planning Department at the national level and the Planning Commissions at the state level. The Gender Budget Statement is a component of the annual "Union Budget of India", being India's national budget, which is issued by the Ministry of Finance. There are two parts to the Gender Budget Statement. Part 'A' lists "schemes" for which the beneficiaries are solely women and girls, while Part 'B' lists the schemes for which at least 30 per cent of the expenditure flows to women and girls. Thus, the Gender Budget Statement indicates the quantity of public financial resources for which women and girls are the sole and partial beneficiaries. In this respect, India's Gender Budget Statement is a quantitative form of gender budgeting. To support ministries and departments in undertaking gender budgeting, in 2007, the Ministry of Women and Child Development issued a handbook explaining gender budgeting and providing guidance on the practical steps to be followed.[23]

Twelfth Five Year Plan has been entitled as Faster, Sustainable and More Inclusive growth. It has addressed the shortcomings of the Eleventh Five Year Plan including the decline in women employment. Recognising that economic independence is the key to improving the position of women within the family and in society, the Plan would need to focus on enhancing women's access to control over resources. Amongst others, this would entail not only increasing their presence in the work force but, more importantly, improving the quality of women's work and ensuring their upward mobility on the economic ladder.

The theory of patriarchy puts the question of women empowerment in a proper perspective.[24] The Planning Commission is pushing for special dispensation for single women, particularly those who are single by choice, under various government schemes in the 12th Plan. In addition to reserving a certain percentage of jobs for single women under centrally sponsored schemes, the plan has proposed promoting and strengthening federations of single women at the block and district level.[25]

It is observed in the Census of 2011 that 833 million people continue to live in rural India. A very large proportion of them are either wholly or significantly dependent on their livelihood on farm activity be it crop agriculture, horticulture, animal husbandry or fisheries. Women participation in favour related work, both in agriculture and in animal husbandry in framing policies/schemes for the 12th five year plan, the special needs of women are taken care of. The Mahila Kisan Sashaktikaran Pariyojana (MKSP) which is a sub-component of NRHM (National Rural Health Mission) has been recently launched to meet the specific needs and to give leverage to the enormous potential of empowering rural women in the farm sector, and also in the rural sector and also in the rural non-farmer sector.[26]

It became pertinent to mention here that the work-participation of women couldn't earned the attention of the Indian leadership and policy-makers. One would be shocked to know that the domestic work and allied activities of women couldn't get the category of unpaid work in the census of India until 1970s. It means that the absolute majority of the Indian women work was not considered as a work or work participation by the Indian leadership and policy-makers.

The inception of women studies in India in 1970s questioned the state sponsored welfare measures of the state of women development and urged the authorities concerned to evolve new alternatives for women development in India. It is to be noted that in 1960s and specially before the advent of specialised women's studies decline in femalework participation had been noticed, but it was generally thought to be transitory phenomena as the economy moved from subsistence agriculture and house-hold industry to modern Industry.[27] It was also assumed that the decline would be automatically corrected by a "countervailing force", identified with the increase in income.[28] Analysis of historical trends in developed countries, particularly in Europe, had given rise to the development of the view which held that income increase initially aggravated the downward trend in female work participation; further gains in income reversed the decline.[29] Such assumptions and perspectives were, of course, proven to be erroneous in case of India on several counts.

It was after the Report of the Committee on the Status of Women in India (CSWI) in 1974 that the decline in the women work participation was thought to be the problem of developmental process in India. The long term overall decline, both in percentage of workers to total female population and in their percentage to the total labour force, began to be viewed as evidence that women's economic participation had been adversely affected by the nature of the development process in India. The CSWI postulated that ruination of domestic industry from the colonial period onwards (with relatively greater ruin in the female labour intensive sectors) had eroded the non-agricultural occupations of women, while externally the process of limited modernisation had excluded them from the limited opportunities in the modern sector. The result was a permanent shift of women to the periphery of the economy.[30]

From the latter half of the 1970s and throughout the 1990s studies on the Women Work Participation Rate (WPR) attempted to further explain the processes of underpinning the decline in female employment in India while simultaneously focusing on the question of actual underenumeration or undercounting of women's work in national data sets.

There were sufficient and observable evidences to show that the vast majority of women were not idle but were actively contributing to their household economy. The question, therefore, arose as to why and how their work was not being counted. Considerable attention was paid to problems in measurement of the extent of decline in the Female Work Participation Rate (FWPR), especially in the context of changes in the definition of workers across censuses and the ensuing problems of comparability.[31]

At the conceptual level, the need to evolve alternative methods of capturing women's work and the inadequacy of the existing modes of data collection on women's work were linked to the invisibility of a large part of women's productive labour and its contribution to family subsistence labour in both the monetised and non-monetised segments of the economy.[32] The two sectors where such invisibility prevailed to a great extent were agriculture and household industry. The two decades of discussion and debates contributed to generating a greater awareness of the need to make women's work more visible in the macro data, particularly in agriculture.[33]

The census as the primary source of historical trends was the databased at the heart of these initial discussions and it is only from the 1990s onwards that the quinquennial National Sample Survey Office (NSSO) became more central. In the 1990s, there was an understandable eagerness to assess the impact of the structural shift in the policy framework towards liberalisation, without having to wait for the 2001 census report, the National Sample Survey (NSS), which is thought to be more amenable to capturing women's economic activities, has continued to be the principle data source for most of the studies and analyses of women's work and employment trends even after 2001.

A continue debate on the invisibility of women's work, including issues of definitional limitations in data sources, was in a sense circumscribed during the 1990s by a wave of discussions on the informal sector that came into its own in the 1980s. Arguably, it could be said that the new preoccupation with the informal sector shifted the focus from the classical developmental dualistic approach comprising agriculture (As the backward subsistence sector) and industry (as the modern sector) to a more diffused set of occupations and employments that could always be catalogued and categorised within the dualistic framework. While there were clear failings in the formulaic assumptions of traditional developmental approaches, which were brought out by empirical evidence on informal and unorganised sector employment, the discussions on the informal sector contributed little to the great question of agrarian social relations. In relation to women, home-based work became a primary point of discussion that united the earlier discourses on the invisibility of women's work and the later preoccupation with the informal sector.[34]

Further evidence of the uncounted labour of women in economic activities came from the 1998 'time use survey' conducted by the Central Statistics Office (CSO) in some states, which showed that the Women Participation Rate Survey (WPRS) for women as per the time use data was 58.2 per cent and 30 per cent for rural and urban areas respectively against 25.3 per cent and 12.8 per cent according to current weekly status in the closest NSSO employment survey. The time use survey was used to press a case for computing a value to women's unpaid labour on the grounds of giving it visibility in official statistics and providing a base for unpaid workers to claim their due share from the state exchequer to improve their conditions. Implicit to the valuation argument was a critique of the gross domestic product (GDP) in its present form as "a limited variable to project the status of well-being in an economy."[35]

National Sample Survey Office's report, "Key indicator of employment and unemployment in India, 2009-10" shows that the distributing trend of a steep fall in the Female Work Participation Rate (FWPR) that began in 2007-08 has continued. With an increase of 22.3 million in the male workforce between 2004-05 and 2009-10 being virtually cancelled out by a fall of more than 21 million in the female workforce, of employment trend in India acquired a new urgency. Between 38th (1983) and 43rd (1987-88) rounds of NSSO, the percentage share of rural female Labour Force Participation Rate has increased by 0.2 per cent and urban female LFPR remained at the same level according to the principal status while rural and urban male LFPR has declined as the corresponding rates i.e. 0.8 per cent and 0.3 per cent according to the (ps). Labour force of rural female decreased by 1.1 per cent, urban female labour force increased by 0.3 per cent and rural male labour force decreased by 0.8 per cent, urban male labour force decreased by 0.6 per cent according to principal status and subsidiary status taken together (psss).

Between 50th (1993-94) and 55th (1999-2000) rounds of NSSO,

labour force of rural female decreased by 2.8 per cent, urban female labour force decreased by 1.8 per cent and rural male labour force decreased by 1.6 per cent and urban male labour force decreased by 0.1 per cent according to principal status and subsidiary status taken together (psss).

Between 62nd (2005-06) and 64th (2007-08) rounds of NSSO, labour force of rural female decreased by 2.2 per cent, labour force of urban female 0.6 per cent and labour force of rural male decreased by 0.2 per cent but urban male labour force increased by 1.0 per cent according to principal status and subsidiary status taken together (psss).

Between 66th (2009-10) and 68th (2011-12) rounds of NSSO, rural female labour force decreased by 1.2 per cent, urban female labour force increased by 0.9 per cent and rural male labour force decreased by 0.3 per cent, urban male labour force increased by 0.4 per cent according to principal status and subsidiary status taken together (psss).

Between two Survey rounds of Labour Bureau 2013-14 to 2015-16, LFPR has increased by 3.1 per cent for males and decreased by 2.4 per cent for females in the rural areas according to principal status. In the urban areas LFPR has decreased by 4.7 per cent for males and 2.3 per cent for females according to (ps). LFPR of Rural female declined from 36.4 per cent to 31.7 per cent and urban female labour force declined from 19.7 per cent to 16.6 per cent. While rural male labour force increased by 1.6 per cent and urban male labour force declined from 74.0 per cent to 69.1 per cent according to usual principal subsidiary status during the same period

It can be said that the vicious circle of poverty is continuing in India and the women face worst of poverty, they lack access to the resources, education as well as the mainstream labour market. Unfortunately, the women labour-force is still working under social conservatism and their economic contribution to the family income is still considered as secondary.

The immediate increase in women's work participation after the globalisation has declined within the small span of a decade. The government attempts to improve the women's skills through education has also met with its worst as the women work participation has shown a decreasing trend with the rise of female education in India.

The indicators like workforce participation rate shift in the pattern of employment in different sectors, employment status, unemployment rates and increased number of women in the unorganised sector point out towards the marginalisation of women labour in India. The conditions and position of women's work participation in the unorganised sector of the Indian economy also show the adverse. The government's efforts and claims to improve women's work participation are proving contradictory. The defeminisation of the labour market and the use of capital intensive techniques have forced the unskilled women labour to leave their traditional work and join the domestic and allied domestic work.

No doubt there are laws to protect women and prevent exploitation of women in the inside and the outside home, but these laws have not been strictly implemented. Being a vast country, the scattered nature of women workers, the lack of education and legal illiteracy and the indifferent attitude of the government, bureaucracy and the general status of women in society have caused vulnerability to women.

The rise of global feminism, Beijing Platform for Action, Millennium Development Goals along with the efforts of the World Bank and other international agencies to increase women's participation and empowerment has been viewed as a positive development for the empowerment of women in India. Since the Beijing Platform of Action many strategies and declarations have been adopted by the UN and the National parties have been advised to enhance the work participation of women. Irrespective of the global and national efforts, many women organisations are still working at the grass-root level to make women aware of their rights and importance of their work participation.

After analysing the government policies, programmes and legislation on the socio-economic and political development and empowerment of women in gloablised India, some suggestions can be made to improve the work participation of women.

The need of the hour is that only joint efforts and co-ordination of both the government and non-governmental organisations can help to improve the socio-economic and political position of women. The wholehearted and serious efforts are required to eradicate the problem of the vicious circle of poverty and violence against women at all levels. The problems of poverty, crime against women, prevalence of social conservatism and women backwardness can be controlled through the policy framework, education, awareness and the development of scientific temper among the citizens of all ages.

This awakening can be brought about by launching education campaign among youth and by making them aware of existing social evils and the means to eradicate the same. Mass media can play an active role here as these days it has reached every corner of the country. NGOs can help to spread the concept of gender sensitisation for both the male and female population of India. Women can be trained into new professions and they can work collectively under the self-help groups run by trained women professionals and they can be guided to manage the sale and marketing aspects of their products by the experts.

Notes

1. "Introduction to the challenges of achieving gender equality", *https://www.globalcitizen.org/.../content/introduction-to-the-challenges-of-achieving,* Accessed: 18-6-2018, 9:32 am.
2. "The effects of women in the workforce Essay Example for Free", *https://studymoose.com/?the-effects-of-women-in-the-workforce-essay.* Accessed: 13-6-2018, 8:58 am.
3. "World Bank Gender Data Portal", *http://datatopics.worldbank.org/gender/key%20gender%20employment%20indicators,* Accessed: 18-6-2018, 7:38 am.
4. World Bank, *World Development Report 2012*, p. 79.
5. International Labour Organisation (2014), "Global Employment Trends 2014: Risk of a jobless recovery?", p. 45, *http://www.ilo.org/wcmsp5/groups/public/—dgreports/—dcomm/—publ/documents/publication/wcms_233953.pd,* Accessed: 17-6-2018, 7:30 am.
6. "International Women's Day: The way forward-True...-unicef.org.tr", *www.unicef.org.tr/basinmerkezidetay.aspx?id=2180&dil=en&d,* Accessed: 13-6-2018, 8:58 am.
7. Government of India, "Towards Equality", *Report of the Committee on the Status of Women in India,* Ministry of Human Resources and Development, New Delhi, 1975, p. 356.
8. *Ibid.*
9. M.K. Widge, "Gender Issue in Development", *Yojana,* vol. XXXVII, no. 10, 15 June, 1992, p. 12.

10. Kalbagh Chetana, "A Better Deal for Women by 2000 AD", Kalbagh Chetana (ed.), *Social and Economic Dimensions of Women's Development*, Discovery Publishing House, New Delhi, 1992, p. 124.
11. Barbare Epstein, "What Happened to the Women's Movement", *Monthly Review*, vol. XXXXXIII, no.1, 2001, pp. 1-13.
12. Vibhuti Patel, *Women's Challenges of the New Millennium*, Gyan Publishing House, New Delhi, 2002, pp. 21-25.
13. Geeta Sen and Carer Grown, "Development *Alternative with Women*", *DAWN Network*, Monthly Review Press, Delhi, 1987, p. 87.
14. *Ibid.*
15. Shirin Kudchetkar and Sabiha Al-Issa, *Women against Violence, Violence against Women*, Pencraft International Press, New Delhi, 1998, p. 68.
16. Arvind Gupta, *Social Movements in India*, Patriot Publishers, New Delhi, 2013, pp. 73-75.
17. Patel, n. 12, p. 49.
18. Government of India, "National Perspective Plan for Women 1988-2000 AD", *Report of the Core Groups*, Department of Women and Child Development, Ministry of Human Resource Development, New Delhi, 1986, p. 14.
19. Kanakalatha Mukund, *Women Welfare Programmes in A.P.*, 1990, Centre of Economic and Social Studies, Hyderabad, 1990, p. 204.
20. Government of India, *Eighth Five Year Plan (1992–97)*, Planning Commission, New Delhi, 1992, pp. 291-292.
21. Government of India, *Tenth Five Year Plan (2002-2007)*, Planning Commission, New Delhi, 2002, pp. 202-209.
22. Government of India, *Twelfth Five Year Plan* (2012-2017), Planning Commission, New Delhi, 2012, pp. 192-197.
23. Bhumika Jhamb, *et al.*, "The Paradox of Gender Responsive Budgeting", *Economic and Political Weekly*, vol. XLVIII, no. 20, May, 2013, pp. 36-38, also see: Yamini Mishra and Navanita Sinha, "Gender Responsive Budgeting in India", *Economic and Political Weekly*, vol. XLVII, no. 17, April, 2012, pp. 50-56.
24. Editorial, "Good News for Single Women in 12th Plan", *The Hindu*, 14 May, 2013.
25. *Ibid.*
26. *Ibid.*, pp. 124-125.
27. *Ibid.*
28. Kamalanath Naryana, "Women in Working Force in India", *Economic and Political Weekly*, vol. III, no. 2, 1968, p. 927.
29. J.N. Sinha, "How to Use 1961 Census Working Force Data: A Comment", *Economic and Political Weekly*, vol. II, no. 15, April, 1967, p. 89.
30. Nirmala Benerjee, "Whatever Happened to the Dreams of Modernity,

The Nehruvian Era and Women's Position", *Economic and Political Weekly*, vol. XXXIII, no. 17, April, 1998, pp. 2203-05.

31. Devaki Jain, "Domestic Work: Its Implication for Enumeration on Women's Work and Employment", K. Saradamoni (ed.), *Women, Work and Society*, Indian Statistical Institute, Calcutta, 1995, pp. 79-82.
32. *Ibid.*, p. 81.
33. *Ibid.*
34. Government of India, *Report on the Conditions of Work and Promotion of Livelihood in the Unorganised Sector*, National Commission for Enterprises in the Unorganised Sector, New Delhi, 2007, pp. 132-136.
35. *Ibid.*

Bibliography

Primary Sources

Government of India, Ministry of Human Resource Development, *Report of the Core Group*, Department of Women and Child Development, New Delhi, 1986.

Government of India, Ministry of Finance, *Economic Survey: 2007–08*, New Delhi, 2008.

Government of India, Ministry of Home Affair, *National Crime Record Bureau (NCRB)*, New Delhi, 2011.

Government of India, Ministry of Home Affair, *National Crime Record Bureau (NCRB)*, New Delhi, 2012.

Government of India, Ministry of Home Affair, *National Crime Record Bureau (NCRB)*, New Delhi, 2013.

Government of India, Ministry of Human Resource Development, *Annual Report, 2010-11*, Department of Higher Education, New Delhi, 2011.

Government of India, Ministry of Human Resource Development, *Country Report Fourth World Conference on Women, Beijing 1995*, Department of Women and Child Development, New Delhi, 1995.

Government of India, Ministry of Human Resource Development, *National Plan of Action for Girl Child (2005)*, New Delhi, 2005.

Government of India, Ministry of Human Resource Development, *XII Five Year Plan: Report of the Working Group on Women's Agency and Empowerment*, Ministry of Women and Child Development, New Delhi, 2012.

Government of India, Ministry of Human Resources Development, *All India Survey on Higher Education (2010-2011) and (2011-2012)*, Department of Higher Education, New Delhi, 2013.

Government of India, Ministry of Human Resources Development, *Annual Report 2011-12*, Ministry of Women and Child Development, New Delhi, 2012.

Government of India, Ministry of Human Resources Development, *Report of the Committee on the Status of Women in India*, New Delhi, 1975.

Government of India, Ministry of Labour and Employment, Labour Bureau 4th annual Employment-Unemployment Survey Round, Chandigarh, 2013-14.

Government of India, Ministry of Labour and Employment, Labour Bureau 5th Annual Employment-Unemployment Survey Round, Chandigarh, 2015-16.

Government of India, Ministry of Statistics and Programme Implementation, NSSO 38th Employment and Unemployment Survey Round, 1983.

Government of India, Ministry of Statistics and Programme Implementation, NSSO 43rd Employment and Unemployment Survey Round, 1987-88.

Government of India, Ministry of Statistics and Programme Implementation, NSSO 50th Employment and Unemployment Survey Round, 1993-94.

Government of India, Ministry of Statistics and Programme Implementation, NSSO 55th Employment and Unemployment Survey Round, 1999-2000.

Government of India, Ministry of Statistics and Programme Implementation, NSSO 62nd Employment and Unemployment Survey Round, 2005-06.

Government of India, Ministry of Statistics and Programme Implementation, NSSO 64th Employment and Unemployment Survey Round, 2007-08.

Government of India, Ministry of Statistics and Programme Implementation, NSSO 66th Employment and Unemployment Survey Round, 2009-10.

Government of India, Ministry of Statistics and Programme Implementation, NSSO 68th Employment and Unemployment Survey Round, 2011-12.

Government of India, Ministry of Statistics and Programme Implementation, *Women and Men in India, 2012*, New Delhi, 2013.

Government of India, National Commission for Enterprises in the Unorganised Sector, *Report on the Conditions of Work and Promotion of Livelihood in the Unorganised Sector*, New Delhi, 2007.

Government of India, National Commission for Women, *Domestic Violence Act, 2005*, New Delhi, 2005.

Government of India, National Commission for Women, *Sexual Harassment at Work Place Act, 2013*, New Delhi, 2013.

Government of India, Planning Commission, *Eighth Five Year Plan (1992-97)*, New Delhi, 1992.

Government of India, Planning Commission, *Eleventh Five Year Plan (2007-2012)*, New Delhi, 2002.

Government of India, Planning Commission, *Seventh Five Year Plan (1985-90)*, New Delhi, 1985.

Government of India, Planning Commission, *Tenth Five Year Plan (2002-2007)*, New Delhi, 2002.

Government of India, Planning Commission, *Twelfth Five Year Plan (2012-2017)*, New Delhi, 2012.

Government of India, Press Information Bureau, *National Commission for Women Act, 1992*, New Delhi, 1992.

United Nations, UN Women, *Beijing Declaration and Platform for Action*, New York, 2014.

United Nations, UN Women, *Strategic Plan 2014-2017*, New York, 2014.

United Nations, UNDP, *Gender Dimensions of Millennium Development Goals Report 2013*, United Nations, New York, 2014.

United Nations, UNDP, *The Millennium Development Goals Report 2014*, United Nations, New York, 2014.

World Bank, "Gender Equality and Development", *World Development Report 2014*, Washington, DC, 2015.

World Health Organisation, United Nations Children's Fund, *Progress on Drinking Water and Sanitation: 2012 Update*, Geneva, 2012.

World Health Organisation, United Nations Office on Drug and Crime, *World Development Report 2014*, Washington DC, USA.

World Health Organisation, United Nations Office on Drug and Crime, *Women Health in Prison: Correcting Gender Inequalities in Prison Health*, Denmark, 2009.

World Health Organisation, United Nations Office on Drug and Crime, *Homicide Data by Sex, United Nations (2013)*, Denmark, 2013.

Secondary Sources

Books

Aggarwal, H.O., *Human Rights*, Central Law Agency, Allahabad, 2005.

Aggarwal, Nomita, *Women and Law in India*, Women Studies and Development Centre, University of Delhi, 2002.

Agles, Flavia, *Law and Gender Inequality: The Politics of Women's Rights in India*, Oxford University Press, Delhi, 1999.

Agnew, Vijay, *Elite Women in Indian Politics*, Vikas Publishing House Pvt. Ltd., New Delhi, 1979.

Ahluwalia, M., *State Level Performance under Economic Reforms in India*, Centre for Research on Economic Development and Policy Reform, Stanford University, Stanford, 2001.

Altekar, A.S., *The Position of Women in Hindu Civilisation*, Mohit Banarsidass Publishers Private Limited, New Delhi, 1978.

Anguestine, E.A., *Working Women and Maternity Benefits*, Indian Social Institute, New Delhi, 1989.

Asthana, Pratima, *Women's Movement in India*, Vikas Publishing Pvt. Ltd., New Delhi, 1974.

Bader, Clarisse, *Women in Ancient India: Moral and Literary Studies*, Anmol Publications, New Delhi, 2000.

Bagal, J.C., *Women's Education in Eastern India: The First Phase*, The World Press Pvt. Ltd., Calcutta, 1956.

Bala, Raj, *The Legal and Political Status of Women in India*, Mohit Publications, New Delhi, 1999.

Baral, J.K. and Kumudini Patnaik, *Gender Politics*, Discovery Publishing House, New Delhi, 1990.

Bawa, R.S., and Manjit Singh, "Globalisation, Development and India", Ranjit Singh Ghuman, *et al.* (eds.), *Globalisation and Change*, Rawat Publication, New Delhi, 2010.

Bhargava, B.S. and V. Venkatakirshna, "Panchayati Raj Movement: An Analysis of Its Phases", G. Palanithurai (ed.), *Empowering People: Issues and Solutions*, Kaushik Publishers, New Delhi, 1999.

Biju, M.R., "Globalisation, Democracy and Gender Justice", M.M., Verma (ed.), *Globalisation, India and Third World*, New Century Publications, New Delhi 2012.

—, "Women Empowerment in India: Changing Socio-Political Equation", M.R. Biju (ed.), *Women Empowerment Politics and Policies*, Mittal Publication, New Delhi, 2005.

Chadha, G.K., "World Agriculture Under Strain: Are Developing Countries Heading towards Technological Orphanage?" Ranjit Singh Ghuman, *et al.*, (eds.), *Globalisation and Change*, Rawat Publications, New Delhi, 2010.

Chadwick, H.M., *The Heroic Age*, Cambridge University Press, Cambridge, 1912.

Chawla, Monica, *Gender Justice: Women and Law in India*, Deep & Deep Publications, New Delhi, 2013.

—, *Women and Protective Laws*, Regal Publications, New Delhi, 2006.

Chetana, Kalbagh, "A Better Deal for Women by 2000 AD", Kalbagh Chetana (ed.), *Social and Economic Dimensions of Women's Development*, Discovery Publishing House, New Delhi, 1992.

Chopra, P.N., *Society and Culture in Mughal Age*, Oxford University Press, New Delhi, 1955.

Das, A.N., *Global Campaign for Women Human Rights*, MD Publication Pvt. Ltd., New Delhi, 2010.

Das, S., *The Status of Indian Women*, ESS Publications, New Delhi, 1979.

Desai, Neera and Amit Kumar Gupta, *Women and Society in India*, Ajanta Publications, Delhi, 1987.

Devendra, Kiran, *Changing Status of Women in India*, Vikas Publishing House Pvt. Ltd., New Delhi, 1994.

—, *Status and Position of Women in India*, Vikas Publishing House Pvt. Ltd., New Delhi, 1985.

Dubey, Jayshree and Anuradha Sharma, "Women and Hinduism", Anil Dutta Mishra (ed.), *Women and Religion: An Encyclopedia on Women in Different Religion of the World*, vol. 1, Regal Publications, New Delhi, 2011.

Dutt, G.S., *A Woman of India*, Vikas Publishing House Pvt. Ltd., New Delhi, 1977.

Forbes, Geraldin, *Women in Modern India*, Cambridge University Press, New Delhi, 1998.

Franceschet, Susan, *et al.*, "Conceptualizing the Impact of Gender Quotas", Susan Franceschet, *et al.* (ed.), *The Impact of Gender Quotas*, Oxford University Press, New York, 2012.

Ganesamurthy, V.S., "Women in India: A Situational Report", V.S. Ganesamurthy (ed.), *Women in Indian Economy*, New Century Publications, New Delhi, 2008.

Giri, P.K., *Crime against Women*, Sublime Publication, Jaipur, 2009.

Gupta, Arvind, *Social Movements in India*, Patriot Publishers, New Delhi, 2013.

Habib, Irfan, *Agrarian System in Mughal India*, Asia Publishing House, London, 1963.

Hafner, Burton Emilie and Mark, A. Pollack, *Mainstreaming Gender in Global Governance*, University of Wisconsin, Madison, 2000.

Hasan, Ibn, *Central Structure of the Mughal Empire* (2nd edition), Asian Publication, New Delhi, 1970.

Hazra, Anupam, *India's Social Sector and Millennium Development*, Rawat Publications, New Delhi, 2013.

Heimsath, Charles H., *Indian Nationalism and Hindu Social Reforms*, Princeton University Press, Princeton, 1964.

Heyzer, N., *Daughters in Industry: Work, Skills and Consciousness of Women Workers in Asia*, Asian and Pacific Development Centre, Kuala Lumpur, 1988.

Husain, Yusuf, *Educational System in Medieval India*, Gyan Publishing House, Delhi, 1956.

—, *Glimpses of Medieval Indian Culture*, vol. 30, Asia Publishing House, Delhi, 1956.

Jain, Devaki, "Domestic Work: Its Implication for Enumeration on Women's Work and Employment", K. Saradamoni (ed.), *Women, Work and Society*, Indian Statistical Institute, Calcutta, 1995.

Jain, J.C., *Life in Ancient India as Depicted in Jain Canons*, Vikas Publishing House, New Delhi, 1947.

Janapathy, V., *Indian Women: Through the Ages*, Gyan Publishing House, New Delhi, 2002.

Joshi, M.C., *Princes and Polity in Ancient India*, Kusumanjali Prakashan, Meerut, 1986.

Kanakalatha Mukund, *Women Welfare Programmes in A.P. 1990*, Centre of Economic and Social Studies, Hyderabad, 1990.

Kang, Tajpreet Kaur, "Globalisation and Employment Status of Women in India", Rameswari Pandya (ed.), *Women Welfare and Employment in India*, New Century Publications, New Delhi, 2008.

Kant, Anjali, *Women and Law*, APH Publication, New Delhi, 2003.

Kardam, Nuket. *Bringing Women in India: Women's Issues in International Development*, CO-Lynne Rienner, Boulder 1991.

Kaur, Manmohan, *Women in India's Freedom Struggle*, Sterling Publishers Pvt. Ltd., Delhi, 1968.

Kaushik, Vijay and Bela Rani Sharma, *Indian Women through Ages*, Sarup and Sons, New Delhi, 2005.

Kenneth, W. Jones, *Arya Dharm: Hindu Consciousness in Nineteenth Century Punjab*, Manohar Publication, Delhi, 1976.

Klausen, Jytte, *et al.*, *Has liberalism failed Women Representation in Europe and the US*, Palgrave Publishers, New York, 2001.

Kudchetkar, Shirin and Sabiha Al-Issa, *Women against Violence, Violence against Women*, Pencraft International Press, New Delhi, 1998.

Mahapatra, Padmalaya and Bijoyini Mohanty, *Elite Women of India*, APH Publishing Corporation, New Delhi, 2002.

Mark, Pollack, *Mainstreaming Gender in Global Governance*, University of Wisconsin, Madison, 2000.

Mary, K. Meyer and Prugl Elisabeth, *Gender Politics in Global Governance*, MD: Rowman & Littlefield, Lanham, 1999.

Mathew, P. D, and Shalu Nigam, *Law Relating to Dowry Offences*, Indian Social Institute, New Delhi, 1986.

—, and Bakshi, P.M., *Hindu Marriage Act*, Indian Social Institute, New Delhi, 1986.

Mathur, Y.B., *Women's Education in India, 1813-1966*, Asia Publishing House, Bombay, 1973.

Mazumda, Annu Menon, *Social Welfare in India*, Asia Publishing House, Bombay, 1964.

Mazumdar, Vina, *Symbols of Power: Studies on the Political Status of Women in India*, Allied Publishers Pvt. Ltd., Bombay, 1979.

Mehta, Asha Kapur, "Globalisation and Women", Raj Mohini (ed.), *Globalisation, Culture and Women's Development"*, Rawat Publications, Jaipur, 1999.

Misra, Rekha, *Women in Mugal India*, Munsiram Manoharlal Publisher, New Delhi, 1967.

Mukherjee, Roma, *Legal Status and Remedies for Women in India*, Deep & Deep Publications, New Delhi, 1998.

Narula, Uma, *Indian Women Across Generations*, Atlantic Publishers, New Delhi, 2005.

Naryan, Iqubal, "Panchayati Raj-Democracy and Development", Ramesh Arora (ed.), *Peoples Participation in Development Process*, State Institute of Public Administration, Jaipur, 1979.

Nayyar, Deepak, "Toward Global Governance", Deepak Nayyar (ed.), *Governing Globalisation: Issues and Institutions,* Oxford University Press, New Delhi, 2006.

Desai, Neera, "Changing Status of Women, Policies and Programmes", Amit Kumar Gupta (ed.), *Women and Society, Development Perspective,* Quiterion Publishers, New Delhi, 1986.

Nelhercot, Arthur H., *The Last Four Lives of Annie Besant,* University of Chicago Press, Chicago, 1963.

Ojha, P.N., *Some Aspects of Northern Indian Social Life,* Gyan Publishing House, New Delhi, 1975.

Onimoda, Bade, "Adjustment Policies: Policy Options Before the Developing Nations", Pam Rajput and Hem Lata Swarup (eds.), *Women and Globalisation,* Asish Publishing House, New Delhi, 2002.

Padmavthi, D., "Empowerment of Women Through Micro Finance", Rameswari Pandya (ed.), *Women Welfare and Empowerment in India,* New Century Publications, New Delhi, 2008.

Palit, Mriducchanda, "Power Behind the Throne: Women in Early Mughal Politics", Mandakranta Bose (ed.), *Women and Power,* Deep & Deep Publications, New Delhi, 1985.

Panda, Rohini and Deanna Ford, *Gender Quotas and Female Leadership: A Review,* Background Paper for the World Development Report on Gender, Cambridge Massachusetts, Harvard University, Harvard, 2011.

Pandit, Madhudan, *Human Rights and Social Justice,* Swastik Publications, New Delhi, 2011.

Pandya, Rameshwari and Sarika Patel, *Women in the Unorganised Sector of India,* New Century Publications, New Delhi, 2010.

Pardia Subhas, C., and Samita Nayak, *Empowerment of Women India,* Northern Book Centre, New Delhi, 2009.

Parmar, Y.S., *Polyandry in the Himalayas,* Vikas Publishing House Pvt. Ltd., New Delhi, 1973.

Patel, Vibhuti, *Women's Challenges of New Millennium,* Gyan Publishing House, New Delhi, 2002.

Paul, Tinku, "Rural Women Work Force", Rameshwari Pandya, *Women Welfare and Empowerment in India,* New Century Publications, New Delhi, 2008.

Poonia, Meenakshi and Virender S., *Women and Human Rights in India,* Sonali Publications, New Delhi, 2011.

Prasad, Rajeshwar, "Globalisation, Culture and Women's Development", Mohini Raj Sethi (ed.), *Globalisation, Culture and Women's Development,* Rawat Publications, Jaipur, 1999.

Querashi, I.H., *Administration of the Sultans of Delhi,* Atlantic Publishers, New Delhi, 1990.

Rajput, Pam, "Women's Political Participation in ındia: An Agenda for Empowerment", Pramila Kapur (ed.), *Empowering the Indian Women*, Ministry of Information and Broadcasting, Government of India, New Delhi, 2000.

Rao, N.V. Jagannatha and Godavari D. Patil, "Changing Role and Status of the Indian Women", J.P. Singh (ed.), *The Indian Women: Myth and Reality*, Gyan Publishing House, New Delhi, 1996.

Ray, S.C., *History of Mughal India*, Oxford University Press, New Delhi, 1986.

Reddy, N. Anugula and Shantha, Sinha, *School Dropouts or Pushouts? Overcoming Barriers for Right to Education*, NUEPA, New Delhi, 2010.

Sarkar J.N., *Studies in Mughal India*, Atlantic Publishers & Distributors Ltd., Bombay, 1975.

Sen, Geeta and Carer Grown, *Development Alternative with Women: DAWN Network*, Monthly Review Press, New Delhi, 1987.

Shaheed, F., "Women, State and Power: The Dynamics of Variation and Convergence across East and West", N. Hussain, *et al.* (eds.), *Engendering the Nation-State*, Simorgh Publications, Lahore, 1997.

Sharma, Anuradha and Jayshree Dubey, "Women and Buddhism", Anil Dutta Mishra (ed.), *Women and Religion: An Encyclopedia on Women in Different Religions of the World*, vol. 2, Regal Publication, New Delhi, 2011.

Sharma, R.S., *Material Culture and Social Formulations in Ancient India*, Macmillan India Ltd., Madras, 1983.

Sharma, Sangeeta, *Women Liberation*, Rawat Publications, New Delhi, 2010.

Sharma, Tripal, *Women in Ancient India (From 320 AD to 1200 AD)*, ESS Publication, New Delhi, 1987.

Shastri, Shakuntala Rao, *Women in Vedic Age*, Bharatiya Vidya Bhavan, New Delhi, 1954.

Singh, Sita Ram, *Nationalism and Social Reforms in India*, Vikas Publishing House, New Delhi, 1968.

Singh, V.S., *Indian History*, Allahabad Law Agency, Faridabad, 1986.

Sinha, Niroj, "Women's Participation in National Freedom Struggle", Niroj Sinha (ed.), *Women in Indian Politics*, Gyan Publishing House, New Delhi, 2006.

—, *Women in Indian Politics, Empowerment of Women through Political Participation*, Gyan Publishing House, New Delhi, 2000.

Srivastva, Rashmi, "Empowerment of Women through Political Participation: With Special Reference to Madhya Pradesh", Niroj Sinha (ed.), *Women in Indian Politics*, Anmol Publications, New Delhi, 2009.

Subhas, C. Pardia and Samita Nayak, *Empowerment of Women India*, Northern Book Centre, New Delhi, 2009.

Suchinmayee, Rachna, *Human Rights and Environment*, Atlantic Publication, New Delhi, 2008.

Suguna, B., *Women's Movements*, Discovery Publishing House, New Delhi, 2009.

Swarup, Hem Lata and Pam Rajput, "Political Economy: Some Critical Gender Issues", Pam Rajput and Hem Lata Swarup (eds.), *Women and Globalisation*, Ashish Publishing House, New Delhi, 1994.

Thakur, Sadhana, *et al.*, "Women and Jainism", Anil Dutta Mishra, *Women and Religion: An Encyclopedia on Women in Different Religion of the World*, Vol. 3, Regal Publications, New Delhi, 2011.

Thangmani, K., "Education for Women", Rameshwari Pandya (ed.), *Women Welfare and Empowerment in India*, New Century Publications, New Delhi, 2010.

Thomas, P., *Indian Women Through Ages*, Asia Publication, Bombay, 1964.

Upadhyay, Neelam and Rekha Pandya, *Women in India: Past and Present*, APH Publishing, Delhi, 1990.

V. Rajendra, Raju, *Role of Women in India's Freedom Struggle*, Discovery Publishing House, New Delhi, 1994.

Vishalakshmi, R. and Nedunchezi ar "Education of Girls and Women in Tamil Nadu", R. Vishalakshmi (ed.), *Status of Women Souvenir 1973*, Task-force Sub-Committee on Education, Madras, 1985.

Vishnoi, Savita, *Economic Status of Women in Ancient India*, Kusumanjali Prakashan, Meerut, 1993.

Visram, Rozina, *Women in India and Pakistan: The Struggle for Independence from British Rule*, Cambridge University Press, Cambridge, 1992.

Whittington, *Early Travels*, Oxford University Press, Delhi, 1975.

Yadav, Ravi Prakash, *et al.*, "Empowerment of Women in India", Rameshwari Pandya (ed.), *Women Welfare and Empowerment in India*, New Century Publication, New Delhi, 2008.

Zollinger, Giele and Leslie F., *Women and Equality in the Workplace*, ABC-CLIO Publication, California, 2003.

Journals

Abraham, Vinod, "Missing Labour or Consistent Defeminisation", *Economic and Political Weekly*, vol. XVIII, no. 31, 3 August, 2013.

AIR 1953 Madh. Bharat.

AIR 1979 SC.

AIR 1983 SC.

AIR 1986 SC.

AIR 1989 SC.

AIR 1992 SC.

Akerkar, S., "Theory and Practice of Women's Movement in India: A Discourse Analysis", *Economic and Political Weekly*, vol. XXX, no. 27, 1995.

Arora, Banarsi, "Women in Politics: Governance in Patriarchal and Non-participatory Culture", *Guru Nanak Journal of Sociology*, vol. XX, no. 2, 1999.

Arora, Rashmi Umesh, "Bank Credit and Development: A Study of Uttar Pradesh", *The Journal of Developing Areas*, vol. VI, no. 1, 2012.

—, "Gender Inequality, Economic Development and Globalisation: A State Level Analysis of India", *The Journal of Developing Areas*, vol. XXXXVI, no. 1, 2012.

Banerjee, Sikata "Gender and Nationalism: The Masculinisation of Hinduism and Female Political Participation in India", *Women's Studies International Forum*, vol. XXVI, n. 2, 2003.

Barbara, Southard, "Colonial Politics and Women's Rights: Woman Suffrage Campaigns in Bengal, British India in the 1920s", *Modern Asian Studies*, vol. XXVII, no. 2, 1993.

Basu, A.M., "Why Does Education lead to lower fertility? A Critical Review of Some of the Possibilities", *World Development*, vol. XXX, no.10, 2002.

Basu, Kaushik, "India and the Global Economy: Role of Culture, Norms and Beliefs", *Economic and Political Weekly*, vol. XXXVI, no. 40, October, 2001.

Benerjee, Nirmala, "Whatever Happened to the Dreams of Modernity, The Nehruvian Era and Women's Position", *Economic and Political Weekly*, vol. XXXIII, no. 17, September, 1998.

Bhattacharji, Sukumari, "Economic Rights of Women in Indian", *Economic and Political Weekly*", vol. XXVII, no. 9, March, 1991

Braveman, P.N., *et al.*, "Health Inequalities and Social Inequalities in Health", *Bulletin of the World Health Organisation*, vol. XXXXXXXVIII, no. 2, 2000.

Chen, Li-Ju, "Do Gender Quotas Influence Women's Representation and Policies?" *The European Journal of Comparative Economics*, vol. III, no. 1, 2010.

Childs, Sarah and Krook, Mona Leena, "Critical Mass Theory and Women's Representation", *Political Studies*, vol. XXXXXVI, no. 32, September, 2012.

Deshpande, Rajeshwari, "How Did Women Vote in Lok Sabha Elections 2009?" *Economic and Political Weekly*, vol. XXXXIV, no. 39, October, 2009.

—, "How Gendered Was Women's Participation Women in Election 2004", *Economic and Political Weekly*, vol. XXXIX, no. 51, December, 2004.

Epstein, Barbare, "What Happened to the Women's Movement", *Monthly Review*, vol. XXXXXIII, no. 1, 2001.

Eumeyer, E. and Plumper, T., "The Gendered Nature of Natural Disasters: The Impact of Catastrophic Events on the Gender Gap in Life Expectancy, 1981–2002", *Annals of the Association of American Geographers*, vol. XXXXXXXXXVII, no. 3, 2007.

Fadia, Kuldeep, "Women's Empowerment through Political Participation in India", *Indian Journal of Public Administration*, vol. LX, no. 3, July to September 2014.

Gangoli, Geetanjali, "Reproduction, Abortion and Women Health", *Social Scientist*, vol. XXVI, no 1, January-April 1998.

Hagaragi, Ambaraya, "Policies, Programmes, and Women's Status in India", *Third Concept*, vol. XXVI, no. 30, August, 2012.

Harrigan, Jane and Mosley Paul, "Evaluating the Impact of World Bank Structural Adjustment Leading: 1980-87", *The Journal of Development Studies*, vol. II, no. 3, January 1991.

Himanshu, "Employment Trends in India: A Re-examination", *Economic and Political Weekly*, vol. XXXXVI, no. 37, October, 2011.

Hooshang, Amirahmadi and Weiping Wu, "Export Processing Zones in Asia", *Asian Survey*, vol. XXXV, no.9, 1995.

James, K.S., "Recent Shifts in Infant Mortality in India: An Exploration", *Economic and Political Weekly*, vol. XLIX, no. 3, January, 2014.

Jhamb, Bhumika, *et al.*, "The Paradox of Gender Responsive Budgeting", *Economic and Political Weekly*, vol. XLVIII, no. 20, May, 2013.

Kannan, K.P. and G. Reveendren,"Counting and Profiling the Missing Labour Force", *Economic and Political Weekly*, vol. XXXXVII, no. 6, February, 2012.

Kishwar, Madhu, "Women and Politics: Beyond Quotas", *Economic and Political Weekly*, vol. XXXI, no. 43, November, 1996.

Kitchlu, T.N., "Women Rights, Legislative Measures", Yojana, vol. XXXV, no. 20, November, 1991.

Kotvi, Naryan S., "The Myth of Gender Equity", *World Affairs*, vol. V, no. 3, July-September, 2001.

Lang, P. and Young, S., "Foreign Direct Investment and Technology Transfer: A Case Study of Foreign Direct Investment in North East China", *Transnational Corporations*, vol. V, no.1, 1996.

Manjreker, Nandini, "Contemporary Challenges to Women's Education: Towards an Exclusion Goal", *Economic and Political Weekly*, vol. XXXXIII, no. 43, October, 2003.

Manu, Bhaskar, "Women Panchayat Members in Kerala", *Economic and Political Weekly*, vol. XXXII, no. 17, April, 1997.

Mathew, George and Ramesh Nayak, "Panchayat at Work: What it Means for the Oppressed", *Economic and Political Weekly*, vol. XXXI, no. 27, July, 1996.

Mathur, Kanchan, "Gender Hierarchies and Inequalities: Taking Stock of Women's Sexual and Reproductive Health", *Economic and Political Weekly*, vol. XLIII, no. 49, December, 2008.

Matthai, Raichel, "Political Status of Indian Women: Progress in Since Independence", *Mainstream*, vol. XLV, no. 1, December, 2006.

Mazumdar, Indrani, "Women Unpaid Labour in Neo-liberal India", *Indian Historical Review*, vol. XXXV, no. 2, 2009.

Mazumdar, Veena, "Reservation for Women", *Economic and Political Weekly*, vol. XXIV, no. 50, June, 1989.

Mittal, Neha, "Women Workers in Unorganised Sector: Socio-Economic Perspective", *Asian Journal of Multidimensional Research*, vol. 1, no. 3, August, 2012.

Mohanty, Biduyat, "Panchayati Raj, 73rd Constitutional Amendment and Women", *Economic and Political Weekly*, vol. XXXIX, no. 49, December, 1995.

Mukherjee, Mukul, "Towards Gender-Aware Data Systems–Indian Experience", *Economic and Political Weekly*", vol. XXX1, no. 43, October, 2001.

Naidu, Gurappa, "Globalisation and its Impact on Indian Society", The *Indian Journal of Political Science*, vol. XXXXXXVII, no. 1, JAN.-MAR., 2006.

Nair, Jayshree Ramkrishan and Heema, "Engendering Health: A Brief History of Women's Involvement in Health Issues", *SAMYUKTA: A Journal of Women Studies*, vol. II, no. 1, January, 2002.

Narayanan, Harini, "Women's Health, Population Control and Collective Action", *Economic and Political Weekly*, vol. XLVI, no. 8, February, 2011.

Naryana, Kamalanath, "Women in Working Force in India", *Economic and Political Weekly*, vol. III, no. 2, August, 1968.

Pai, Sudha, "Pradhanis in New Panchayat: Field Notes from Meerut District", *Economic and Political Weekly*, vol. XXXIII, no. 18, May, 1998.

Pal, Mahi, "Women in Panchayat", *Economic and Political Weekly*, vol. XXXIII, no. 4, January, 1998.

Pal, Satarupa, "Women in Twelfth Five Year Plan in India: An Analysis", *A Journal of Humanities and Science*, Vol. II, no. 1, July, 2013.

Patel, Vibhuti, "Getting a Foot Hold in Politics, Women in Political Decision Making Process", *Social Action*, vol. XXXXXXV, no. 1, January-March, 2005.

Philip, Musgrove, "Public Spending on Health Care: How is Different Criteria Related?" *Health Policy*, vol. XXXVII, no. 3, 2011.

Rai, Praveen, "Electoral Participation of Women in India: Key Determinants and Barriers", Economic *and Political Weekly*, vol. XLVI, no. 3, January, 2011.

Rawal, Vikas, "Ownership holdings of land in Rural India: Putting the Record Straight", *Economic and Political Weekly*, vol. XXXXIII, no. 10, March, 2008.

Sengupta, Chandan "Conceptualising Globalisation: Issues and Implications", *Economic and Political Weekly*, vol. XXXVI, no. 33, August, 2011.

Sharma, Sanjeev Kumar, "Demystifying the Globalisation Myth", *The Indian Journal of Political Science*, vol. XXXXXXV, no. 4, Oct.-Dec., 2004.

Shettar, Rajeshwari, "A Study on Issues and Challenges of Women Empowerment in India", *Journal of Business and Management*, vol. XVII, no. 4, April, 2015.

Sinha, J.N., "How to Use 1961 Census Working Force Data: A Comment", *Economic and Political Weekly*, vol. II, no. 15, May, 1967.

Southard, Barbara, "Colonial Politics and Women's Rights: Woman Suffrage Campaigns in Bengal, British India in the 1920s", *Modern Asian Studies*, vol. XXVII, no. 2, 1993.

Tharakan, Sophie M., and, Michael, Tharakan, "Status of Women in India: A Historical Perspective", *Social Scientist*, vol. IV, no. 1, November-December, 1975.

Widge, M.K., "Gender Issue in Development", *Yojana*, vol. XXXVII, no. 10, June, 1992.

Unpublished Works

Bhattacharya, D. and Mustafizur Rahman, "Female Employment under Export-Propelled Industrialisation: Prospects for Internalizing Global Opportunities in the Apparel Sector in Bangladesh", *Occasional paper 10*, The United Nations Research Institute for Social Development (UNRISD), Geneva. 1999.

Chaudhary, Devendra Kumar, *Arya Samaj in Punjab 1877-1901*, M. Phil Dissertation (Unpublished), Punjabi University, Patiala, 1979.

Ghosh, Jayati, *Globalisation and Economic Empowerment of Women: Emerging Issues in South Asia*, paper presented for Intergovernmental Meeting on Beijing Platform for Action, UN-ESCAP, and September, 2004.

Newspapers

Anand, Anitha, "Engendering the Plan", *The Hindu*, 6 April, 1997.

Deswal, D., "Ladoo and Jalebis: The Code of Killer Doctors of Jatland", *Times of India*, 8 April, 2011.

Editorial, "Good News for Single Women in 12th Plan", *The Hindu*, 14 May, 2013.

Editorial, "Infant Mortality Rate Shows Slight Decline", *The Hindu*, 28 December, 2011.

Editorial, "Drop Out Rate by Stages", *Times of India*, 01 April, 2012.

Gupta, V.S., "Nation Building and Empowerment of Women", *Employment News*, 11-17 August, 2009.

Tandon, Aditi, "Oops, sorry, we've killed you", *The Sunday Tribune,* 23 November, 2014.

Internet Websites

"Beedi and Cigar Workers (Conditions of Employment) Act, 1966", *www.advocatekhoj.com/.../bareacts/beediandcigar/index.phd?...Beedi%2....*

"Chief Executives Board | United Nations Educational on 18", *IndianKanoon.org/doc/86124,*

"Development agenda beyond 2015/UNDESA/United", *www.un.org/en/development/desa/development-beyond-2015.htm,*

"Equal Remuneration Act 1976", *www.excelconsultancyservices.co.in/EqualRemuneration.htm.*

"General's Message for 2015", www.onwomen.org/en.s

"ILO, Global Employment Trends, 2014", *http://www.ilo.org/wcmsp5/groups/public/—dgreports/—dcomm/—publ/documents/publication/wcms_233953.pdf.*

"International labour organisation, 1919", *en.wikipedia.org/wiki/international-labour-organisation.*

"The First Factories Act-Indian History", www.*indhistory.com/factory-act.html,*

"Tokenism or Agency: The Impact of Women's Reservations on Panchayats in South India", http:*//www.econ.vt.edu/seminars/seminarpapers/2006/rao_reservations_0313_wtables.pdf*

"WEF, Women's Employment: Measuring the Global Gender Gap', World Economic Forum", *http://www.weforum.org/pdf/Global_Competitiveness_Report/Report/gender_gap.pdf*

"Women's Reservation Bill-Wikipedia, free encyclopedia", *https://en.wikipedia.org/wiki/Women's _Reservation_ Bill.*

Index